Easy WordPerfect®
(for Version 6)

Shelley O'Hara

que

Easy WordPerfect (for Version 6)

Easy WordPerfect (for Version 6)
Copyright ©1993 by Que® Corporation

All rights reserved. Printed in the United States of America. No part of this book may be used or reproduced in any form or by any means, or stored in a database or retrieval system, without prior written permission of the publisher except in the case of brief quotations embodied in critical articles and reviews. Making copies of any part of this book for any purpose other than your own personal use is a violation of United States copyright laws. For information, address Que Corporation, 11711 N. College Ave., Carmel, IN 46032.

Library of Congress Catalog No.: 93-84129

ISBN: 1-56529-087-9

This book is sold *as is*, without warranty of any kind, either express or implied, respecting the contents of this book, including but not limited to implied warranties for the book's quality, performance, merchantability, or fitness for any particular purpose. Neither Que Corporation nor its dealers or distributors shall be liable to the purchaser or any other person or entity with respect to any liability, loss, or damage caused or alleged to have been caused directly or indirectly by this book.

95 94 93   6 5 4 3 2 1

Interpretation of the printing code: the rightmost double-digit number is the year of the book's printing; the rightmost single-digit number, the number of the book's printing. For example, a printing code of 93-1 shows that the first printing of the book occurred in 1993.

Screen reproductions in this book were created using Collage Plus from Inner Media, Inc., Hollis, NH.

Easy WordPerfect (for Version 6) is based on WordPerfect Version 6.0.

Publisher: David P. Ewing

Associate Publisher: Rick Ranucci

Operations Manager: Sheila Cunningham

Publishing Plan Manager: Thomas H. Bennett

Marketing Manager: Ray Robinson

Book Designer: Scott Cook

Indexer: Jeanne Clark

Production Team: Danielle Bird, Julie Brown, Heather Kaufman, Bob LaRoche, Jay Lesandrini, Tim Montgomery, Michelle Worthington

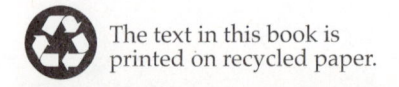

The text in this book is printed on recycled paper.

Credits

Acquisitions Editor
　　Chris Katsaropoulos

Production Editor
　　Barbara K. Koenig

Technical Editor
　　Chris Pichereau

Novice Reviewer
　　Bruce Meyer

WordPerfect is a registered trademark of WordPerfect Corporation.

About the Author

Shelley O'Hara is a Title Manager at Que Corporation. She is the author of most of the books in the *Easy* series, including the best-selling *Easy Windows 3.1* and *Easy 1-2-3, 2nd Edition*. She also is the coauthor of *Real Men Use DOS*. Shelley received her bachelor's degree from the University of South Carolina and her master's degree from the University of Maryland.

Contents

The Basics 1

    A Letter from the Author 2

    An Introduction to WordPerfect 3

    How To Use This Book 6

    How To Follow an Exercise 7

    Important Stuff To Remember 10

Task/Review 15

    Alphabetical Listing of Tasks 16

    Entering and Editing Text 19

        Start WordPerfect 20

        Select a menu command 22

        Exit WordPerfect 24

        Change to Graphics mode 26

        Get help 28

        Add text 30

        Overwrite text 32

        Insert a blank line 34

        Combine paragraphs 36

        Insert a page break 38

        Go to a page 40

        Delete a character 42

        Delete a word 44

        Select a block 46

        Select a paragraph 48

        Delete a block 50

Contents

Undelete text 52

Undo a command 54

Copy a block 56

Move a block 58

Files 61

Save a document for the first time 62

Save a document with a new name 64

Save and clear a document 66

Abandon a document 68

Open a document 70

Create a new document 72

Open more than one document 74

Switch to another open document 76

Display all open documents 78

Basic Formatting 81

Reveal codes 82

Center text 84

Right-justify text 86

Indent text 88

Create a hanging indent 90

Make text bold 92

Underline text 94

Italicize text 96

Change the font 98

Change the font size 100

Change the initial font 102

Easy WordPerfect for Version 6

Contents

More Editing 105
- Change the case of a block 106
- Search for text 108
- Search and replace text 110
- Insert the current date 112
- Check spelling 114
- Look up a word in the thesaurus 116
- Display document information 118
- Save a block 120
- Retrieve a block 122
- Sort text 124

More Formatting 127
- Set left tabs 128
- Align numbers at the decimal point 130
- Double space a document 132
- Add a paragraph border 134
- Shade a paragraph 136
- Center text on a page 138
- Number pages 140
- Add a page border 142
- Set margins 144
- Change to Page mode 146
- Create a header 148
- Edit a header 150
- Create a footer 152

Contents

Edit a footer 154

Insert a special character 156

Draw a horizontal line 158

Insert a graphic 160

Insert a table 162

Enter text into a table 164

Add a row to a table 166

Delete a row from a table 168

Create a two-column document 170

Type text in the second column 172

Printing 175

Preview a document 176

Print a document 178

Print a block 180

More Files 183

Start the File Manager 184

Use the File Manager to open a file 186

Create a directory 188

Display a different directory 190

Change the default directory 192

Copy a file 194

Rename a file 196

Delete a file 198

Find a file 200

Contents

    Merging 203

        Create a merge letter 204

        Create a form file 206

        Enter text into a form file 208

        Save the form file 212

        Create a data file 214

        Enter a record into the data file 218

        Enter other records into the data file 220

        Save the data file 222

        Merge the files 224

Reference 227

    Guide to Using the Mouse 228

        Moving the Cursor 229

        Selecting a Menu Command 229

        Blocking Text 229

    Where To Get More Help 230

    Glossary 231

Index 235

The Basics

A Letter from the Author

An Introduction to WordPerfect

How To Use This Book

How To Follow an Exercise

Important Stuff To Remember

Easy WordPerfect for Version 6

The Basics

A Letter from the Author

Dear Reader:

If you are a beginning computer user and are intimidated by computers, this book is written for you. This book is set up to make it as easy as possible to learn how to use a program such as WordPerfect.

First, this book explains all terms and concepts so that they are easy to understand. The book doesn't assume that you know all the buzzwords of computing.

Second, this book doesn't cover every single WordPerfect feature. It starts with the basics and then moves on to cover the features you'll use most often in your day-to-day work.

Third, this book includes easy-to-follow steps for each procedure. It's simple to follow along with each sample exercise or to use the steps as a review.

Fourth, you don't need to worry that you might do something wrong and ruin a document or the computer. This book points out mistakes you might make and shows you how to avoid them. This book explains how to escape from a situation when you change your mind during a procedure.

I hope that you learn a lot from this book—enough to get started and build your confidence. Armed with that confidence, you'll be ready to create any type of document.

Sincerely,

Shelley O'Hara

An Introduction to WordPerfect

WordPerfect is one of the world's most popular word processing software programs. You can use the program to create a variety of documents, including

- Letters
- Memos
- Reports
- Manuscripts
- Term papers
- Resumes
- Form letters

You can create these documents with a typewriter, but WordPerfect makes writing, editing, and printing easier.

Specifically, you can use WordPerfect to perform these functions:

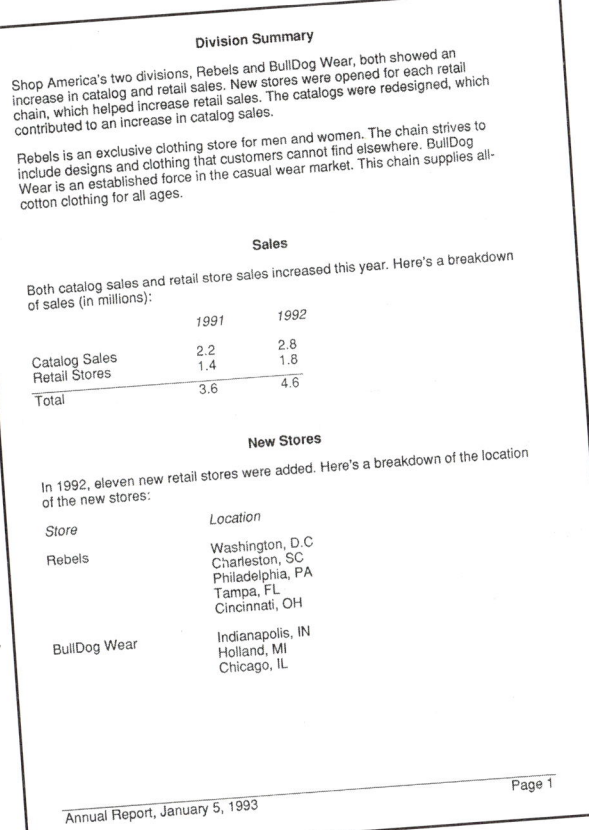

Correct errors. With a typewriter, after you press a key, that character is committed to paper. To correct a mistake, you have to use correction fluid or retype the document. With WordPerfect, you see the text on-screen. You can easily correct your typographical errors before you print the document.

Move around quickly. With the document on-screen, you can move from one sentence, paragraph, or page to another. You can move quickly from the top of the document to the bottom and vice versa.

Make editing changes. You can insert text into any location in your document. You also can quickly delete any amount of text, such as a character, a word, a sentence, or a paragraph.

Rearrange your text. When you sit down to write, you don't always write in order, from the introduction to the summary. Ideas might occur to you in a different order. As you're writing the summary, you might think of an idea that belongs in the introduction. With WordPerfect, you can easily move and copy text from one location to another.

Restore deleted text. When you accidentally delete text you meant to keep, you don't have to retype it. Instead, you can just restore the text.

Check your spelling. Before you print, you can run a spelling check to search for misspellings and double words. If you are a poor typist, this feature lets you concentrate on your writing and leave spelling errors for WordPerfect to catch.

Search for text. You can search your document for a particular word or phrase. For example, you can move quickly to the section of your document that discusses expenditures by searching for the word *expenditures.*

Search and replace text. You can make text replacements throughout the document quickly and easily. For example, you can change all occurrences of the name *Smith* to *Smythe* in a document.

Make formatting changes. WordPerfect enables you to change margins, tabs, and other formatting options easily. You can experiment with the settings until the document appears the way you want it. Then you can print it.

Change how text is printed. You can boldface, italicize, and underline text. You also can use a different typeface, depending on your printer.

Preview your document. You can preview your document to see how it will look when you print it. If you want to make changes before you print, you can.

How To Use This Book

This book is set up so that you can use it several different ways:

- You can read the book from start to finish.
- You can start reading at any point in the book.
- You can experiment with one exercise, many exercises, or all exercises.
- You can flip through the book and look at the Before and After pictures to locate specific tasks.
- You can look through the alphabetical task list at the beginning of the "Task/Review" part of this book to find the task you want.
- You can read only the exercise, only the review, or both the exercise and review portions. As you learn the program, you might want to follow the exercises. After you learn the program, you can refer to the review portion to remind yourself of how to perform a certain task.
- You can read any part of the exercises that you want. You can read all the text to see both the steps to follow and the explanation of those steps. You can read only the text in red to see the keystrokes to press. You can read only the explanation to understand what happens during a particular step.

How To Follow an Exercise

WordPerfect is flexible because it enables you to perform a task many different ways. For consistency, this book makes certain assumptions about how your computer is set up and how you use WordPerfect. As you follow along with each exercise, keep the following key points in mind:

- This book assumes that you have a hard drive and that you followed the basic installation. This book also assumes that you have installed a printer and that you have not changed any program defaults.

- This book assumes that you use the keyboard—rather than the mouse—to choose menu commands. For information on using the mouse, see the "Reference" in the back of this book.

- This book is based on WordPerfect 6.0, which is quite different from versions 5.1 and 5.0.

- In the exercise sections, this book assumes that you are starting from the Before screen. If this screen contains any text, you should type the text as it appears in the screen.

- Only the Before and After screens are illustrated. Screens are not shown for every step within an exercise.

- In the Before and After screens, a large font size has been chosen so that the text is easy to read. Your screen will look different, depending on what font you've chosen.

Task section

The Task section includes numbered steps that tell you how to accomplish tasks such as saving a document or indenting a paragraph. The numbered steps walk you through a specific example so that you can learn the task by doing it. Blue text below the numbered steps explains the concept further.

Oops! notes

You may find that you performed a task, such as underlining text, that you do not want after all. The Oops! notes tell you how to undo each procedure. By showing you how to reverse nearly every procedure or get out of every mode, these notes allow you to use WordPerfect more confidently.

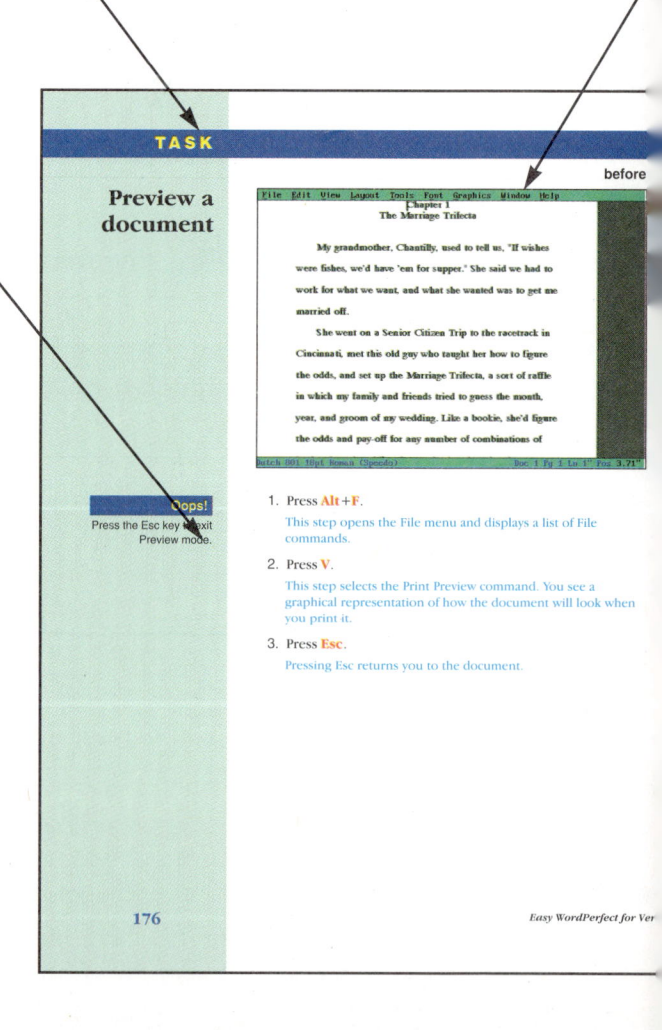

TASK

Preview a document

before

Oops!
Press the Esc key to exit Preview mode.

1. Press **Alt**+**F**.
   This step opens the File menu and displays a list of File commands.
2. Press **V**.
   This step selects the Print Preview command. You see a graphical representation of how the document will look when you print it.
3. Press **Esc**.
   Pressing Esc returns you to the document.

176

Easy WordPerfect for Ver

8

Easy WordPerfect for Version 6

Before and After Screens

Each exercise includes Before and After pictures that show how the computer screen will look before and after you follow the numbered steps in the Task section.

Review section

After you learn a procedure by following the specific example given in the Task section, you can refer to the Review section for a quick summary of the task. The Review section gives you generic steps for completing a task so that you can apply those steps to your own work. You can use these steps as a quick reference to refresh your memory about how to perform a procedure.

after

Zoom and other options

For more information on other print preview options, see Que's *Using WordPerfect 6, Special Edition.*

REVIEW

To preview a document

Press **Alt+F** to open the File menu.
Press **V** to select Print Preview.
Press **Esc** to return to the document.

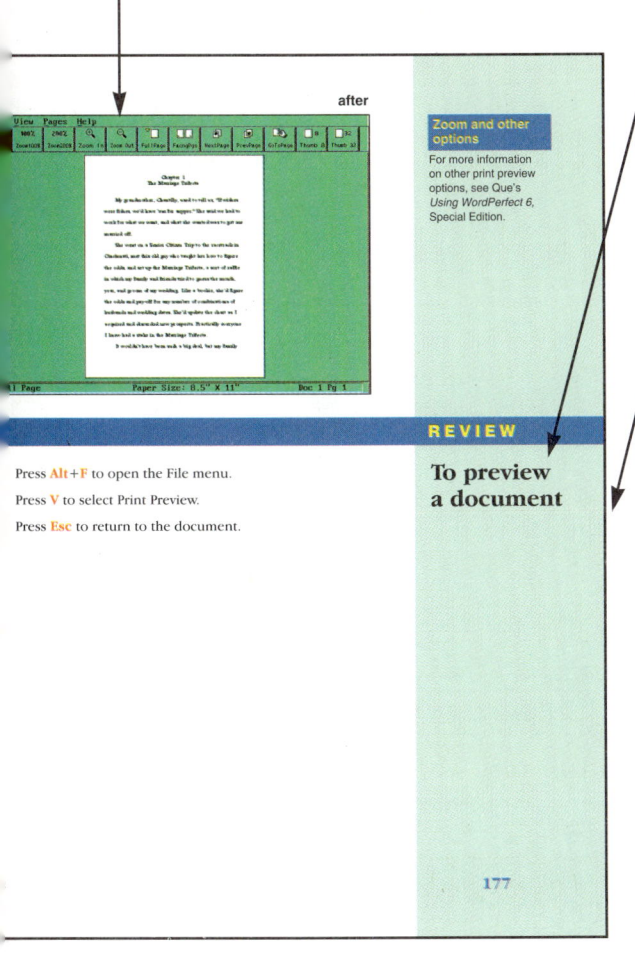

Other notes

Each exercise contains other short notes that tell you a little more about each procedure. These notes define terms, explain other options, refer you to other sections when applicable, and so on.

The Basics

Important Stuff To Remember

Now that you know the key to the book, there are just a few other things you should keep in mind. The information covered in the following sections pertains to the basics of using WordPerfect—the do-it-all-the-time kind of things. Take a quick look through this section before you get started.

Reviewing the Editing Screen

After you start the program, you see a blank editing screen. For information on starting the program, see *TASK: Start WordPerfect*. Depending on what mode you've selected, you might see something slightly different. See *TASK: Change to graphics mode*.

Don't let this screen intimidate you. Think of the screen as a blank piece of paper. You can write anything you want—just start typing.

The top line of the screen displays the menu bar. For information on accessing menu commands, see *TASK: Select a menu command*.

Easy WordPerfect for Version 6

WordPerfect displays a blinking cursor in the editing screen. The cursor indicates where text will appear when you start typing.

The bottom left side of the editing screen displays the current font.

The bottom right side of the editing screen displays the following information about your document:

Indicator	Description
Doc	Document number
Pg	Page number
Ln	Line number in inches (the cursor's vertical position)
Pos	Column number in inches (the cursor's horizontal position)

WordPerfect displays the line and column position in inches. You can change this measurement if you want. See Que's *Using WordPerfect 6,* Special Edition, for more information.

Using Your Keyboard

You type on a computer keyboard just like you do on a typewriter; however, there are a few important differences:

- On a typewriter, you press the Return key when you reach the end of the line. (The Return key is called the Enter key on a computer keyboard.) With Word-Perfect, you don't press Enter at the end of the line. WordPerfect automatically wraps any words that don't fit to the next line.

- You cannot move the cursor around on-screen until you have typed something, pressed the space bar, or pressed Enter. WordPerfect doesn't permit the cursor to move where nothing exists. After you enter text or spaces on-screen or press Enter, you can move the cursor.

- You use the arrow keys and key combinations to move the cursor. The following table lists the most

The Basics

The Basics

common cursor-movement keys and key combinations. If a key combination is joined with a plus sign, you must press and hold the first key and then press the second key. If the key combination is separated by commas, press and release the first key, then press the next key, and so on.

To move...	Press...
One character right	→
One character left	←
One line up	↑
One line down	↓
To previous word	Ctrl + ←
To next word	Ctrl + →
To beginning of line	Home, Home, ←
To end of line	Home, Home, → (or press End)
To beginning of document (before any codes)	Home, Home, Home, ↑
To end of document (after any codes)	Home, Home, Home, ↓
To previous page	PgUp
To next page	PgDn

Saving Your Work

All your work is stored temporarily in memory, which is like having a shopping list in your head. Until you commit the list to paper, you might forget some or all items. The same is true with WordPerfect. Until you save the document, you can lose all or part of the text.

Saving the document doesn't commit it to paper like the shopping list. Saving the document saves the document to your disk. Then when you need the document again, you can retrieve it from the disk.

Easy WordPerfect for Version 6

WordPerfect does not save your work automatically; you need to save it yourself. You should save every five or ten minutes. You will learn how to save and retrieve files in the section "Files."

Task/Review

Entering and Editing Text

Files

Basic Formatting

More Editing

More Formatting

Printing

More Files

Merging

Easy WordPerfect for Version 6

Alphabetical Listing of Tasks

Abandon a document 68
Add a page border 142
Add a paragraph border 134
Add a row to a table 166
Add text 30
Align numbers at the decimal point 130
Center text 84
Center text on a page 138
Change the font 98
Change the font size 100
Change the case of a block 106
Change the default directory 192
Change the initial font 102
Change to Graphics mode 26
Change to Page mode 146
Check spelling 114
Combine paragraphs 36
Copy a block 56
Copy a file 194
Create a data file 214
Create a directory 188
Create a footer 152
Create a form file 206
Create a hanging indent 90
Create a header 148
Create a merge letter 204
Create a new document 72
Create a two-column document 170
Delete a block 50
Delete a character 42
Delete a file 198
Delete a row from a table 168

16

Easy WordPerfect for Version 6

Delete a word 44
Display a different directory 190
Display all open documents 78
Display document information 118
Double space a document 132
Draw a horizontal line 158
Edit a footer 154
Edit a header 150
Enter a record into the data file 218
Enter other records into the data file 220
Enter text into a form file 208
Enter text into a table 164
Exit WordPerfect 24
Find a file 200
Get help 28
Go to a page 40
Indent text 88
Insert a blank line 34
Insert a graphic 160
Insert a page break 38
Insert a special character 156
Insert a table 162
Insert the current date 112
Italicize text 96
Look up a word in the thesaurus 116
Make text bold 92
Merge the files 224
Move a block 58
Number pages 140
Open a document 70
Open more than one document 74
Overwrite text 32

17

Preview a document 176
Print a block 180
Print a document 178
Rename a file 196
Retrieve a block 122
Reveal codes 82
Right-justify text 86
Save a block 120
Save a document for the first time 62
Save a document with a new name 64
Save and clear a document 66
Save the data file 222
Save the form file 212
Search and replace text 110
Search for text 108
Select a block 46
Select a menu command 22
Select a paragraph 48
Set left tabs 128
Set margins 144
Shade a paragraph 136
Sort text 124
Start the File Manager 184
Start WordPerfect 20
Switch to another open document 76
Type text in the second column 172
Undelete text 52
Underline text 94
Undo a command 54
Use the File Manager to open a file 186

Entering and Editing Text

This section covers the following tasks:

Start WordPerfect

Select a menu command

Exit WordPerfect

Change to Graphics mode

Get help

Add text

Overwrite text

Insert a blank line

Combine paragraphs

Insert a page break

Go to a page

Delete a character

Delete a word

Select a block

Select a paragraph

Delete a block

Undelete text

Undo a command

Copy a block

Move a block

TASK

Start WordPerfect

before

```
C:\>
```

Oops!
To exit WordPerfect, see TASK: Exit WordPerfect.

1. Turn on your computer and monitor.

   Every computer has a different location for its power switch. Many systems have the switch on the side, front, or back of the computer. You might need to turn on the monitor separately from the computer system. Check your computer setup manuals for the location of your particular system's on/off or power buttons.

2. If necessary, respond to the prompts for date and time, or simply press **Enter**.

   When you first turn on the computer, some systems ask you to enter the current date and time before you begin your work. (Many of the newer computer models enter the date and time automatically, so don't worry if your system does not ask you for them. Type the current date and press the Enter key. Then type the time and press the Enter key. The `C:\>` (or C prompt) should be on-screen now.

   If you are not concerned with having the current date on your computer, just press the Enter key in response to these prompts.

3. When you see the `C:\>` prompt, type **CD\WP60**.

   Typing *CD\WP60* brings you to the directory where WordPerfect 6 is located.

20 *Easy WordPerfect for Version 6*

after

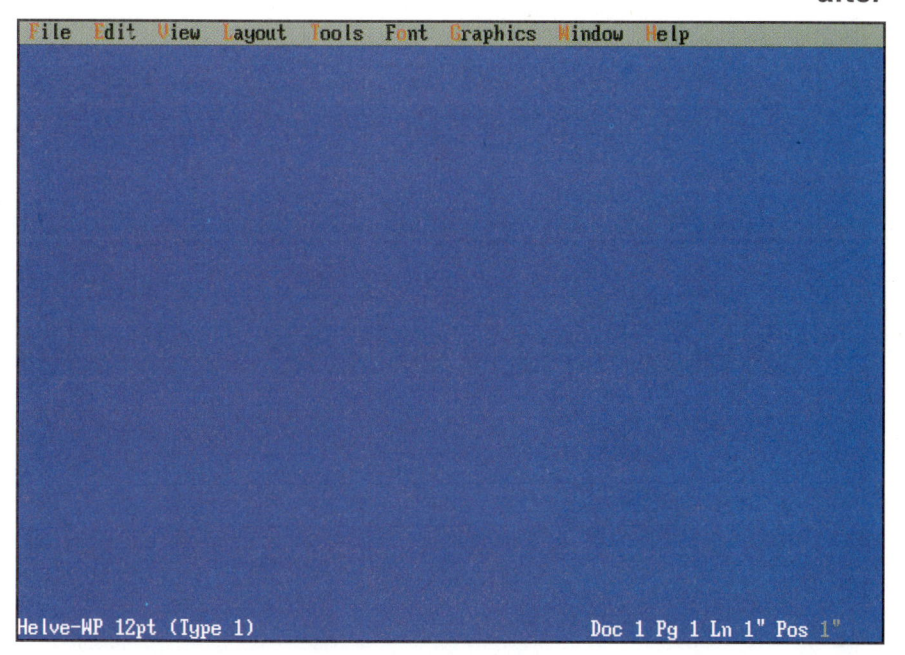

[Screenshot of WordPerfect editing screen with menu bar: File Edit View Layout Tools Font Graphics Window Help. Status line shows: Helve-WP 12pt (Type 1)   Doc 1 Pg 1 Ln 1" Pos 1"]

4. Press **Enter**.

   Pressing the Enter key places you in the WordPerfect directory. You see the `C:\WP60>` prompt.

5. Type **WP**.

   WP is the command to start the program.

6. Press **Enter**.

   You see the opening screen, followed by the editing screen. You are now ready to create a new file or retrieve a file.

When the program will not start...

If the program doesn't start, make sure that both the computer and monitor are turned on and plugged in.

Use the correct directory!

Make sure that the program is stored in the WP60 directory. You might have installed the program in a different directory. If so, type that directory name in step 3.

REVIEW

To start WordPerfect

1. Turn on your computer and monitor.

2. If necessary, respond to the prompts for date and time, or press **Enter**.

3. Type **CD\WP60** at the `C:\>` prompt.

4. Press **Enter**.

5. Type **WP**.

6. Press **Enter**.

Entering and Editing Text

21

TASK

Select a menu command

before

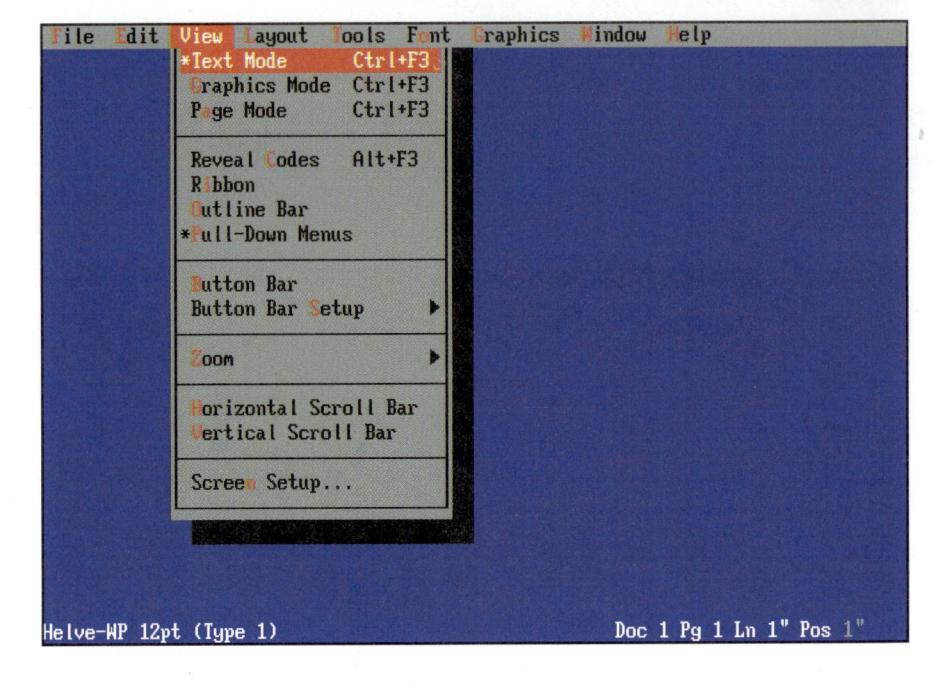

[Screenshot of WordPerfect View menu showing: Text Mode Ctrl+F3, Graphics Mode Ctrl+F3, Page Mode Ctrl+F3, Reveal Codes Alt+F3, Ribbon, Outline Bar, *Pull-Down Menus, Button Bar, Button Bar Setup, Zoom, Horizontal Scroll Bar, Vertical Scroll Bar, Screen Setup...]

Oops!

To close a menu without making a selection, press the Esc key twice.

1. Press **Alt+V**.

   This step opens the View menu. To open a menu, you must press and hold down the Alt key, then press the "key" letter in the menu name. The "key" letter will be in a different color or underlined (depending on your monitor).

2. Press **G**.

   This step selects the Graphics Mode command. To select a menu command, type the "key" letter in the command name. The "key" letter will be in a different color or underlined.

   Some commands are executed as soon as you select them. Other commands prompt for more information in a dialog box. Select the options you want and then press Enter. Other commands display another menu of commands. You select from these menus the same way: press the "key" letter.

Easy WordPerfect for Version 6

after

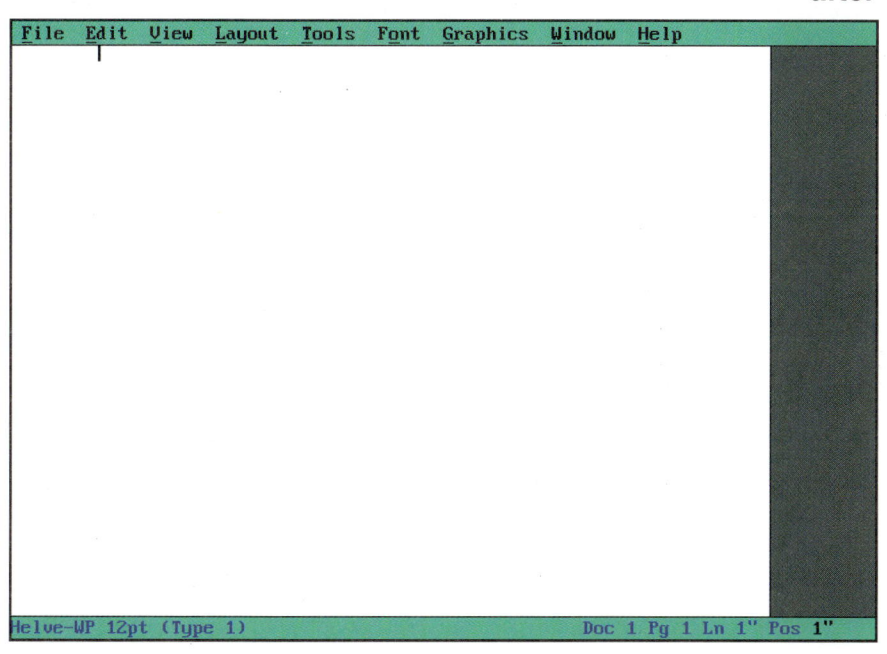

```
File  Edit  View  Layout  Tools  Font  Graphics  Window  Help
```

Helve-WP 12pt (Type 1)   Doc 1 Pg 1 Ln 1" Pos 1"

1. Press and hold down the **Alt** key.
2. Press the key letter in the menu name.
3. Press the key letter in the command name.

Don't see menus?

If you don't see the menus, press Alt+=. Then open the View menu (press Alt+V) and select the Pull-Down Menus command (press P) to have the menus displayed all the time.

REVIEW

To select a menu command

Use the mouse

The steps in this book show you how to use the keyboard to complete tasks, but keep in mind that you also can use a mouse, if you have one. To use the mouse to select a command, click on the menu name to display that menu; then click on the command you want.

TASK

Exit WordPerfect

before

Oops!
To restart the program, see *TASK: Start WordPerfect*.

1. Press **Alt**+ **F**

   This step opens the File menu. You see a list of File commands.

2. Press **X**.

   This step selects the Exit WP command. You see the Exit WordPerfect dialog box, which prompts you to save any open documents.

3. Press **A**.

   This step tells WordPerfect that you don't want to save the document. The check mark next to the first document is removed. (If there isn't a check mark, skip this step. The option is already deselected.)

4. Press **Enter**.

   This step exits WordPerfect.

24

Easy WordPerfect for Version 6

after

```
C:\>
```

1. Press **Alt**+**F** to open the File menu.
2. Press **X** to select the Exit WP command.
3. Press **A** to tell WordPerfect not to save the document.
4. Press **Enter**.

Save the file
If you want to save the file, see the tasks in the section "Managing Files."

REVIEW

To exit WordPerfect

Try a shortcut
Press Home, F7 to select the Exit WP command.

Entering and Editing Text

25

TASK

Change to Graphics mode

before

```
File  Edit  View  Layout  Tools  Font  Graphics  Window  Help
```

Dutch 801 18pt Roman (Speedo)   Doc 1 Pg 1 Ln 1" Pos 1"

1. Press **Alt+V**.

   This step opens the View menu. You see a list of View commands.

2. Press **G**.

   This step selects the Graphics Mode command. Graphics mode displays font and other formatting changes on-screen. This mode is slower than Text mode, but it's the easiest mode for beginners to use. This book shows the screens in Graphics mode.

Oops!

To return to Text mode, press Alt+V to open the View menu. Then Press T to select Text Mode.

Easy WordPerfect for Version 6

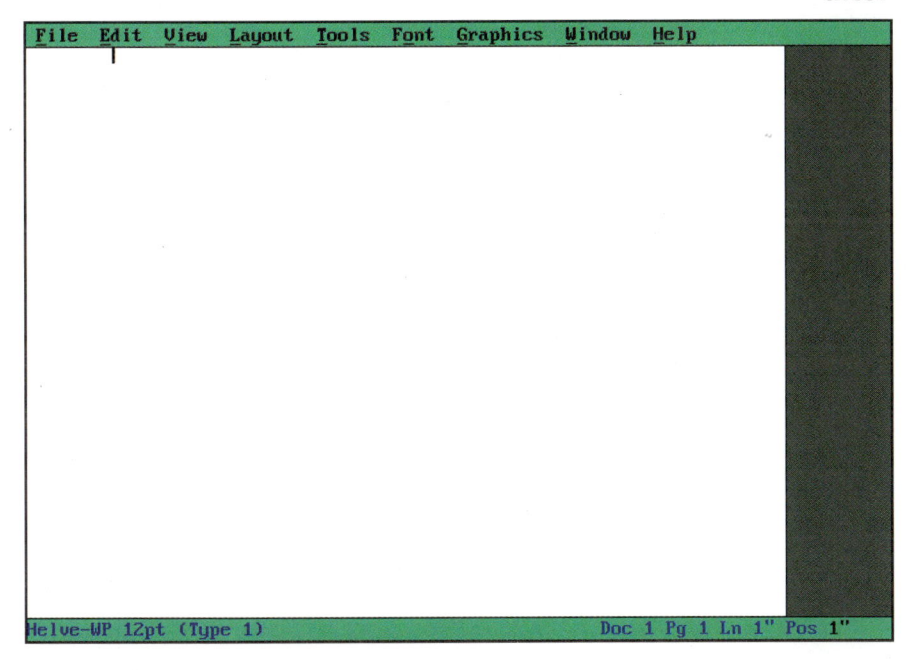

after

1. Press **Alt+V** to open the View menu.
2. Press **G** to select the Graphics Mode command.

REVIEW

To change to Graphics mode

Entering and Editing Text

27

TASK

Get help

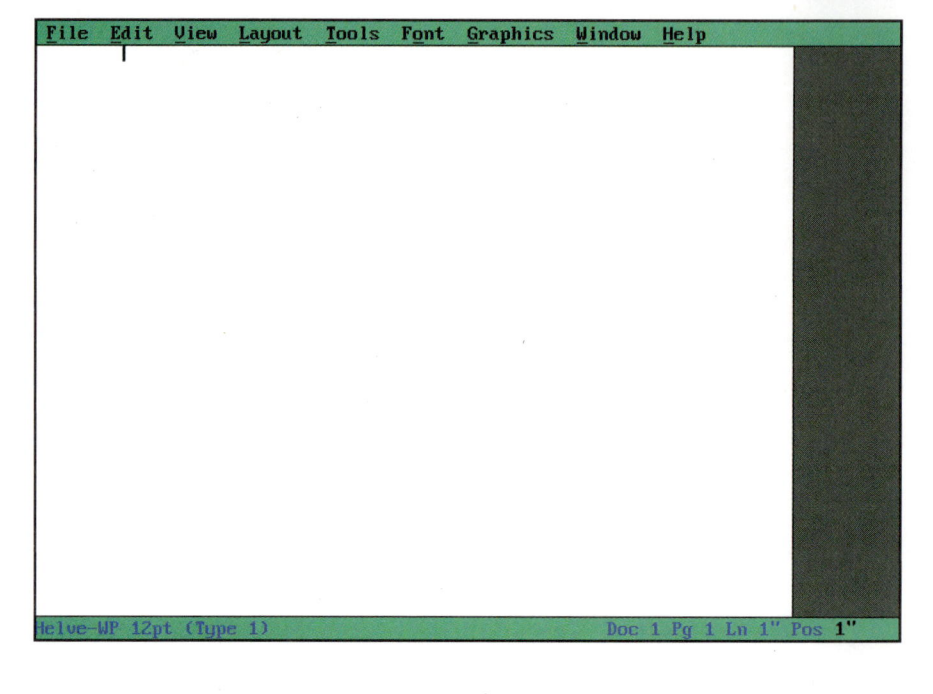

before

[screen image showing WordPerfect menu bar: File Edit View Layout Tools Font Graphics Window Help]

> **Oops!**
> Press the Esc key at any time to exit Help.

1. Press **Alt+H**.

   This step opens the Help menu. You see a list of Help commands.

2. Press **C**.

   This step selects the Contents command. You see a list of Help sections.

3. Press **Enter**.

   This step selects the Index section. You see an index of Help topics.

4. Press the ↓ key until you highlight the **All Merge Codes** topic.

   This step selects the topic you want help on.

5. Press **Enter**.

   This step displays the Help window. The After screen shows this step. When you are finished reading the Help information, close the Help window.

6. Press **Esc**.

   This step closes the Help window.

28   *Easy WordPerfect for Version 6*

after

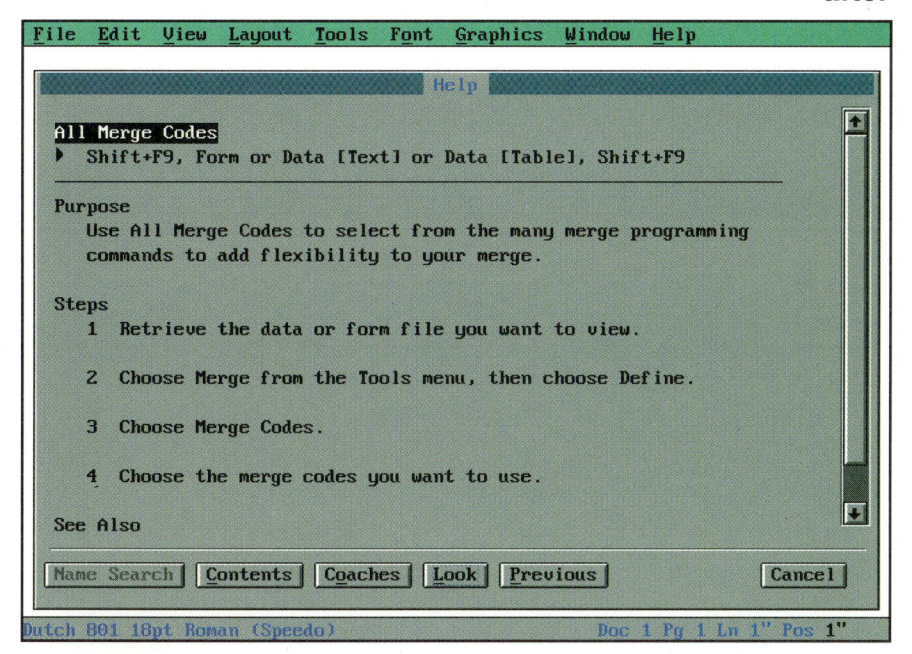

> **Try a shortcut**
>
> Press F1 to select the Contents command.

REVIEW

To get help

1. Press **Alt+H** to open the Help menu.
2. Press **C** to select the Contents command.
3. Press **Enter** to select Index.
4. Use the arrow keys to select the topic you want.
5. Press **Enter**.
6. To exit Help, press **Esc**.

> **Other Help features**
>
> For information on other Help features, see Que's *Using WordPerfect 6.0, Special Edition.*

Entering and Editing Text

29

TASK

Add text

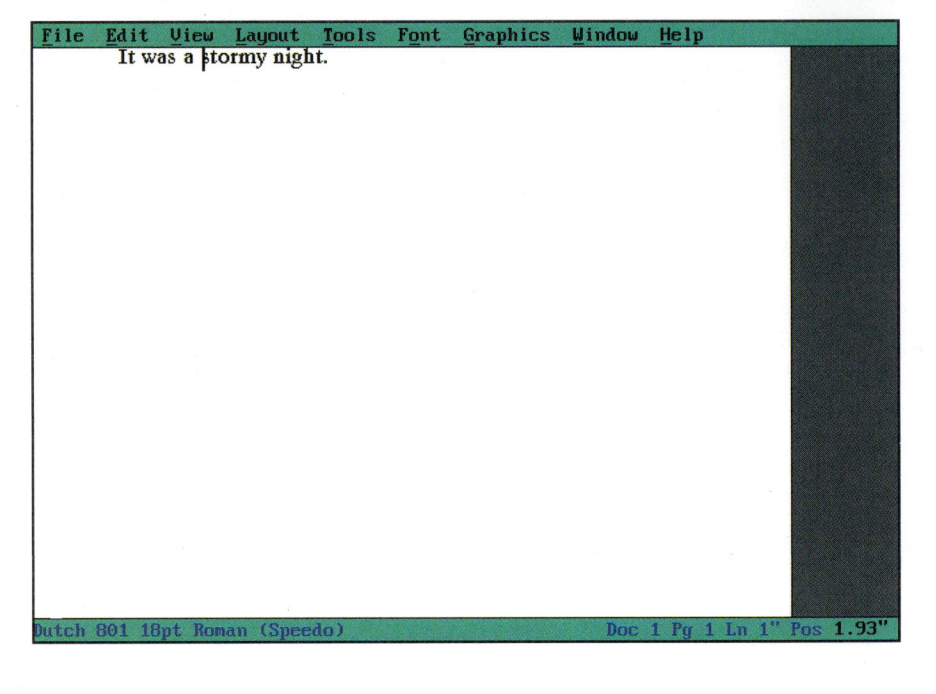

before

```
File  Edit  View  Layout  Tools  Font  Graphics  Window  Help
      It was a |stormy night.




















Dutch 801 18pt Roman (Speedo)              Doc 1 Pg 1 Ln 1" Pos 1.93"
```

Oops!

You can delete a character, a word, a sentence, a paragraph, or any amount of text. See the tasks on deleting text.

1. Use the arrow keys to position the cursor before the word *stormy*.

   You will insert text before this word. Always remember to type any text shown in the Before screen, before you begin the steps.

2. Type **dark and**.

   The text is inserted and pushes existing text right. Note that you do not have to press the Ins key to insert text. Pressing the Ins key puts WordPerfect in Typeover mode. See *TASK: Overwrite text* for more information.

3. Press the **space bar**.

   Pressing the space bar inserts a space after the new text.

Easy WordPerfect for Version 6

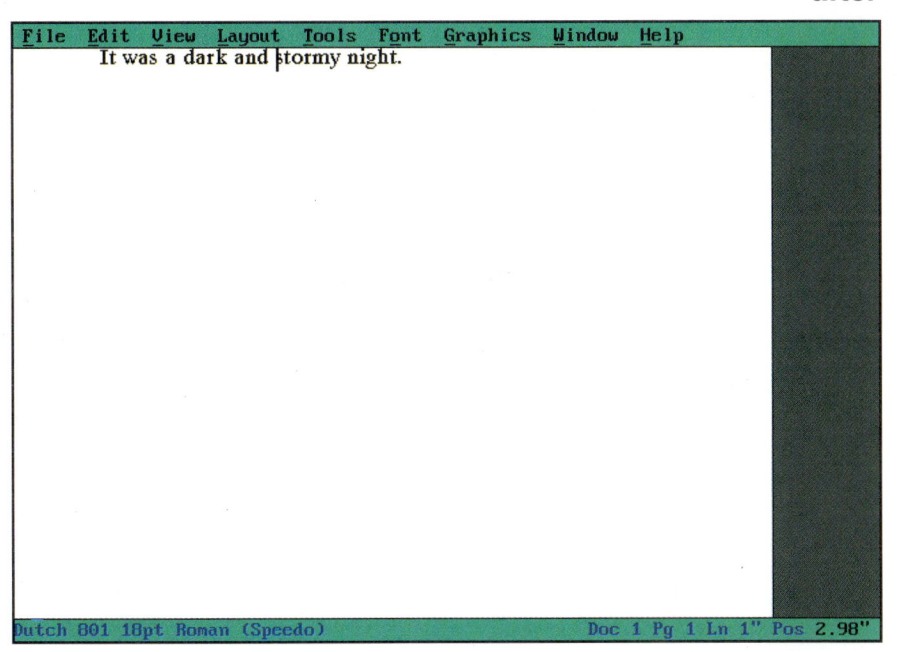

after

1. Position the cursor where you want to insert new text.
2. Type the text.

Overwrite text

To change the existing text, you can type over it with new text. See TASK: Overwrite text.

R E V I E W

To add text

TASK

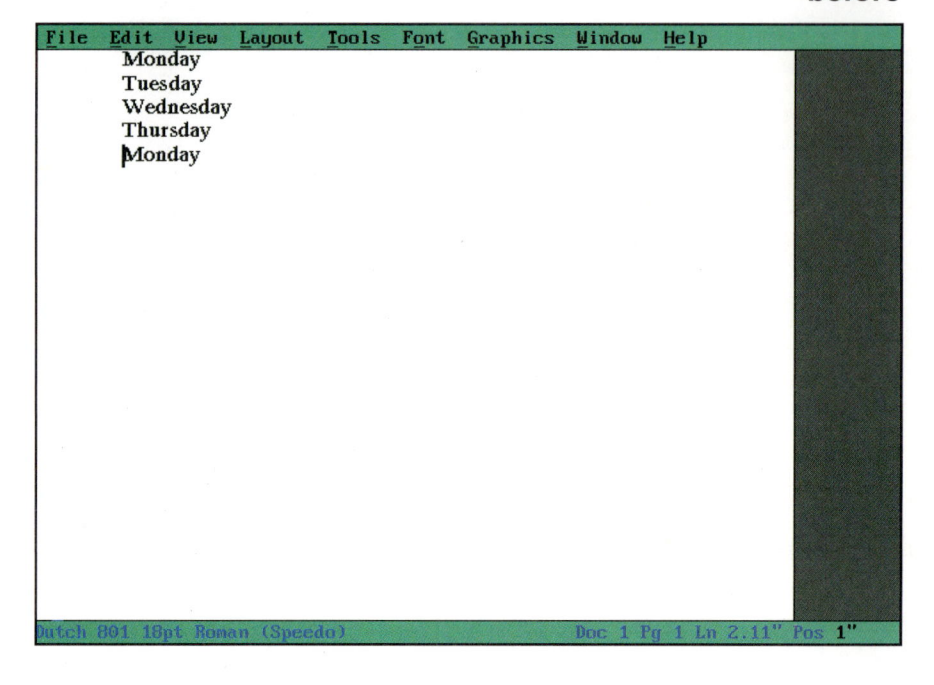

Overwrite text

before

```
File  Edit  View  Layout  Tools  Font  Graphics  Window  Help
     Monday
     Tuesday
     Wednesday
     Thursday
     Monday




Dutch 801 18pt Roman (Speedo)                Doc 1 Pg 1 Ln 2.11" Pos 1"
```

Oops!
If you accidentally overwrite text, press the Ins key to turn off Insert mode. Then retype the original text.

1. Use the arrow keys to move the cursor to the *M* in *Monday* at the bottom of the list of weekdays.

   The *M* is the first letter of the text you want to overwrite.

2. Press **Ins**.

   Pressing the Ins key turns off Insert mode. (WordPerfect automatically uses Insert mode until you turn it off.) The Ins key is a toggle, which means that you press it once to turn off Insert mode, and press it again to turn Insert mode back on again. In the bottom left corner of the screen, you see the message Typeover.

3. Type **Fri**.

   Typing *Fri* replaces *Mon* (the existing text). The word changes from *Monday* to *Friday*.

4. Press **Ins**.

   Pressing the Ins key turns on Insert mode again.

32   *Easy WordPerfect for Version 6*

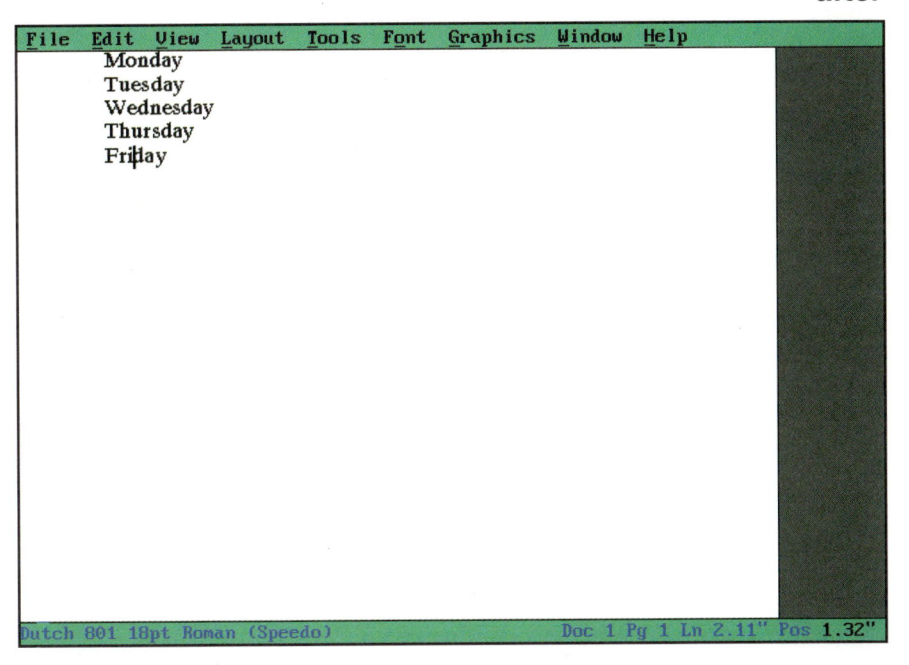

after

```
File  Edit  View  Layout  Tools  Font  Graphics  Window  Help
    Monday
    Tuesday
    Wednesday
    Thursday
    Friday




Dutch 801 18pt Roman (Speedo)                Doc 1 Pg 1 Ln 2.11" Pos 1.32"
```

Insert vs. Typeover mode

In Insert mode (the default mode), WordPerfect inserts new text as you type, but in Typeover mode, WordPerfect overwrites existing text.

REVIEW

To overwrite text

1. Move the cursor to the first character you want to overwrite.
2. Press **Ins**.
3. Type the new text.
4. Press **Ins** again.

Be careful...

Typeover mode can be destructive. Make sure that you do not delete text you want to keep.

Entering and Editing Text

33

TASK

Insert a blank line

before

> File Edit View Layout Tools Font Graphics Window Help
> Dear Loretta:|
>
> Dutch 801 18pt Roman (Speedo)   Doc 1 Pg 1 Ln 1" Pos 2.49"

Oops!
To delete a blank line, move the cursor to that line and press the Del key.

1. Press **Enter**.

   Pressing Enter ends the paragraph and moves the cursor to the beginning of the next line.

2. Press **Enter**.

   Pressing Enter inserts a blank line.

3. Type **Happy Birthday!**.

   This line is the text for the next paragraph.

Easy WordPerfect for Version 6

after

```
File  Edit  View  Layout  Tools  Font  Graphics  Window  Help
      Dear Loretta:

      Happy Birthday!|




Dutch 801 18pt Roman (Speedo)              Doc 1 Pg 1 Ln 1.56" Pos 2.8"
```

1. Move the cursor to the end of the paragraph.
2. Press **Enter twice**.

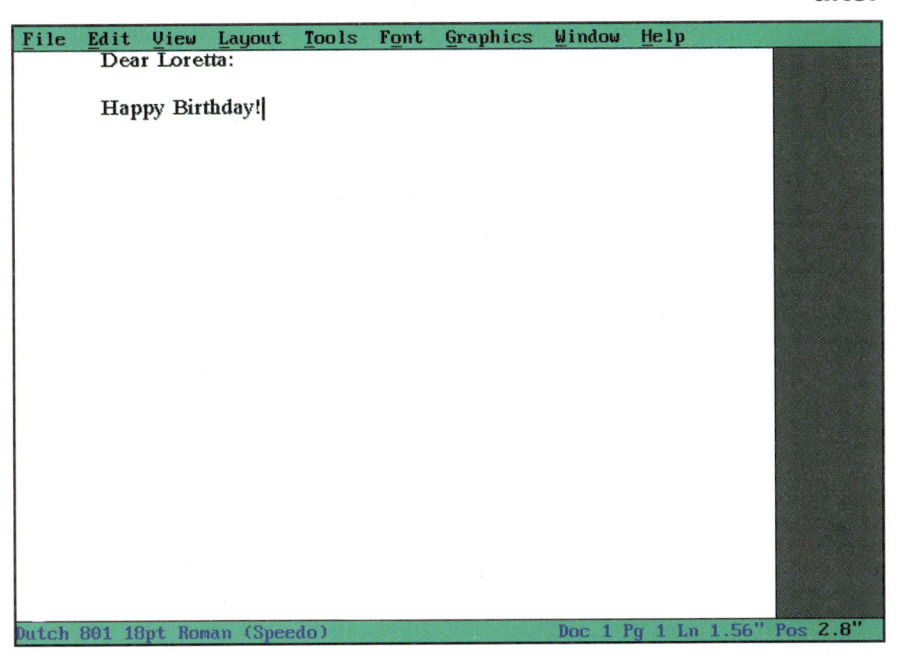

Remember...

You press Enter only to end a paragraph.

REVIEW

To insert a blank line

Entering and Editing Text

TASK

Combine paragraphs

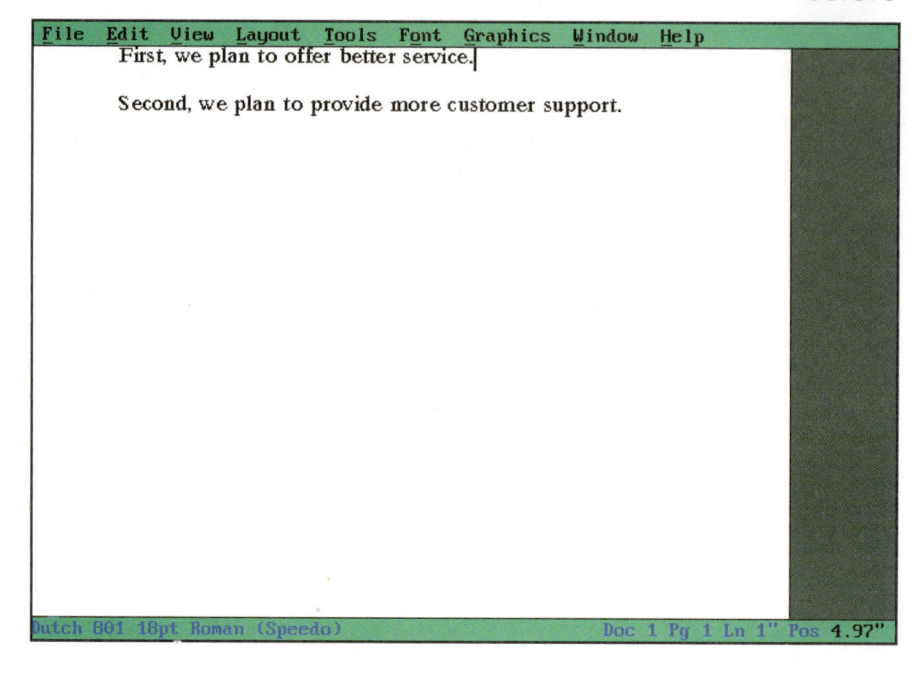

before

> File Edit View Layout Tools Font Graphics Window Help
>
> First, we plan to offer better service.
>
> Second, we plan to provide more customer support.
>
> Dutch 801 18pt Roman (Speedo)   Doc 1 Pg 1 Ln 1" Pos 4.97"

Oops!

To split paragraphs that you have combined, move the cursor to where you want the break. Then press Enter twice.

1. Use the arrow keys to move the cursor anywhere in the line that ends with the word *service*.

   This step moves the cursor to the first paragraph.

2. Press **End**.

   Pressing the End key moves the cursor to the end of the line. The Before screen shows this step.

3. Press **Del twice**.

   Pressing the Del key twice deletes the two hard returns; the second paragraph moves up next to the first paragraph.

4. Press the **space bar**.

   Pressing the space bar inserts a space between the two sentences. WordPerfect readjusts your text on-screen.

Easy WordPerfect for Version 6

after

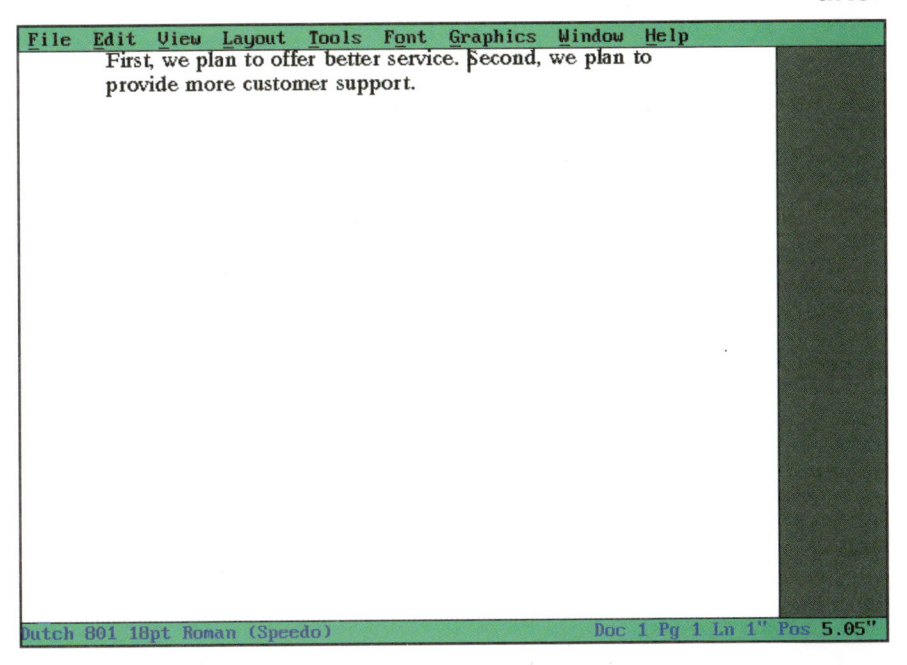

> First, we plan to offer better service. Second, we plan to provide more customer support.

REVIEW

To combine paragraphs

1. Move the cursor to the last line in the first paragraph.
2. Press **End**.
3. Press **Del twice**.
4. Press the **space bar**.

TASK

Insert a page break

before

```
File  Edit  View  Layout  Tools  Font  Graphics  Window  Help
      101 Ways To Drive Your Husband Nuts:
      A Handbook




















Dutch 801 18pt Roman (Speedo)                    Doc 1 Pg 1 Ln 1.28" Pos 2.41"
```

Oops!

To combine pages, move the cursor to just after the page break. Then press Backspace.

1. Use the arrow keys to move the cursor after the words *A Handbook.*

   This step moves the cursor to where you want the new page to begin.

2. Press **Alt**+**L**.

   This step opens the Layout menu. You see a list of Layout commands.

3. Press **A**.

   This step selects the Alignment command. You see another menu with choices.

4. Press **P**.

   This step selects the Hard Page command and inserts a hard page break into the document. You see a double line on-screen. When you print the document, a new page begins where you inserted the page break. WordPerfect does not print the double line.

Easy WordPerfect for Version 6

after

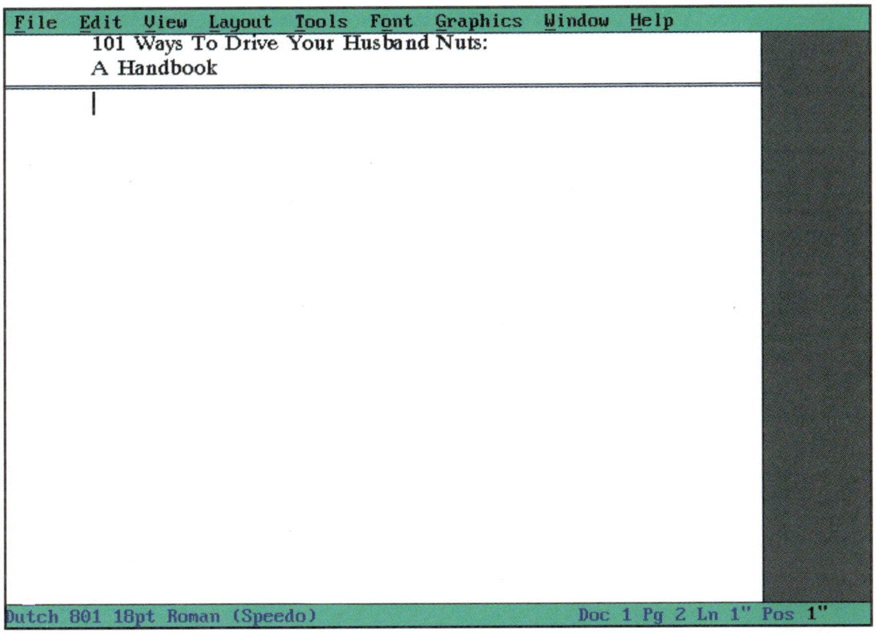
File Edit View Layout Tools Font Graphics Window Help
101 Ways To Drive Your Husband Nuts:
A Handbook
Dutch 801 18pt Roman (Speedo)
Doc 1 Pg 2 Ln 1" Pos 1"

Soft page break vs. hard page break

WordPerfect automatically inserts soft page breaks at the end of each page and adjusts them as you change the text. You insert a hard page break manually, and when you make changes, the break remains in the same place.

REVIEW

To insert a page break

1. Move the cursor to where you want the new page to begin.
2. Press **Alt+L** to open the Layout menu.
3. Press **A** to select the Alignment command.
4. Press **P** to select the Hard Page command.

Try a shortcut

Press Ctrl+Enter to insert a page break.

Go to a page

before

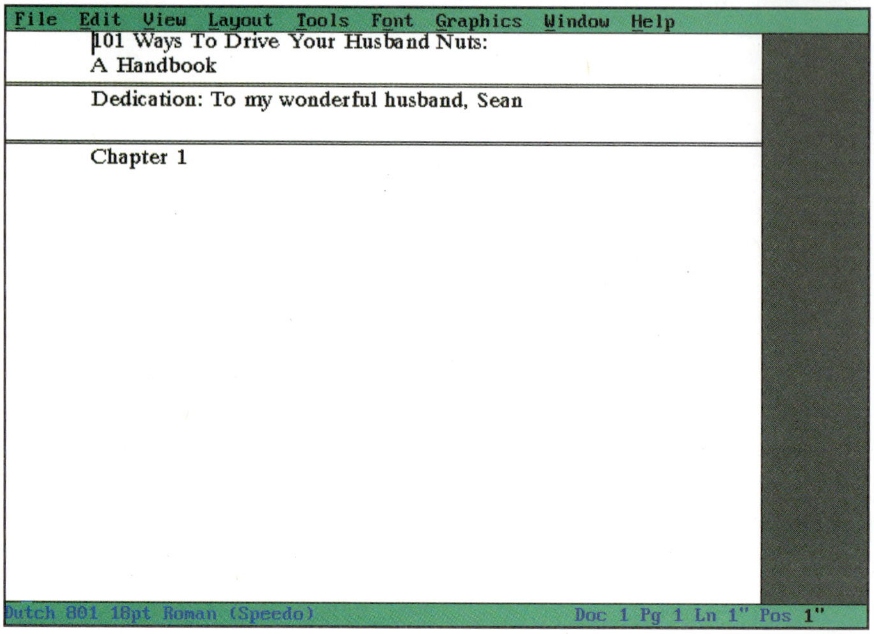
File Edit View Layout Tools Font Graphics Window Help
101 Ways To Drive Your Husband Nuts:
A Handbook
Dedication: To my wonderful husband, Sean
Chapter 1
Dutch 801 18pt Roman (Speedo)
Doc 1 Pg 1 Ln 1" Pos 1"

1. Press **Alt+E**.

   This step opens the Edit menu. You see a list of Edit commands.

2. Press **G**.

   This step selects the Go To command and displays the Go to dialog box.

3. Press **3**.

   Typing *3* tells WordPerfect to go to page 3.

4. Press **Enter**.

   Pressing Enter moves the cursor to page 3. The document is scrolled so that the top of page 3 is at the top of the screen.

Oops!

To go to the top of the document, press Home, Home, Home, ↑ key.

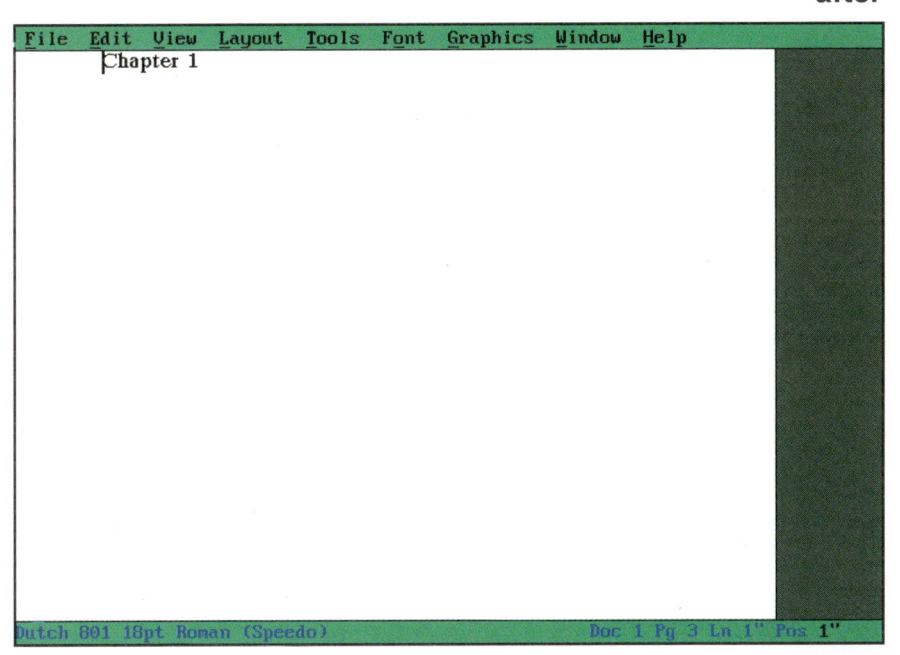

after

1. Press **Alt+E** to open the Edit menu.
2. Press **G** to select the Go To command.
3. Type the page number where you want the cursor to go.
4. Press **Enter**.

Entering and Editing Text

Try a shortcut
Press Ctrl+Home to select the Go To command.

REVIEW

To go to a page

41

TASK

Delete a character

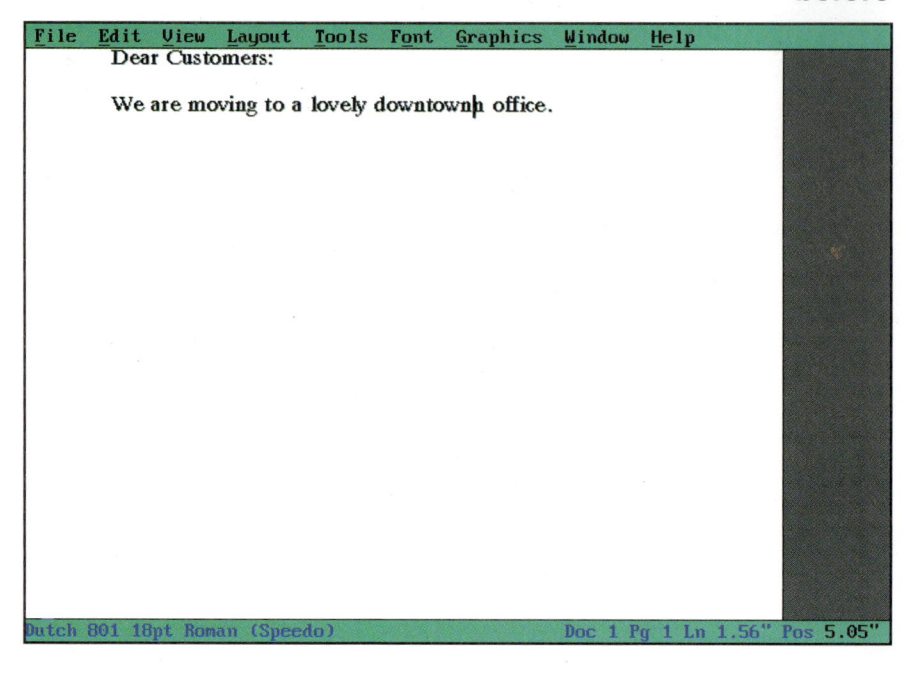

before

```
File  Edit  View  Layout  Tools  Font  Graphics  Window  Help
Dear Customers:

We are moving to a lovely downtownh office.




















Dutch 801 18pt Roman (Speedo)                    Doc 1 Pg 1 Ln 1.56" Pos 5.05"
```

Oops!
To restore a deleted character, see *TASK: Undelete text*.

1. Use the arrow keys to move the cursor before the last *n* in *downtownn*.

   The cursor is located to the left of the character you want to delete (in Graphics mode).

2. Press **Del**.

   Pressing the Del key deletes the character to the right of the cursor.

42

Easy WordPerfect for Version 6

after

[Screenshot: WordPerfect-style document window showing "Dear Customers:" and "We are moving to a lovely downtown office." with cursor between "downtown" and "office". Status bar: Dutch 801 18pt Roman (Speedo)   Doc 1 Pg 1 Ln 1.56" Pos 5.05"]

1. Move the cursor to the left of the character you want to delete.
2. Press **Del**.

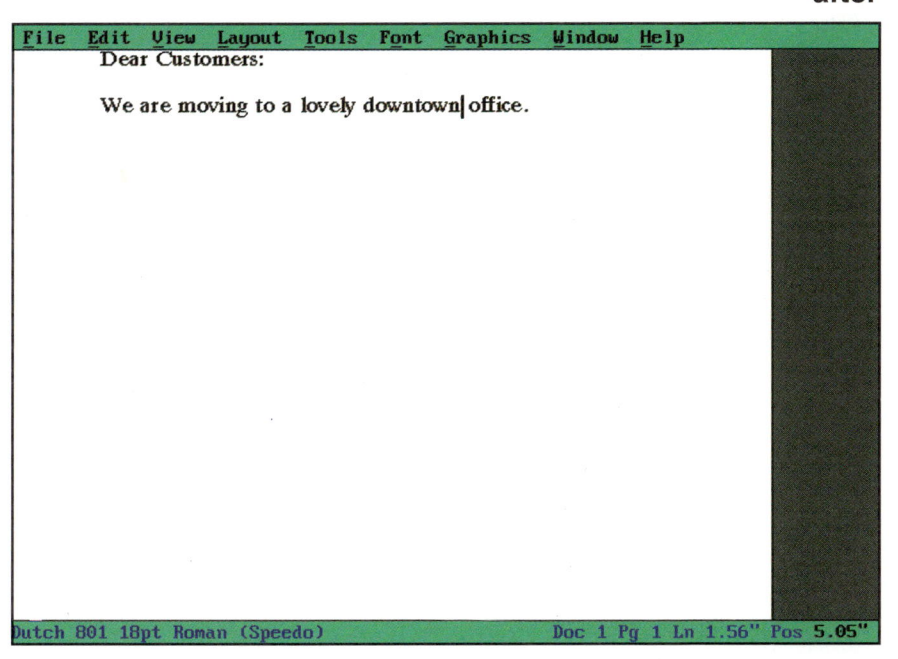

Use another method

You also can position the cursor to the right of the character you want to delete and press the Backspace key.

REVIEW

To delete a character

Delete a block

To delete a block of text, see *TASK: Delete a block*.

Entering and Editing Text

43

TASK

Delete a word

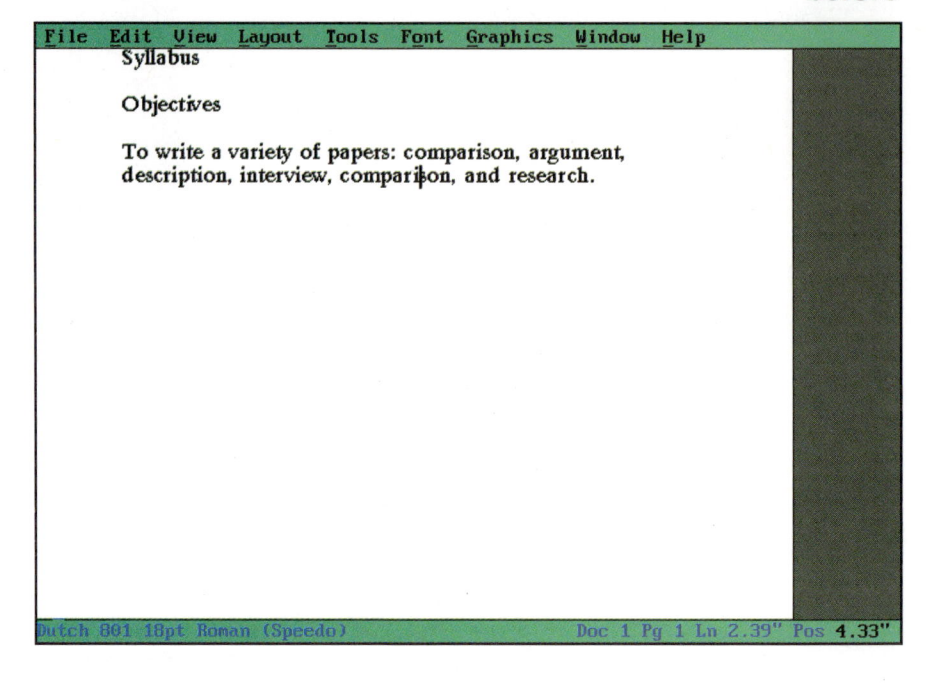

before

> File Edit View Layout Tools Font Graphics Window Help
>
> Syllabus
>
> Objectives
>
> To write a variety of papers: comparison, argument, description, interview, comparison, and research.
>
> Dutch 801 18pt Roman (Speedo)   Doc 1 Pg 1 Ln 2.39" Pos **4.33"**

Oops!
See TASK: Undelete text for instructions on restoring a deleted word.

1. Use the arrow keys to move the cursor anywhere within the word *comparison* on the last line.

   The cursor is positioned on the word you want to delete. You can position the cursor anywhere within the word you want to delete.

2. Press **Ctrl+Backspace**.

   Pressing the Ctrl+Backspace key combination deletes the word *comparison* and the comma and space after it. The remaining text moves left to fill in the gap.

Easy WordPerfect for Version 6

after

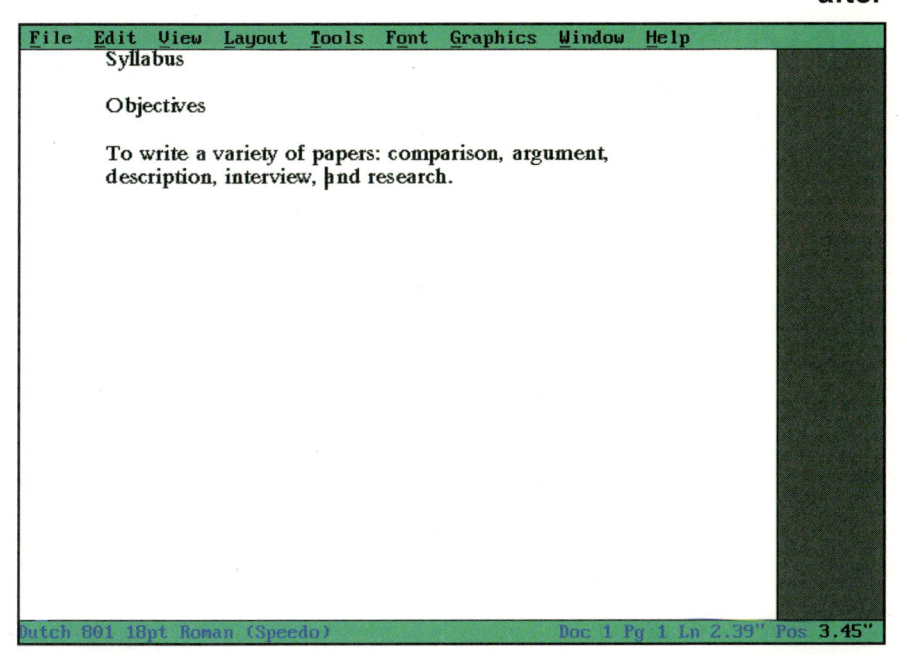

```
File  Edit  View  Layout  Tools  Font  Graphics  Window  Help
      Syllabus

      Objectives

      To write a variety of papers: comparison, argument,
      description, interview, and research.




Dutch 801 18pt Roman (Speedo)              Doc 1 Pg 1 Ln 2.39" Pos 3.45"
```

Delete a block

To delete a block of text, see *TASK: Delete a block.*

REVIEW

1. Move the cursor within the word you want to delete.
2. Press **Ctrl+Backspace**.

To delete a word

Entering and Editing Text

45

TASK

Select a block

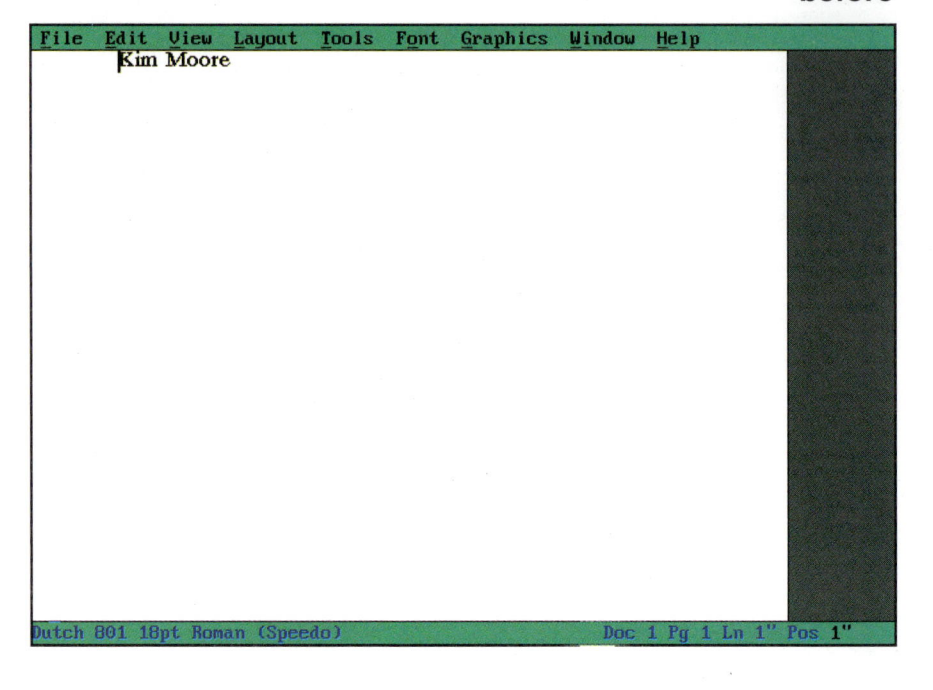

before

```
File  Edit  View  Layout  Tools  Font  Graphics  Window  Help
      Kim Moore













Dutch 801 18pt Roman (Speedo)                    Doc 1 Pg 1 Ln 1" Pos 1"
```

Oops!
To turn off Block mode, press the Esc key.

1. Move the cursor to the left of the *K* in *Kim Moore*.

   This step places the cursor where you want to start blocking text.

2. Press **Alt**+**E**.

   This step opens the Edit menu. You see a list of Edit commands.

3. Press **B**.

   This step selects the Block command.

   You see the message `Block on` in the bottom left corner of the screen, which tells you that you're in Block mode.

4. Press the → key until you highlight the line.

   Pressing the → key highlights the block you want to select. Once a block is selected, you can perform many operations on it—copy it, move it, delete it, change the font, and so on.

46   *Easy WordPerfect for Version 6*

after

Use the mouse

Blocking text with a mouse might be easier, if you have one. Click to the left of the text you want to block, press and hold down the left mouse button, and drag the mouse until the text is highlighted. Then release the mouse button.

REVIEW

To select a block

1. Move the cursor to the first character in the block you want to select.
2. Press **Alt**+**E** to open the Edit menu.
3. Press **B** to select the Block command.
4. Use the arrow keys to highlight the block.

Try a shortcut

Press Alt+F4 to select the Block command.

Entering and Editing Text

TASK

Select a paragraph

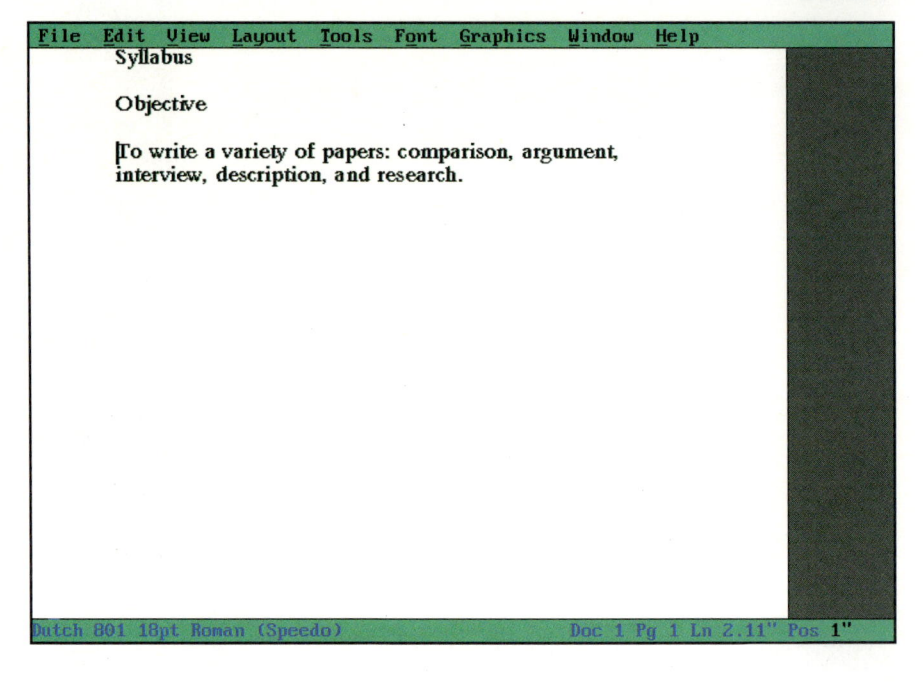

before

```
File  Edit  View  Layout  Tools  Font  Graphics  Window  Help
    Syllabus

    Objective

    |To write a variety of papers: comparison, argument,
    interview, description, and research.
```

Dutch 801 18pt Roman (Speedo)   Doc 1 Pg 1 Ln 2.11" Pos 1"

Oops!
To deselect the paragraph and turn off Block mode, press the Esc key.

1. Move the cursor to the left of the *T* in the paragraph that begins with the words *To write*.

    This step places the cursor where you want to start blocking text.

2. Press **Alt+E**.

    This step opens the Edit menu. You see a list of Edit commands.

3. Press **S**.

    This step selects the Select command. You see a menu of additional choices.

4. Press **P**.

    This step selects the Paragraph command. WordPerfect selects the entire paragraph and turns on Block mode.

Easy WordPerfect for Version 6

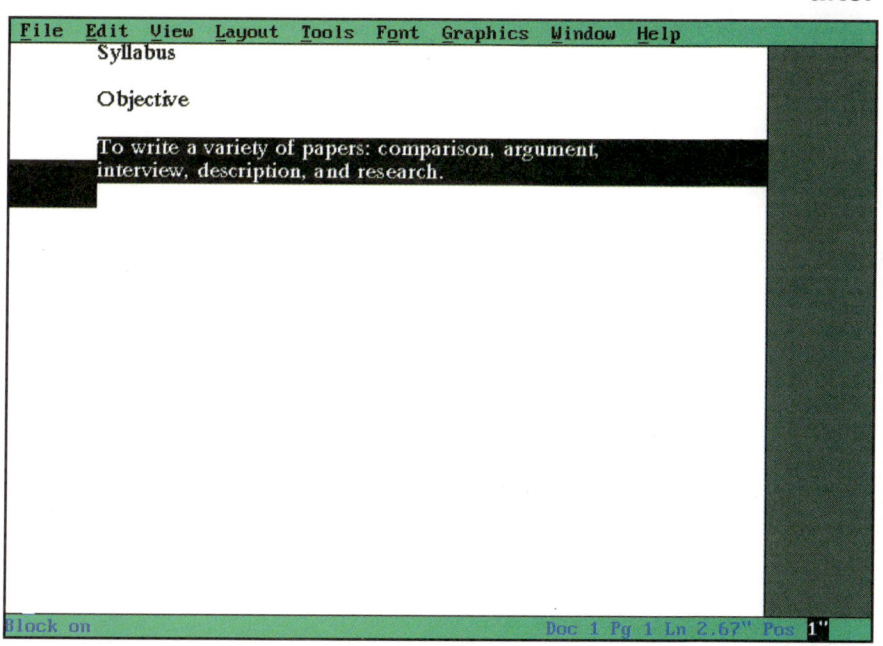

after

REVIEW

To select a paragraph

1. Move the cursor to the first character in the paragraph you want to select.

2. Press **Alt**+**E** to open the Edit menu.

3. Press **S** to select the Select command.

4. Press **P** to select the Paragraph command.

Select a sentence or page

Use this same procedure to select a sentence or page, but in step 4, press S to select a sentence or A to select a page.

Entering and Editing Text

TASK

Delete a block

before

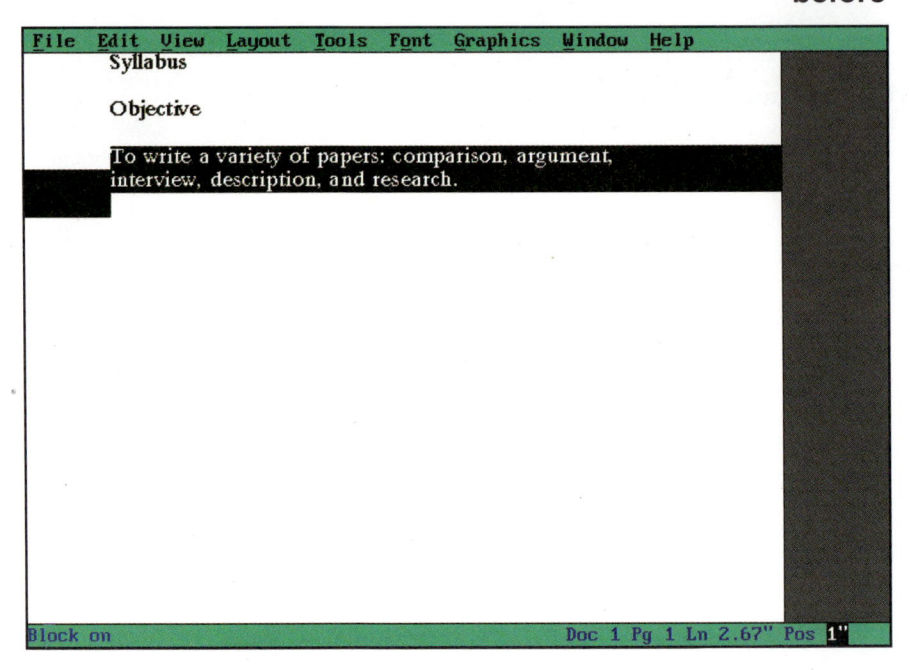

> File Edit View Layout Tools Font Graphics Window Help
> Syllabus
>
> Objective
>
> To write a variety of papers: comparison, argument, interview, description, and research.
>
> Block on   Doc 1 Pg 1 Ln 2.67" Pos 1"

Oops!
To restore deleted text, see *TASK: Undelete text*.

1. Block the paragraph that begins with the words *To write*.

   This step selects the text you want to delete. For help on blocking text, see *TASK: Select a block*.

2. Press **Del**.

   This step deletes the block.

50   *Easy WordPerfect for Version 6*

after

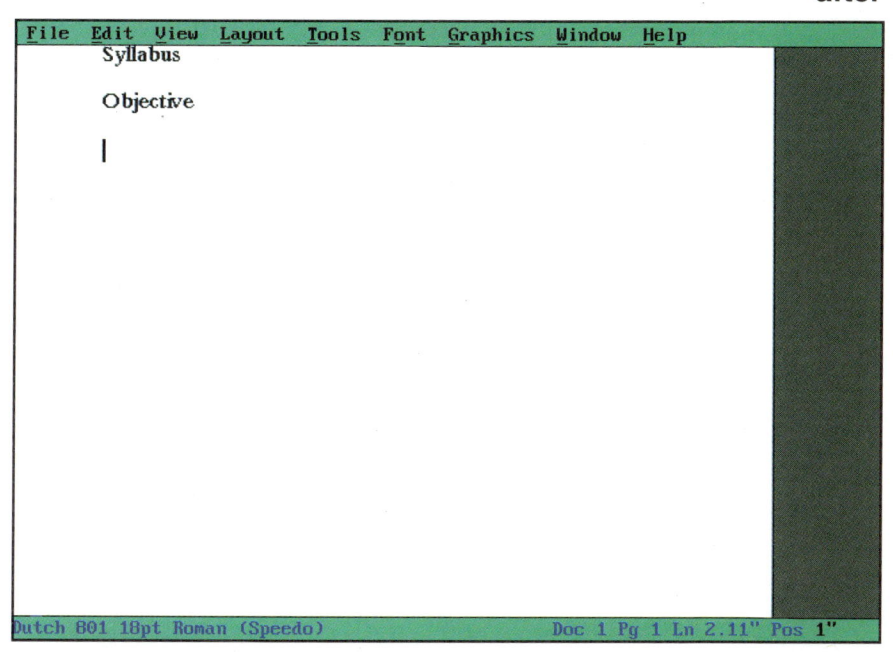

> **Delete a character**
>
> To delete the character left of the cursor, press the Del key. To delete the character right of the cursor, press the Backspace key.

REVIEW

1. Block the text you want to delete.
2. Press **Del**.

To delete a block

Entering and Editing Text

51

TASK

Undelete text

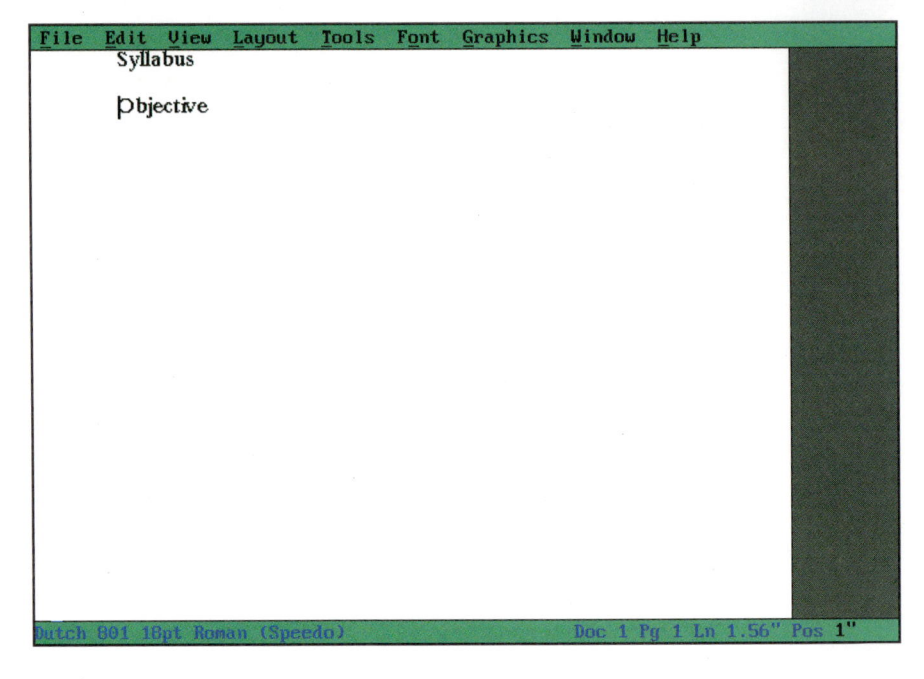

before

[screen showing File Edit View Layout Tools Font Graphics Window Help menu, with "Syllabus" and "Objective" text, status bar: Dutch 801 18pt Roman (Speedo)   Doc 1 Pg 1 Ln 1.56" Pos 1"]

Oops!

If you decide that you don't want to restore the text, simply delete it again.

1. Use the arrow keys to move the cursor to the word *Objective*.

   You will delete the word *Objective* and then undelete it.

2. Press **Ctrl+Backspace**.

   Pressing the Ctrl+Backspace key combination deletes the word *Objective*.

3. Press **Alt+E**.

   This step opens the Edit menu. You see a list of Edit commands.

4. Press **N**.

   This step selects the Undelete command. You see the Undelete dialog box, which enables you to restore this deletion or a previous deletion. The After screen shows this step.

5. Press **R**.

   This step selects the Restore option. The previously deleted text reappears on-screen at the cursor's location.

Easy WordPerfect for Version 6

after

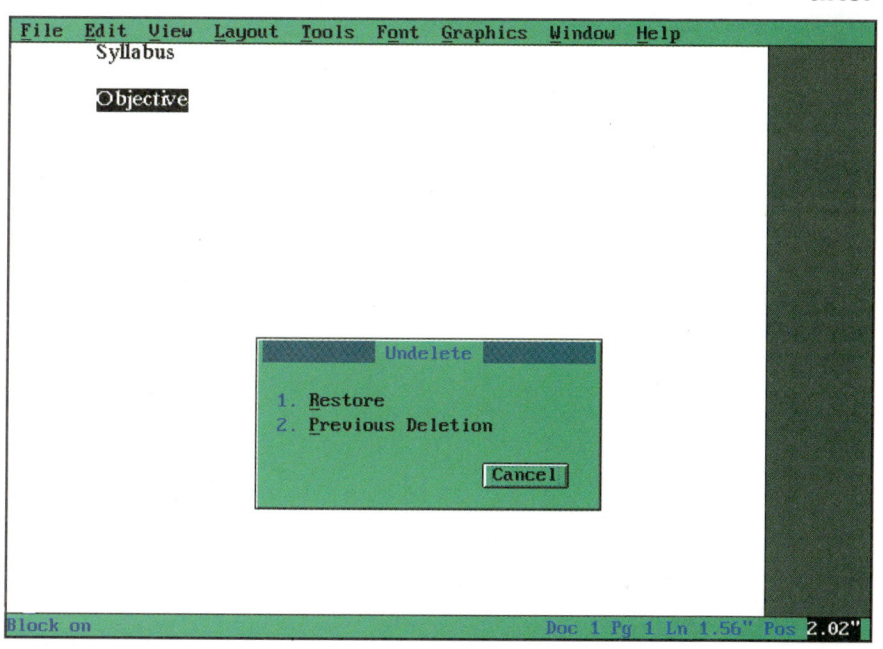

What can you restore?

You can restore the last three sections of text you have deleted. See Que's *Using WordPerfect 6.0, Special Edition.*

REVIEW

To undelete text

1. Move the cursor to the spot where you want the restored text to appear.

2. Press **Alt**+**E** to open the Edit menu.

3. Press **N** to select the Undelete command.

4. Press **R** to select the Restore option.

Try a shortcut

To select the Undelete command, press the Esc key.

Entering and Editing Text

53

TASK

Undo a command

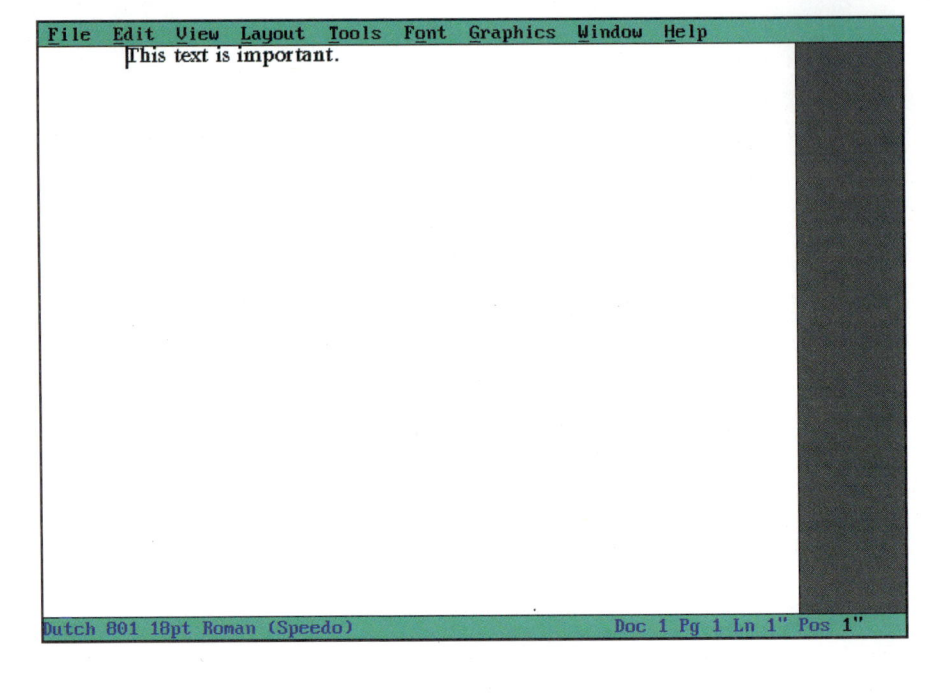

before

```
File  Edit  View  Layout  Tools  Font  Graphics  Window  Help
This text is important.




Dutch 801 18pt Roman (Speedo)              Doc 1 Pg 1 Ln 1" Pos 1"
```

Oops!

To undo the undo, select the Undo command again.

1. Block the text *This text is important*.

   This step blocks text. You will use the Cut command to remove this text from the document; then you will undo that command.

2. Press **Alt**+**E**.

   This step opens the Edit menu and displays a list of Edit commands.

3. Press **T**.

   This step selects the Cut command. WordPerfect cuts the text from the document. To undo the command, follow the next steps.

4. Press **Alt**+**E**.

   This step opens the Edit menu and displays a list of Edit commands.

5. Press **U**.

   This step selects the Undo command. The text is restored to the document.

after

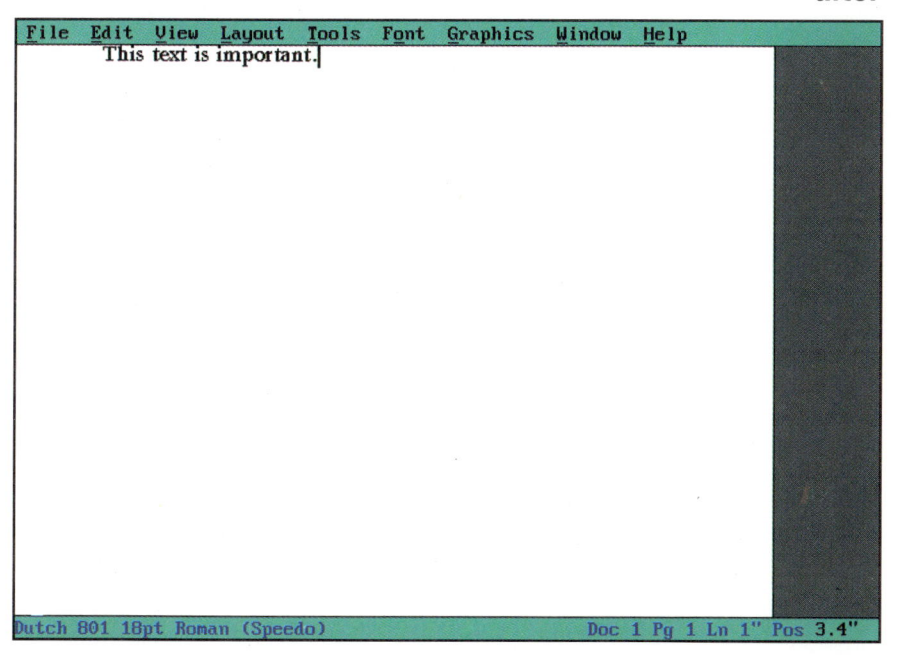

```
File  Edit  View  Layout  Tools  Font  Graphics  Window  Help
      This text is important.




















Dutch 801 18pt Roman (Speedo)                    Doc 1 Pg 1 Ln 1" Pos 3.4"
```

Rules for Undo

You can undo most editing and formatting commands. You cannot undo any File menu commands (such as saving a file). And you can undo only the last command you selected.

REVIEW

To undo a command

1. Press **Alt**+**E** to open the Edit menu.
2. Press **U** to select the Undo command.

Try a shortcut

Press Ctrl+Z to select the Undo command.

Entering and Editing Text

55

TASK

Copy a block

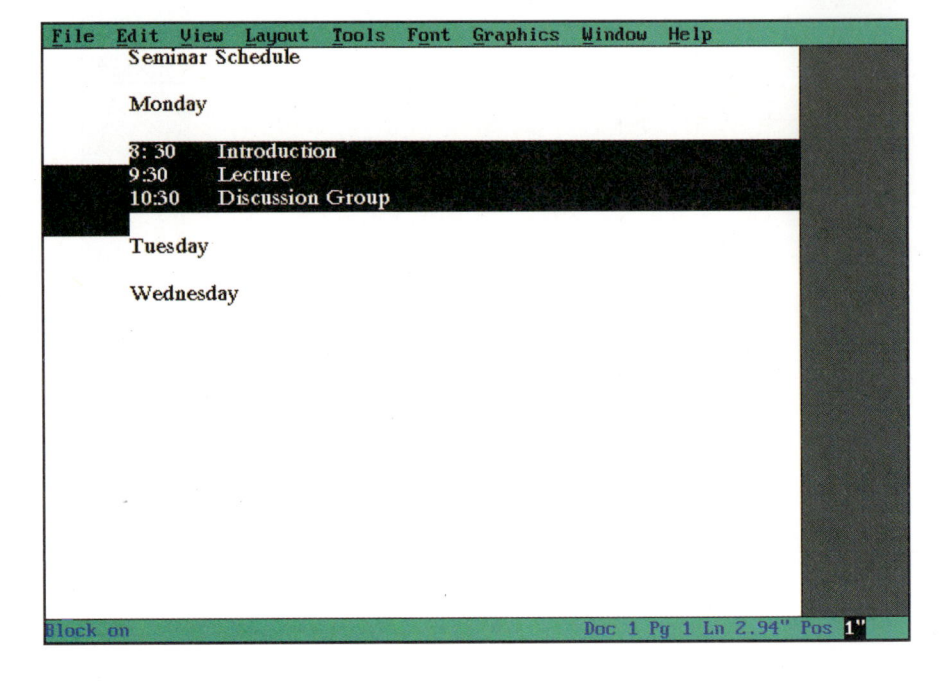

before

```
File  Edit  View  Layout  Tools  Font  Graphics  Window  Help
Seminar Schedule

Monday

    8:30    Introduction
    9:30    Lecture
    10:30   Discussion Group

Tuesday

Wednesday
```

Block on   Doc 1 Pg 1 Ln 2.94" Pos 1"

Oops!
To undo the copy, press Ctrl+Z to select the Undo command. See TASK: Undo a command.

1. Block four lines of text, starting with *8:30*.

   This step blocks the text you want to copy. For help on blocking text, see *TASK: Select a block*.

2. Press **Alt**+**E**.

   This step opens the Edit menu. You see a list of Edit commands.

3. Press **C**.

   This step selects the Copy command and makes a copy of the blocked text.

4. Press the ↓ key **twice**.

   Pressing the ↓ key moves the cursor to the location where you want the copied block of text to appear.

5. Press **Alt**+**E**.

   This step opens the Edit menu, which displays the Edit commands.

6. Press **P**.

   This step selects the Paste command and pastes the copied block of text to the new location.

Easy WordPerfect for Version 6

after

```
File  Edit  View  Layout  Tools  Font  Graphics  Window  Help
     Seminar Schedule

     Monday

     8: 30      Introduction
     9:30       Lecture
     10:30      Discussion Group

     Tuesday

     8: 30      Introduction
     9:30       Lecture
     10:30      Discussion Group

     Wednesday




Dutch 801 18pt Roman (Speedo)        Doc 1 Pg 1 Ln 3.78" Pos 1"
```

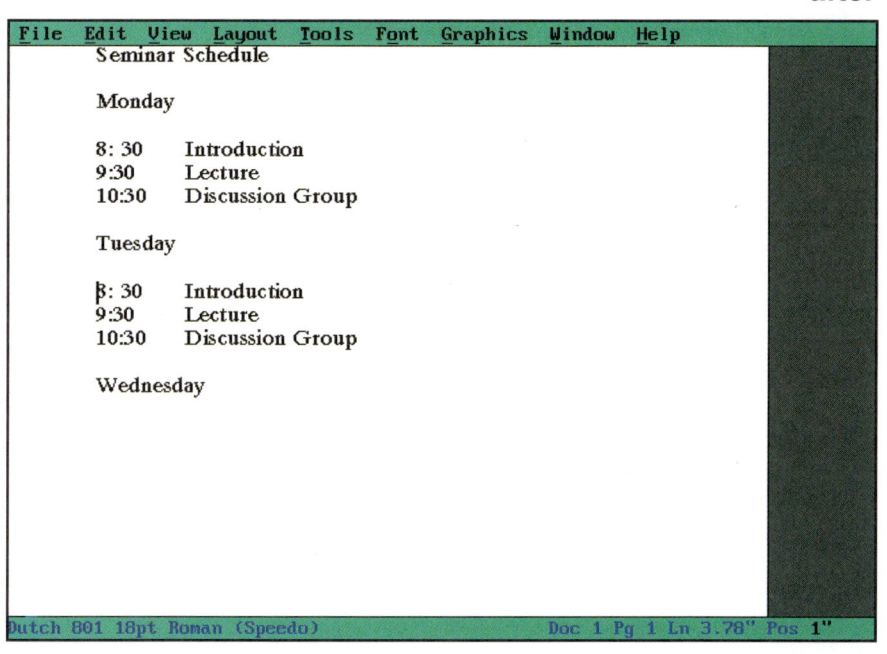

Select the wrong block?

If you select the wrong block, press the Esc key and start again.

REVIEW

To copy a block

1. Block the text you want to copy.
2. Press **Alt**+**E** to open the Edit menu.
3. Press **C** to select the Copy command.
4. Move the cursor to where you want the copy to appear.
5. Press **Alt**+**E** to open the Edit menu.
6. Press **P** to select the Paste command.

Try a shortcut

Press Ctrl+C to select the Copy command. Press Ctrl+V to select the Paste command.

Entering and Editing Text   57

TASK

Move a block

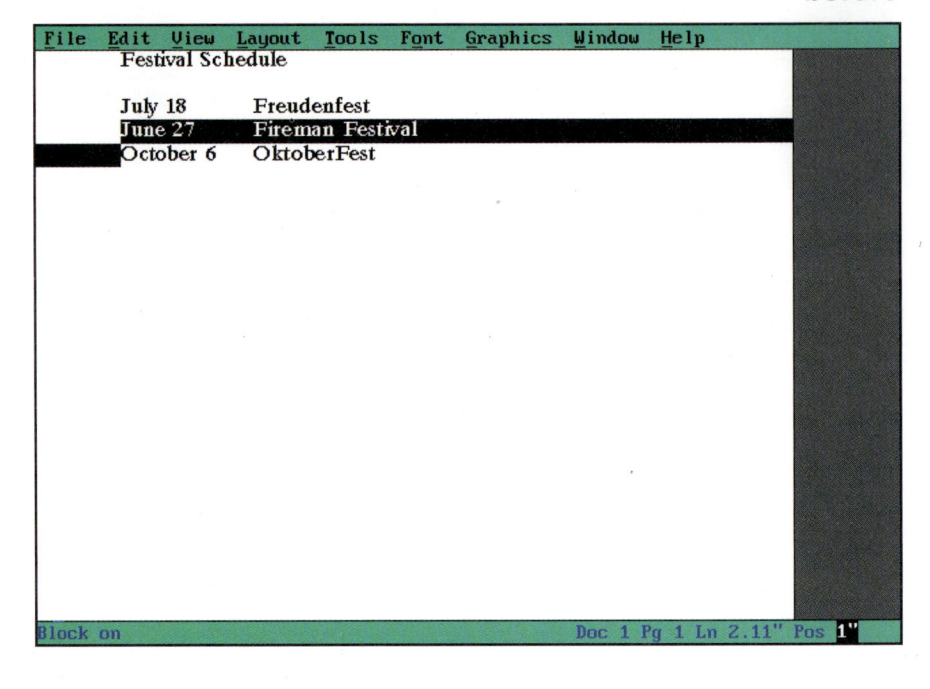

before

Oops!

To undo the cut, press Ctrl+Z to select the Undo command. See *TASK: Undo a command.*

1. Block the paragraph that begins with *June*.

   This step selects the text you want to move. For help on blocking text, see *TASK: Select a paragraph.* Be sure to select the entire paragraph—not just the text.

2. Press **Alt**+**E**.

   This step opens the Edit menu. You see a list of Edit commands.

3. Press **T**.

   This step selects the Cut command and removes the paragraph from the document.

4. Press the ↑ key.

   This step moves the cursor to the location where you want to place the cut block of text.

5. Press **Alt**+**E**.

   This step opens the Edit menu, which displays the Edit commands.

6. Press **P**.

   This step selects the Paste command and pastes the cut block of text to the new location.

Easy WordPerfect for Version 6

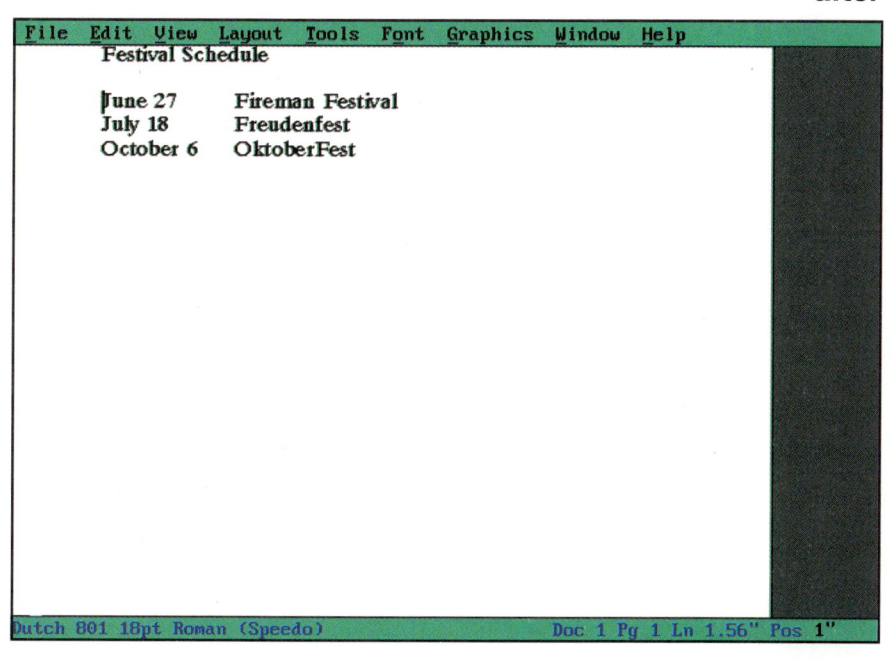

after

> **Select the wrong block?**
>
> If you select the wrong block, press the Esc key and start again.

REVIEW

To move a block

1. Block the text you want to move.
2. Press **Alt**+**E** to open the Edit menu.
3. Press **T** to select the Cut command.
4. Move the cursor to where you want the text to appear.
5. Press **Alt**+**E** to open the Edit menu.
6. Press **P** to select the Paste command.

> **Try a shortcut**
>
> Press Ctrl+X to select the Cut command. Press Ctrl+V to select the Paste command.

Entering and Editing Text   59

Files

This section covers the following tasks:

Save a document for the first time

Save a document with a new name

Save and clear a document

Abandon a document

Open a document

Create a new document

Open more than one document

Switch to another open document

Display all open documents

TASK

Save a document for the first time

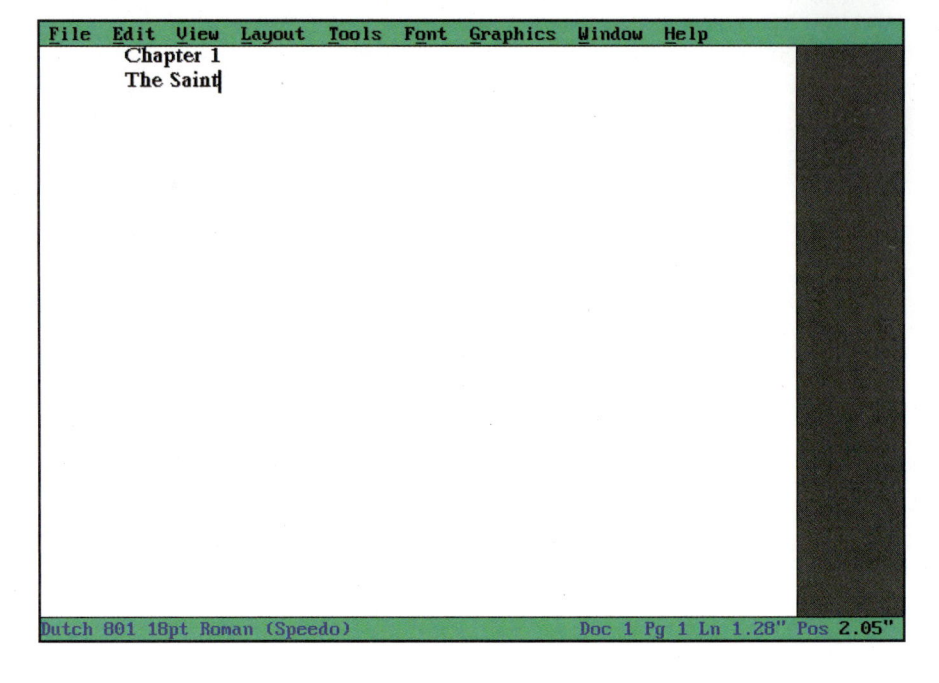

before

[Screenshot of WordPerfect screen showing "Chapter 1" and "The Saint" text]

Oops!
If you do not want to save the file, press the Esc key twice to clear the dialog box.

1. Press **Alt+F**.

   This step opens the File menu. You see a list of File commands.

2. Press **S**.

   This step selects the Save command. You see the Save Document dialog box. Here is where you assign a name to the file.

3. Type **CHAP01.DOC**.

   CHAP01.DOC is the name of the file you are saving. File names consist of two parts: a root name and an extension. The root name can have from one to eight characters; use the root name to describe the file's contents. The optional extension can have from one to three characters. If you use an extension, you must separate it from the root name with a period.

4. Press **Enter**.

   Pressing Enter confirms the name and saves the document to disk. The document remains on-screen so that you can continue working. In the bottom left corner, you see the file name you assigned.

Easy WordPerfect for Version 6

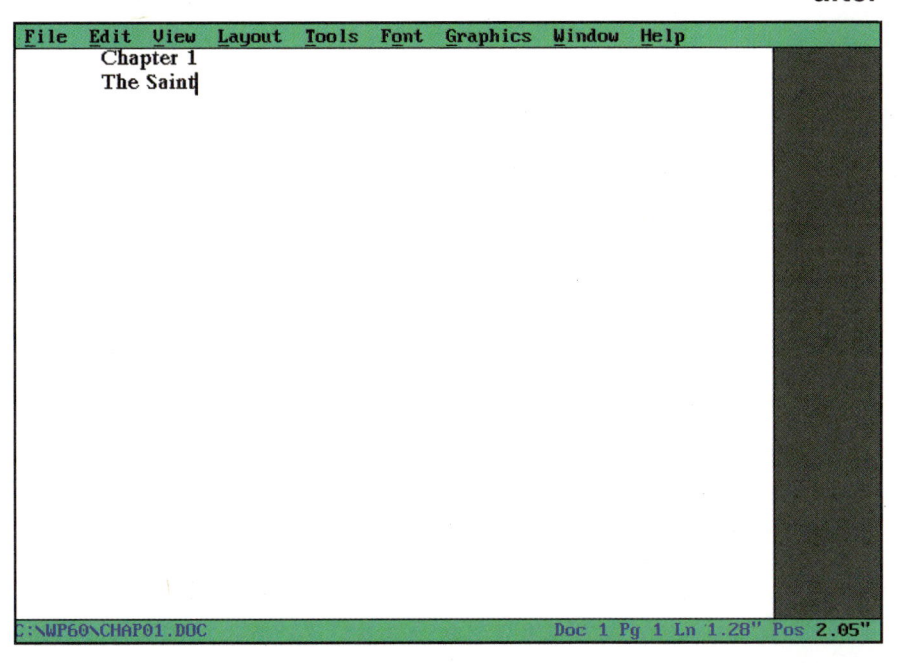

after

1. Press **Alt+F** to open the File menu.
2. Press **S** to select the Save command.
3. Type a file name.
4. Press **Enter**.

Save an existing document

To save a document you've saved before, press Alt+F and then S. This selects the Save command and saves the file. Once you name a file, you aren't prompted to name the file again. The file is saved with the same name and replaces the older version.

REVIEW

To save a document for the first time

Save the document with a different name?

To save the document with a different name, see TASK: Save a document with a new name.

Files

TASK

Save a document with a new name

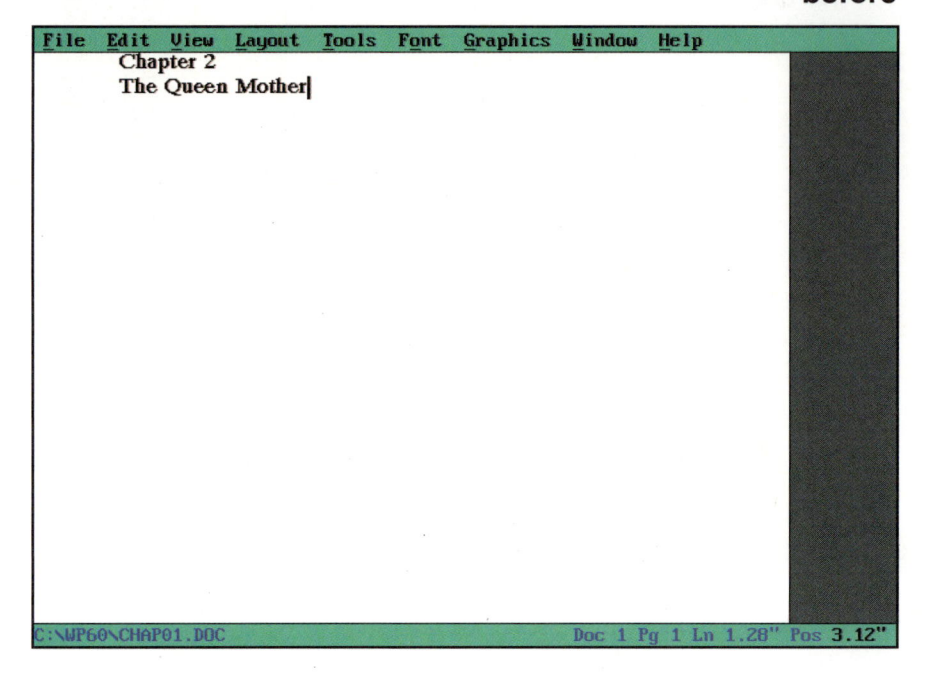

before

[screenshot of WordPerfect showing "Chapter 2 / The Queen Mother" with status bar C:\WP60\CHAP01.DOC]

Oops!
If you do not want to save the file, press the Esc key twice to clear the dialog box.

1. Press **Alt**+**F**.

   This step opens the File menu. You see a list of File commands.

2. Press **A**.

   This step selects the Save As command. You see the Save Document dialog box. The current name is listed in the Filename text box.

3. Type **CHAP02.DOC**.

   CHAP02.DOC is the new name.

4. Press **Enter**.

   Pressing Enter confirms the name and saves the document to disk. The document remains on-screen so that you can continue working. In the bottom left corner, you see the file name you assigned. The original document (the one with the old name) remains intact on-disk.

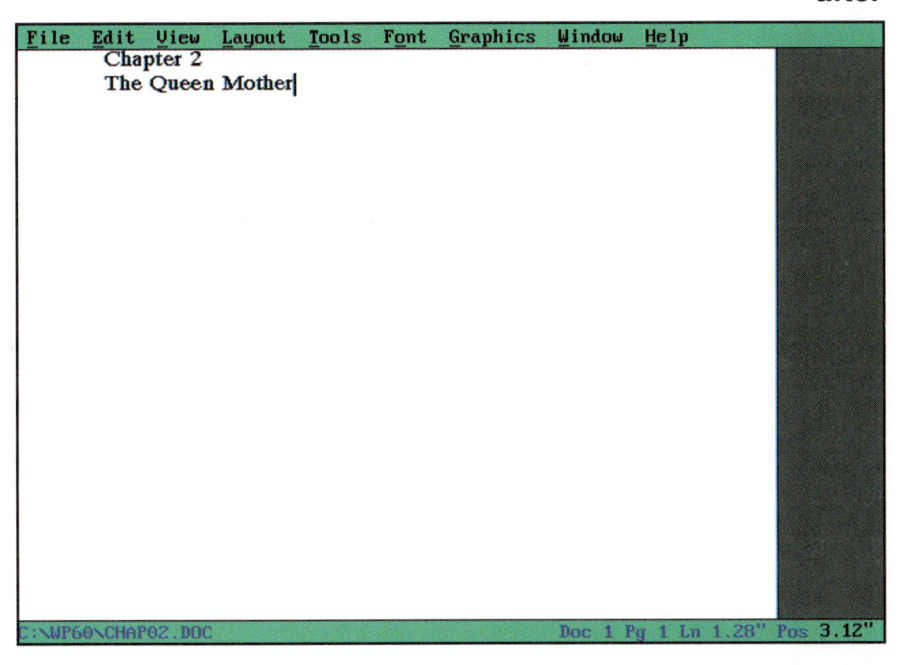

after

```
File  Edit  View  Layout  Tools  Font  Graphics  Window  Help
      Chapter 2
      The Queen Mother|




















C:\WP60\CHAP02.DOC                              Doc 1 Pg 1 Ln 1.28" Pos 3.12"
```

1. Press **Alt**+**F** to open the File menu.
2. Press **A** to select the Save As command.
3. Type a file name.
4. Press **Enter**.

Name already used?

If you type the name of another document, you see a prompt that asks whether you want to replace the file. Press N. Then type a new name.

REVIEW

To save a document with a new name

Try a shortcut

Press F10 to select the Save As command.

Files

TASK

Save and clear a document

before

```
File  Edit  View  Layout  Tools  Font  Graphics  Window  Help
     Chapter 2
     The Queen Mother
```

C:\WP60\CHAP02.DOC   Doc 1 Pg 1 Ln 1.28" Pos 3.12"

Oops!
If you want to keep the document on-screen, press the Esc key.

1. Press **Alt**+**F**.

   This step opens the File menu. You see a list of File commands.

2. Press **E**.

   This step selects the Exit command. You are prompted to save the document.

3. Press **Y**.

   This step tells WordPerfect to save the document. (If you haven't saved it before, you are prompted for a file name. See *TASK: Save a document for the first time.*) If you have saved the document before, you are asked whether you want to exit WordPerfect.

4. Press **N**.

   This step answers No and clears the document. A new blank document appears on-screen.

Easy WordPerfect for Version 6

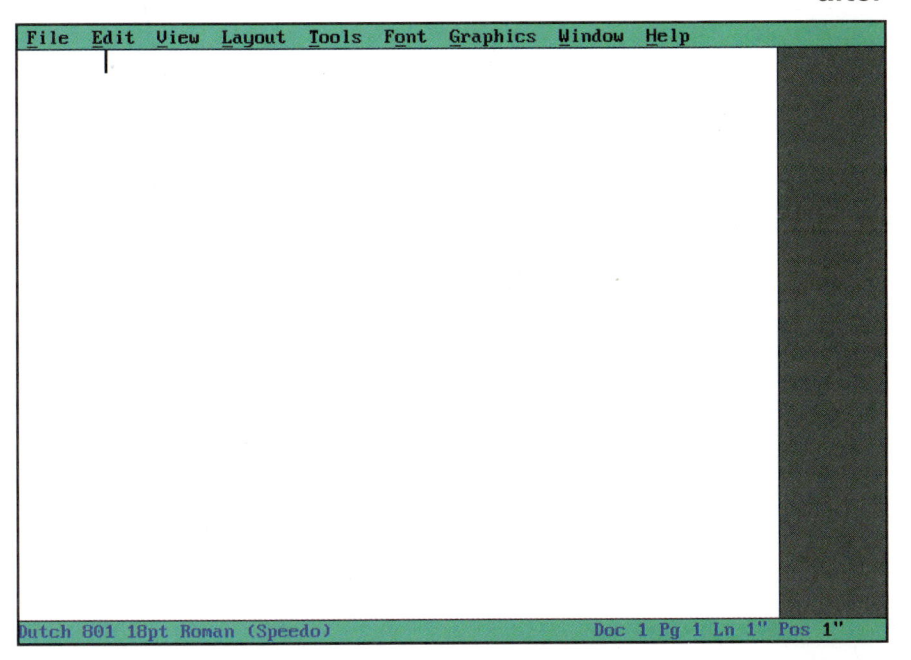

after

REVIEW

To save and clear a document

1. Press **Alt**+**F** to open the File menu.
2. Press **E** to select the Exit command.
3. Press **Y** to save the document.
4. If necessary, type a file name and press **Enter**.
5. Press **N**.

Clear without saving

If you only want to clear the screen, but you don't want to save the document, press N instead of Y in step 3.

Try a shortcut

Press F7 to select the Exit command.

Files

67

TASK

Abandon a document

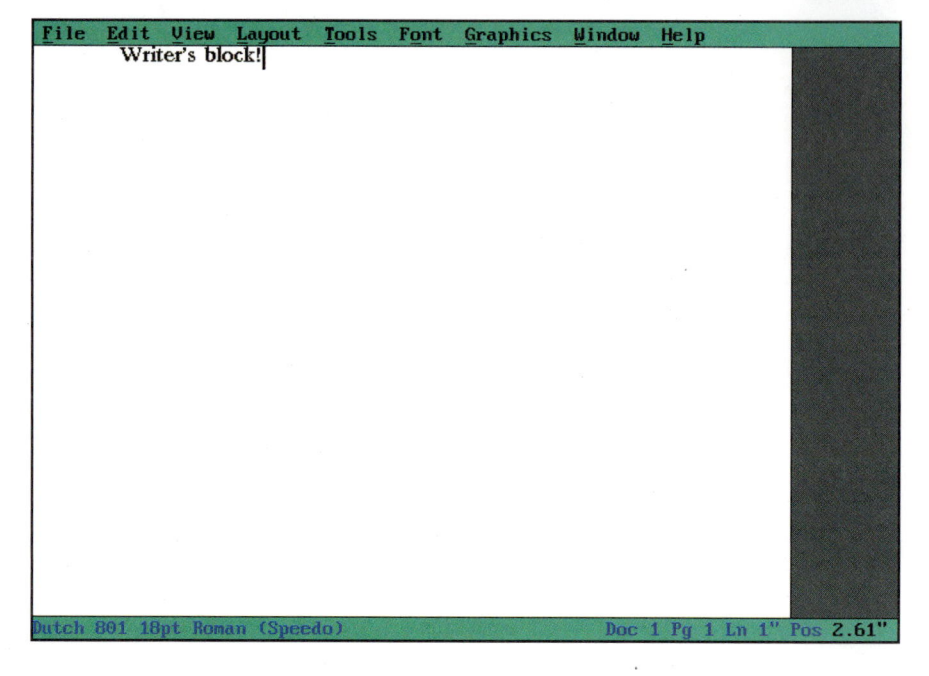

before

```
File  Edit  View  Layout  Tools  Font  Graphics  Window  Help
     Writer's block!
```

Dutch 801 18pt Roman (Speedo)   Doc 1 Pg 1 Ln 1" Pos 2.61"

Oops!
If you want to save the document, press Y instead of N in step 3.

1. Press **Alt+F**.

   This step opens the File menu. You see a list of File commands.

2. Press **E**.

   This step selects the Exit command. You are prompted to save the document.

3. Press **N**.

   This step tells WordPerfect that you don't want to save the document. You are asked whether you want to exit WordPerfect.

4. Press **N**.

   This step answers No and clears the document. A new, blank document appears on-screen.

68

Easy WordPerfect for Version 6

after

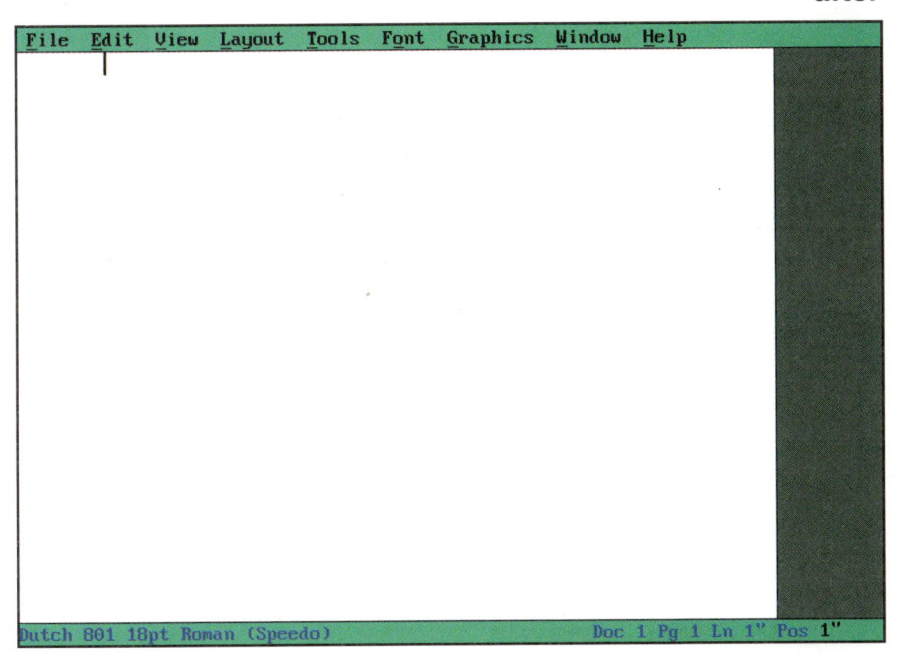

```
File  Edit  View  Layout  Tools  Font  Graphics  Window  Help
```

Dutch 801 18pt Roman (Speedo)   Doc 1 Pg 1 Ln 1" Pos 1"

REVIEW

To abandon a document

1. Press **Alt+F** to open the File menu.
2. Press **E** to select the Exit command.
3. Press **N** to *not* save the document.
4. Press **N**.

Exit WordPerfect?

If you want to exit WordPerfect after abandoning the document, press Y instead of N in step 4.

Try a shortcut

Press F7 to select the Exit command.

Files

69

TASK

Open a document

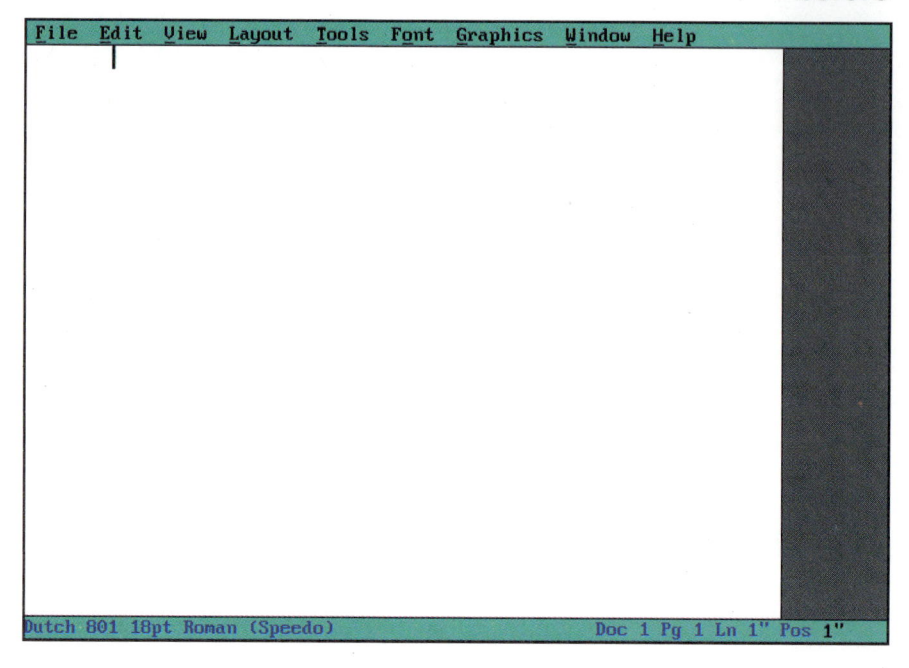

before

```
File  Edit  View  Layout  Tools  Font  Graphics  Window  Help
```

Dutch 801 18pt Roman (Speedo)   Doc 1 Pg 1 Ln 1" Pos 1"

Oops!

If you see the `File not found` message, press Enter to clear the message. Then try typing the file name again. Check your spelling.

1. Start from a blank screen.

   If you have a document on-screen, you must clear it. See *TASK: Save and clear a document.*

2. Press **Alt+F**.

   This step opens the File menu. You see a list of File commands.

3. Press **O**.

   This step selects the Open command. You see the Open Document dialog box.

4. Type **CHAP01.DOC**.

   This is the name of the document you want to open.

5. Press **Enter**.

   The document is displayed on-screen.

70   *Easy WordPerfect for Version 6*

after

```
File  Edit  View  Layout  Tools  Font  Graphics  Window  Help
Chapter 1
The Saint




C:\WP60\CHAP01.DOC                          Doc 1 Pg 1 Ln 1" Pos 1"
```

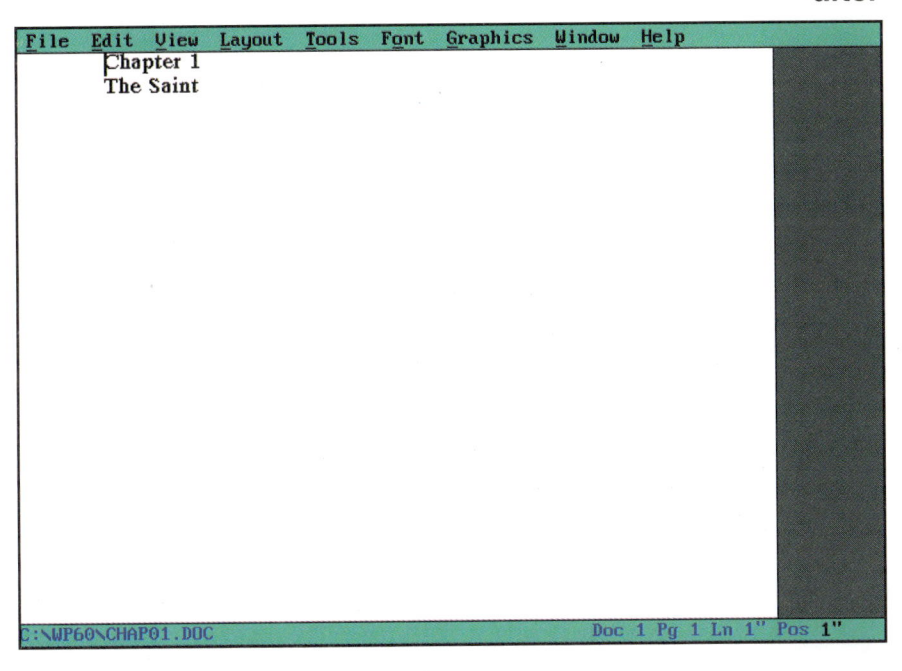

Don't know the file name?

If you can't remember the file name, use the File Manager to display a list of files. See the tasks in the section "More Files."

REVIEW

1. Start from a blank screen.
2. Press **Alt+F** to open the File menu.
3. Press **O** to select the Open command.
4. Type the name of the file you want to open.
5. Press **Enter**.

To open a document

Try a shortcut

Press Shift+F10 to select the Open command.

Files   71

TASK

Create a new document

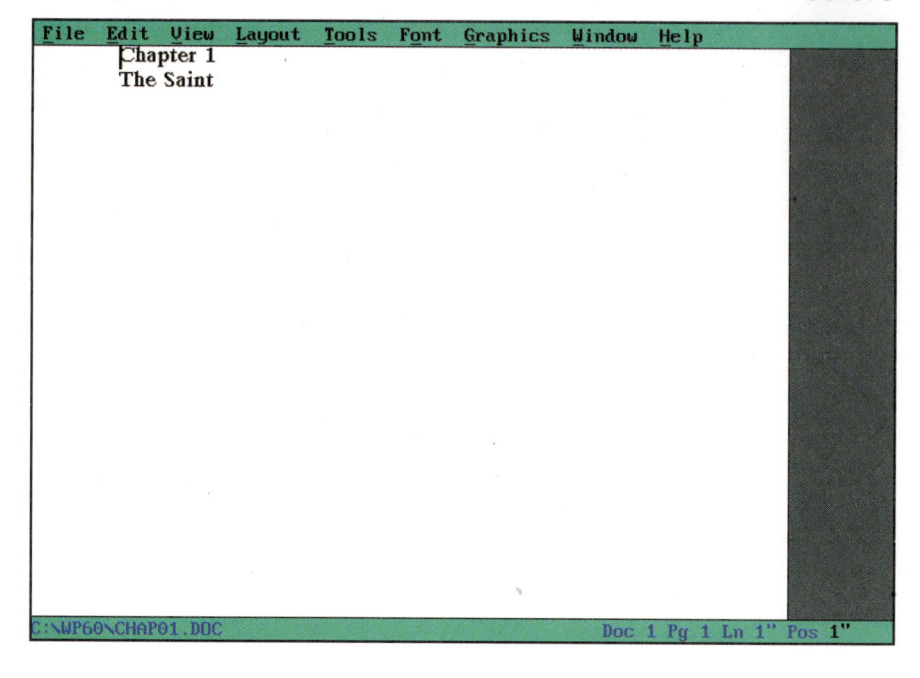

before

Oops!

If you don't want a new document, abandon it. See TASK: Abandon a document.

1. Press **Alt**+**F**.

   This step opens the File menu, which displays the list of File commands.

2. Press **N**.

   This step selects the New command. WordPerfect opens a new document on-screen. The status line displays `Doc 2` to indicate the new, second document. (If you have more than two documents open, you might see a different document number.)

Easy WordPerfect for Version 6

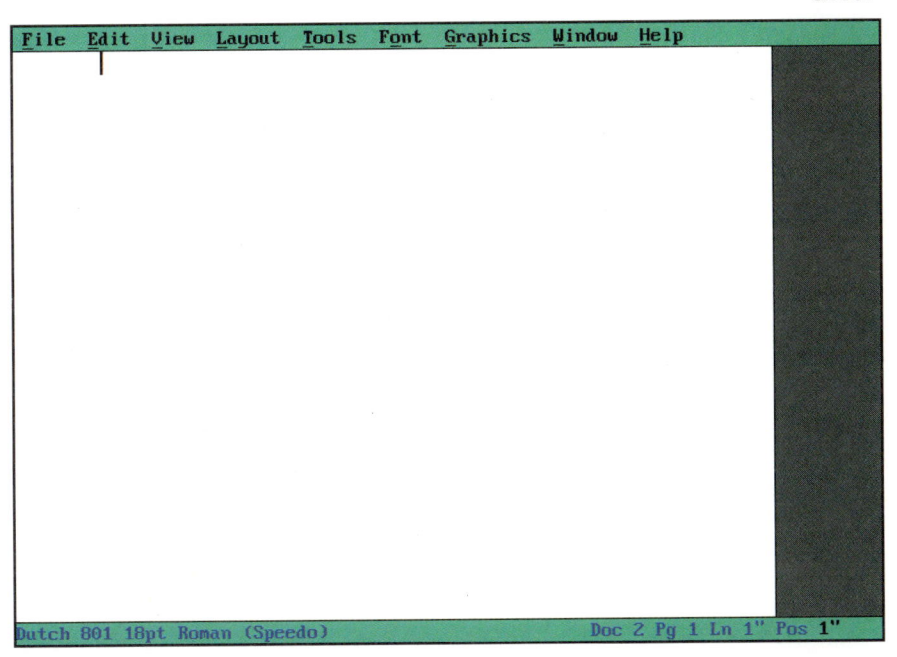

after

1. Press **Alt**+**F** to open the File menu.
2. Press **N** to select the New command.

Clear a document

Each time you clear a document, WordPerfect displays a new document, but you can also use the New command to display a new document.

REVIEW

To create a new document

Files

73

TASK

Open more than one document

before

```
File  Edit  View  Layout  Tools  Font  Graphics  Window  Help
Chapter 1
The Saint




















C:\WP60\CHAP01.DOC                              Doc 1 Pg 1 Ln 1" Pos 1"
```

> **Oops!**
> To close a document, see TASK: Save and clear a document.

1. Press **Alt**+**F**.

   This step opens the File menu, which displays the list of File commands.

2. Press **O**.

   This step selects the Open command. You see the Open Document dialog box.

3. Type **CHAP01.DOC** and press **Enter**.

   This step opens the first document. Now you will repeat steps 1–3 to open the second document.

4. Press **Alt**+**F**.

5. Press **O**.

6. Type **CHAP02.DOC** and press **Enter**.

   You now have two documents open on-screen. The document you opened last is displayed. The status line lists the name of the document. The document indicator (Doc) indicates the number of the document you have open.

74   *Easy WordPerfect for Version 6*

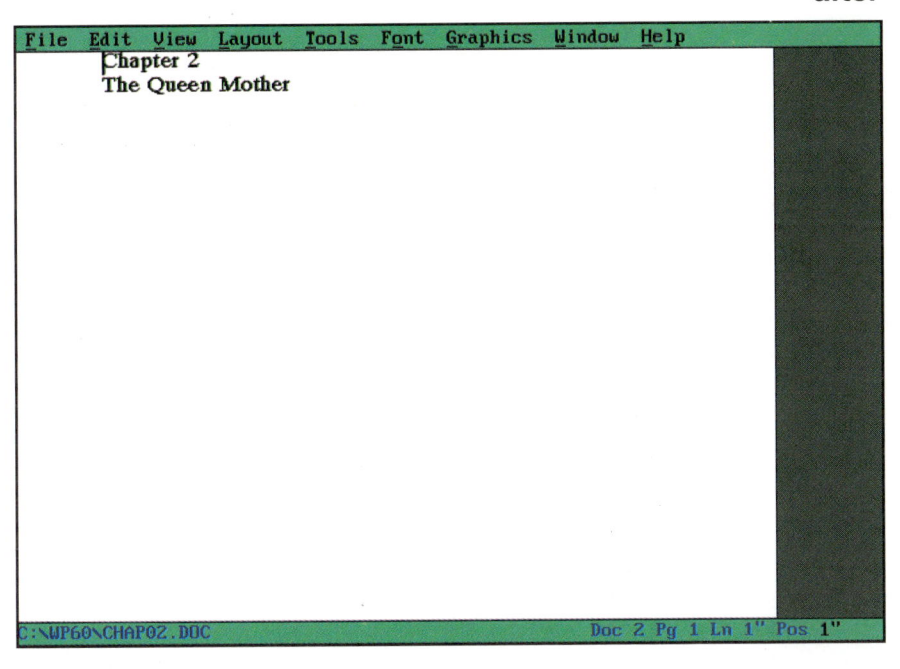

after

1. Press **Alt**+**F** to open the File menu.
2. Press **O** to select the Open command.
3. Type the name of the file you want to open; then press **Enter**.
4. Follow the same steps (1–3) to open the next document.

> **Limit of documents**
>
> WordPerfect lets you have as many as nine documents open at once.

REVIEW

To open more than one document

> **Switch documents**
>
> To switch from one open document to another, see *TASK: Switch to another open document.*

Files

75

TASK

Switch to another open document

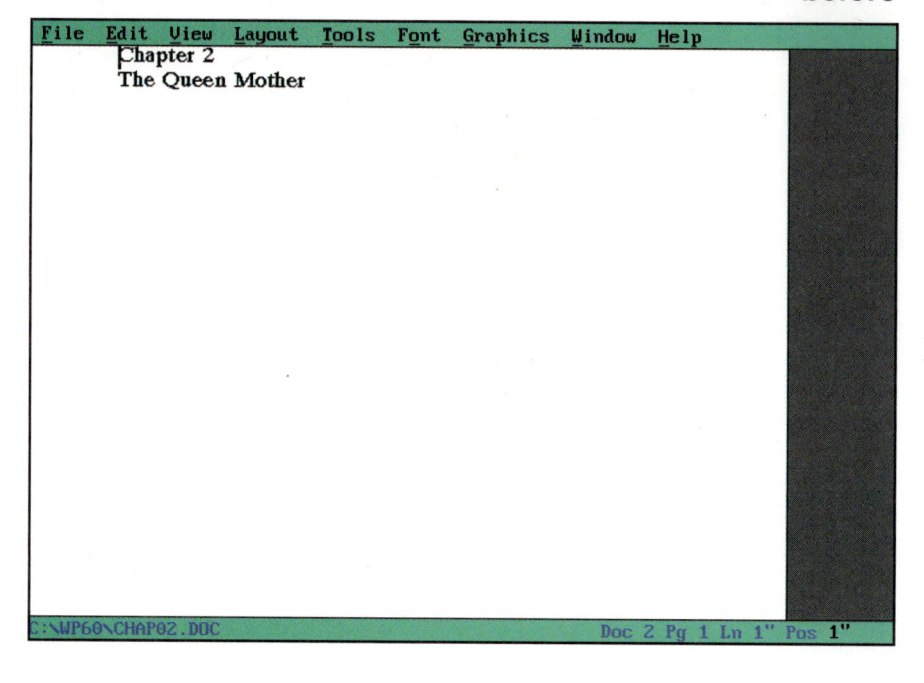

before

```
File  Edit  View  Layout  Tools  Font  Graphics  Window  Help
Chapter 2
The Queen Mother




C:\WP60\CHAP02.DOC                                  Doc 2 Pg 1 Ln 1" Pos 1"
```

Oops!

Follow this same procedure to return to the first document, but type the number next to that document name in the document list.

1. Press **Alt+W**.

   This step opens the Window menu and displays a list of Window commands.

2. Press **W**.

   This step selects the Switch To command. All open documents are listed in a dialog box on-screen.

3. Press **1**.

   This step selects the document to which you want to switch.

76

Easy WordPerfect for Version 6

after

1. Press **Alt+W** to open the Window menu.
2. Press **W** to select the Switch To command.
3. Type the number associated with the document to which you want to switch.

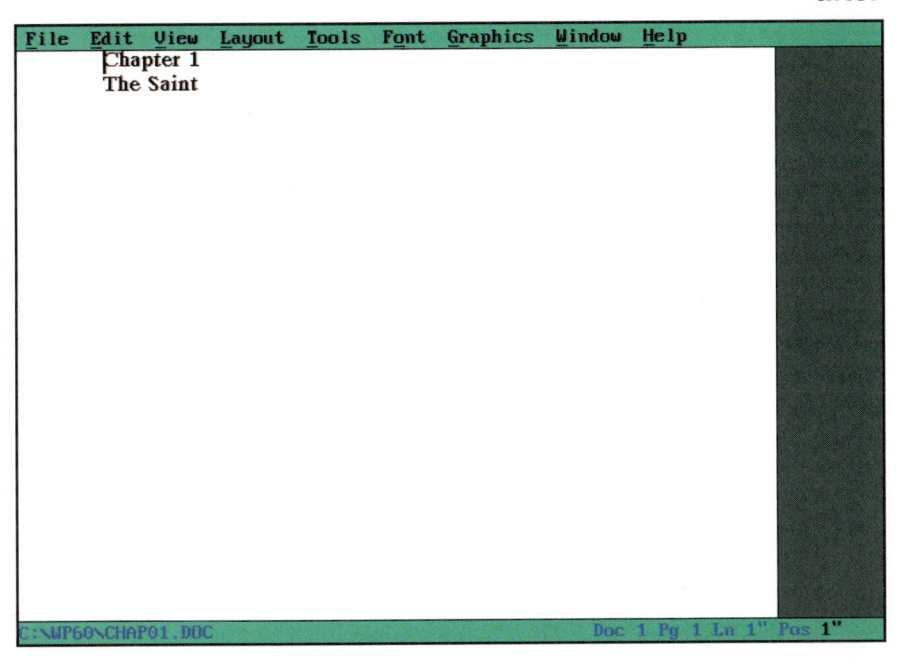

Display open documents

See *TASK: Display all open documents* for help on displaying all open documents.

REVIEW

To switch to another open document

Other options

Instead of pressing W in step 2, you can press N to move to the next document or P to move to the preview window.

Files

TASK

Display all open documents

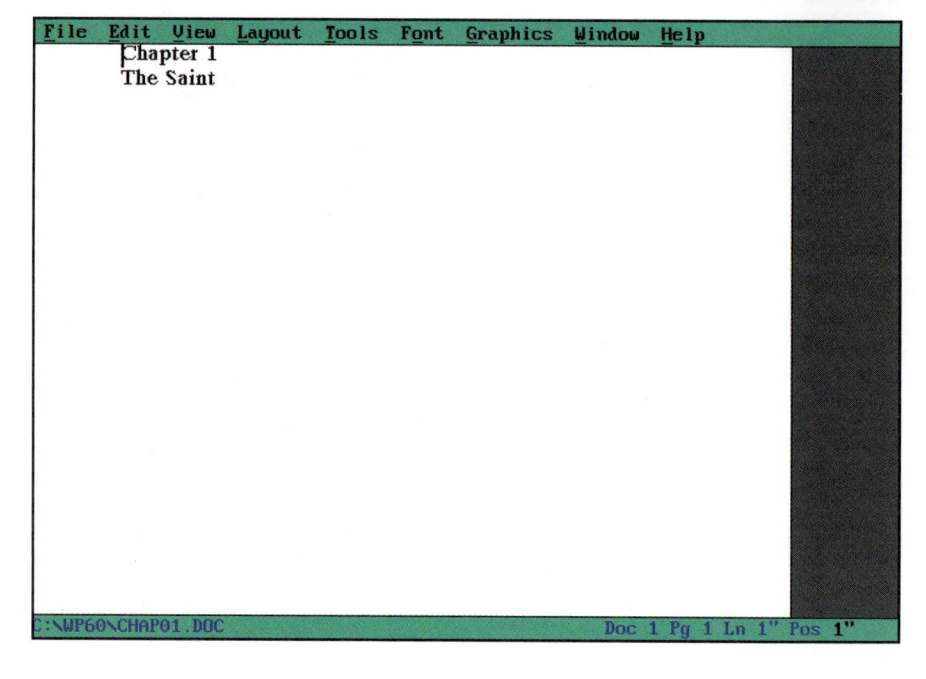

before

```
File  Edit  View  Layout  Tools  Font  Graphics  Window  Help
Chapter 1
The Saint




C:\WP60\CHAP01.DOC                              Doc 1 Pg 1 Ln 1" Pos 1"
```

Oops!

To return to viewing just one document in full-screen, switch to the document you want (see *TASK: Switch to another open document*). Then press Alt+W to open the Window menu. Press M to select the Maximize command.

1. Press **Alt+W**.

   This step opens the Window menu and displays a list of Window commands.

2. Press **T**.

   This step selects the Tile command. WordPerfect arranges all open documents in windows on-screen.

78 *Easy WordPerfect for Version 6*

after

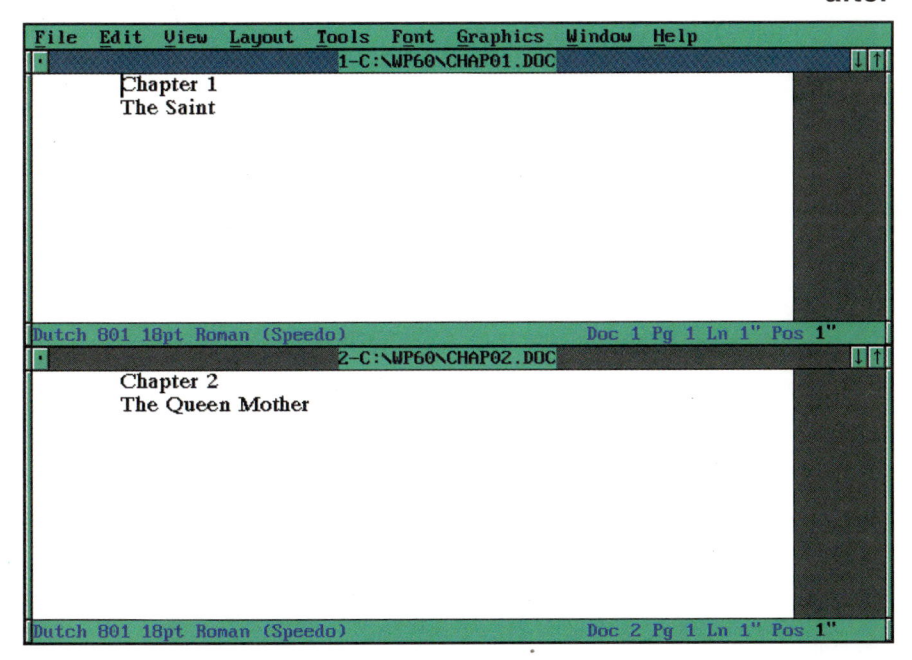

> **Switch between open documents**
>
> See *TASK: Switch to another open document* for help on moving from one open document to another.

REVIEW

1. Press **Alt+W** to open the Window menu.
2. Press **T** to select the Tile command.

To display all open documents

> **Cascade windows**
>
> You can select Cascade instead of Tile in step 2 (press C) to use a different window arrangement.

Basic Formatting

This section covers the following tasks:

Reveal codes

Center text

Right-justify text

Indent text

Create a hanging indent

Make text bold

Underline text

Italicize text

Change the font

Change the font size

Change the initial font

TASK

Reveal codes

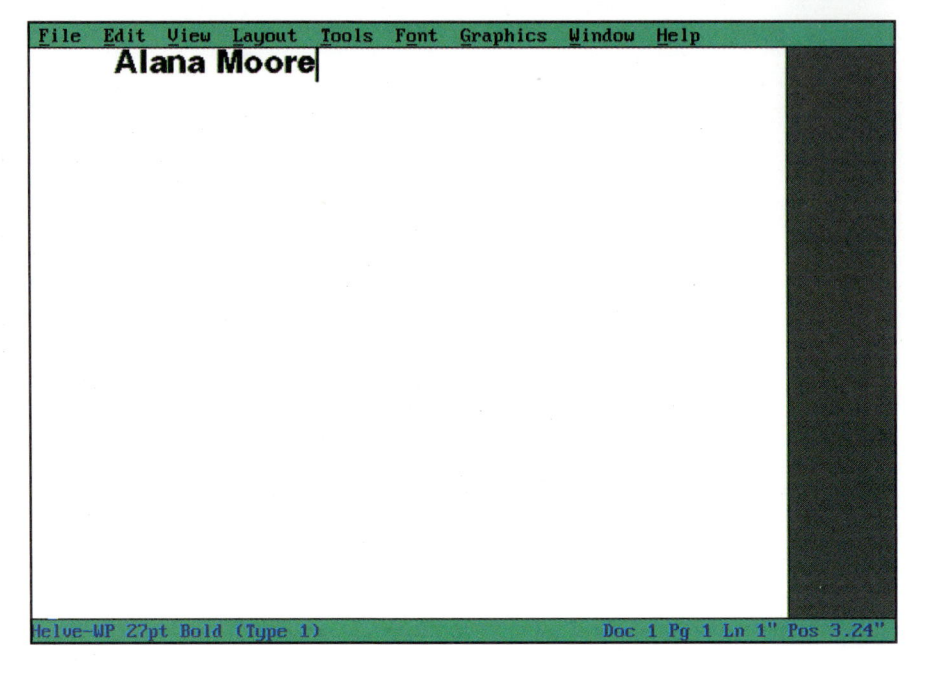

before

```
File  Edit  View  Layout  Tools  Font  Graphics  Window  Help
      Alana Moore|




















Helve-WP 27pt Bold (Type 1)                    Doc 1 Pg 1 Ln 1" Pos 3.24"
```

Oops!
To close the Reveal Codes window, select the command again.

1. Press **Alt**+**V**.

   This step opens the View menu. You see a list of View commands.

2. Press **C**.

   This step selects the Reveal Codes command, which divides the screen horizontally into two windows. You see text in both windows. The lower part of the screen shows the document's hidden codes. These codes indicate tab stops, margin settings, carriage returns, font changes, and so on.

   The cursor appears in both windows. When you move the cursor, both windows move in sync. The cursor expands when you move it to a hidden code, and the entire code is highlighted in the screen's lower half. You can change the formatting of a document by adding or deleting hidden codes.

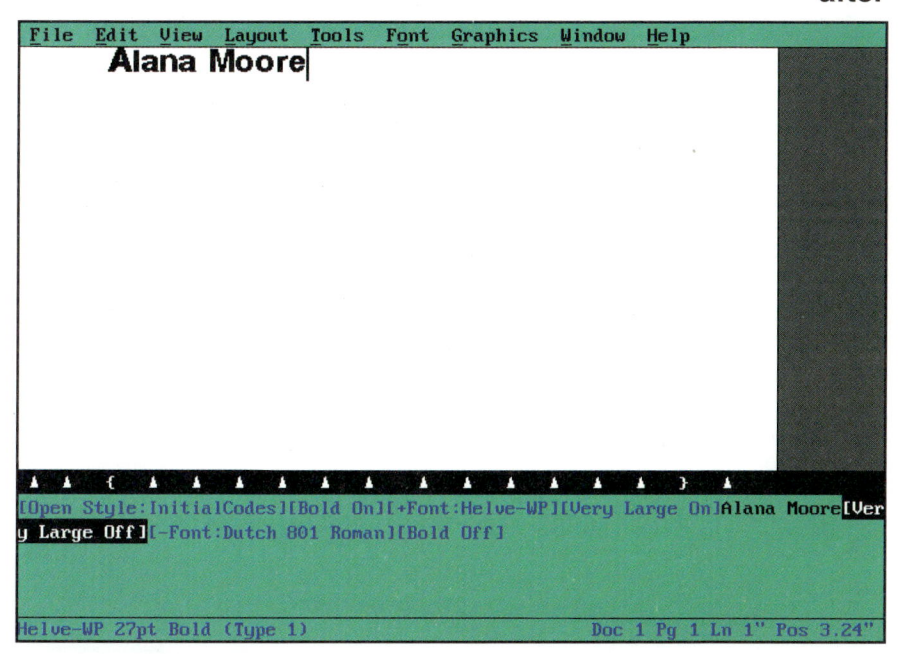

after

1. Press **Alt**+**V** to open the View menu.
2. Press **C** to select Reveal Codes.

Change formatting

To delete a code, first open the Reveal Codes window (press Alt+F3). Then use the arrow keys to highlight the code, and press the Del key.

REVIEW

To reveal codes

Try a shortcut

Press Alt+F3 to open or close the Reveal Codes window.

Basic Formatting

83

TASK

Center text

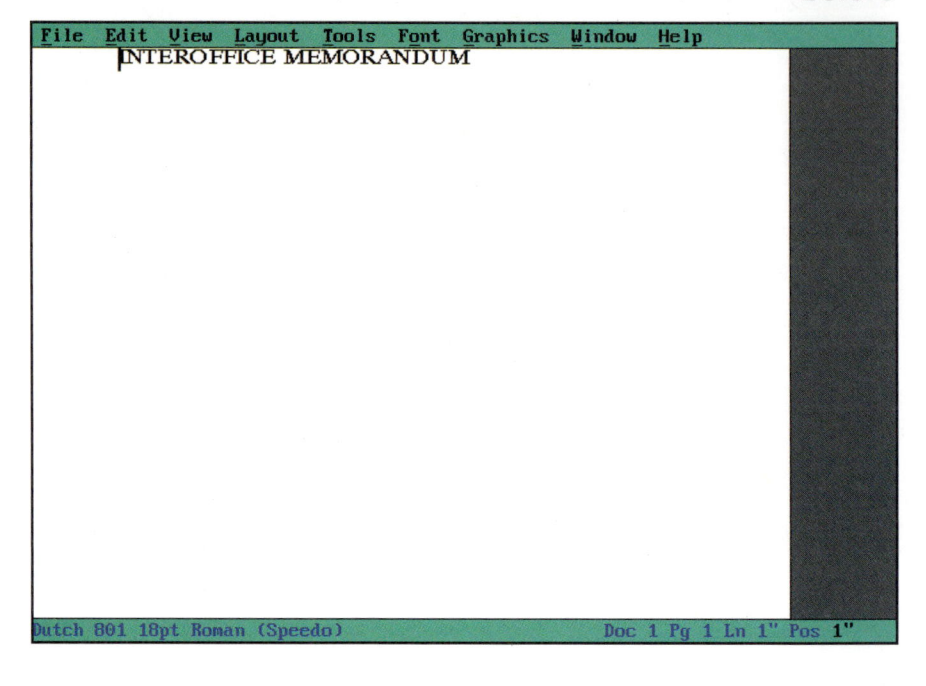

before

```
File  Edit  View  Layout  Tools  Font  Graphics  Window  Help
        INTEROFFICE MEMORANDUM




















Dutch 801 18pt Roman (Speedo)            Doc 1 Pg 1 Ln 1" Pos 1"
```

Oops!

To undo the change, open the Edit menu (press Alt+E) and select the Undo command (press U).

1. Move the cursor to the beginning of the line that says *INTEROFFICE MEMORANDUM*.

   This step moves the cursor to the line you want to center. If you want to center more than one line, block those lines for this step.

2. Press **Alt+L**.

   This step opens the Layout menu. You see a list of Layout commands.

3. Press **A**.

   This step selects the Alignment command. You see a list of alignment choices.

4. Press **C**.

   This step selects the Center command. WordPerfect centers the line on-screen.

84

Easy WordPerfect for Version 6

after

> **Reveal Codes**
>
> If you don't undo the change immediately, you'll have to delete a hidden code to undo the change. Open the Reveal Codes window (press Alt+F3) and delete the `[Cntr on Mar]` code.

REVIEW

To center text

1. Move the cursor to the beginning of the line you want to center.
2. Press **Alt**+**L** to open the Layout menu.
3. Press **A** to select the Alignment command.
4. Press **C** to select the Center command.

> **Try a shortcut**
>
> Press Shift+F6 to select the Center command.

Basic Formatting

85

TASK

Right-justify text

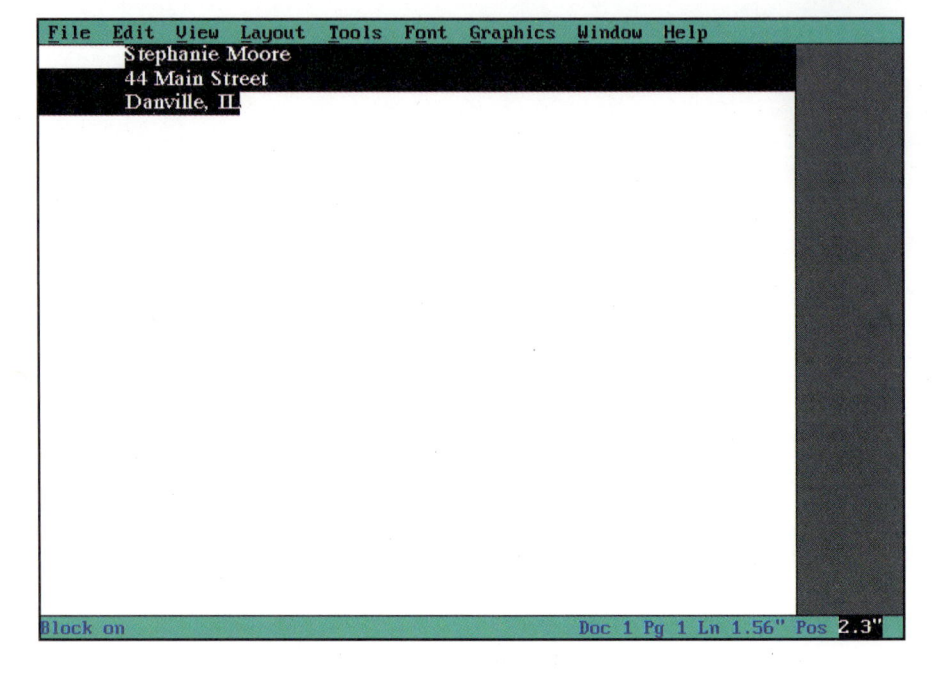

before

```
File  Edit  View  Layout  Tools  Font  Graphics  Window  Help
      Stephanie Moore
      44 Main Street
      Danville, IL
```

Block on   Doc 1 Pg 1 Ln 1.56" Pos 2.3"

Oops!

To undo the change, open the Edit menu (press Alt+E) and select the Undo command (press U).

1. Block the three lines of text that start with *Stephanie Moore*.

   This step selects the text you want to align. For help on blocking text, see *TASK: Select a block*.

2. Press **Alt+L**.

   This step opens the Layout menu. You see a list of Layout commands.

3. Press **A**.

   This step selects the Alignment command. You see a list of alignment choices.

4. Press **F**.

   This step selects the Flush Right command. WordPerfect aligns the text with the right margin.

86

Easy WordPerfect for Version 6

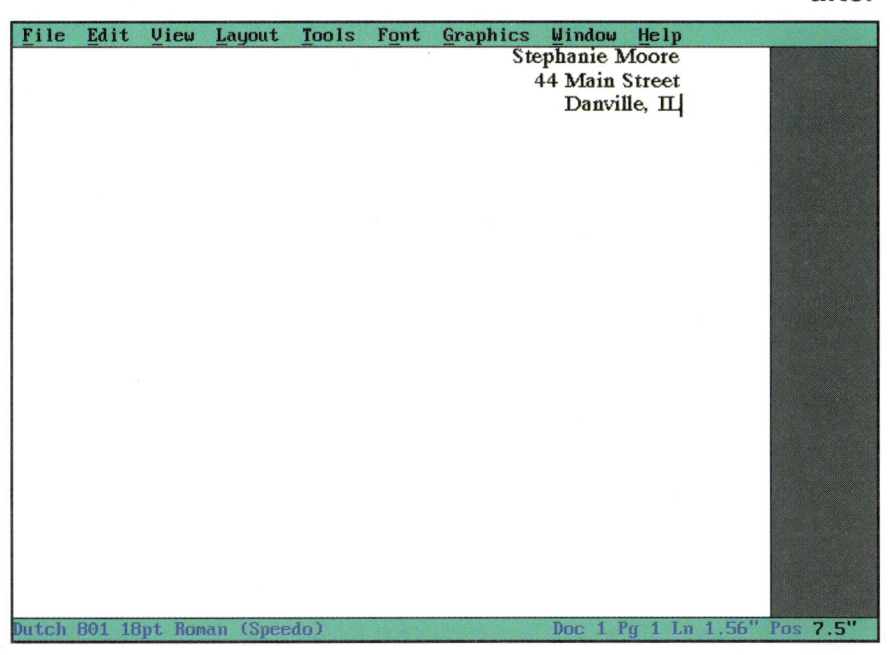

after

```
File  Edit  View  Layout  Tools  Font  Graphics  Window  Help
                                    Stephanie Moore
                                     44 Main Street
                                     Danville, IL
```

1. Block the text you want to align.
2. Press **Alt**+**L** to open the Layout menu.
3. Press **A** to select the Alignment command.
4. Press **F** to select the Flush Right command.

Reveal Codes

If you don't undo the change immediately, you'll have to delete a hidden code to undo the change. Open the Reveal Codes window (press Alt+F3) and delete the `[Flsh Rgt]` code.

REVIEW

To right-justify text

Try a shortcut

Press Alt+F6 to select the Flush Right command.

Basic Formatting

87

TASK

Indent text

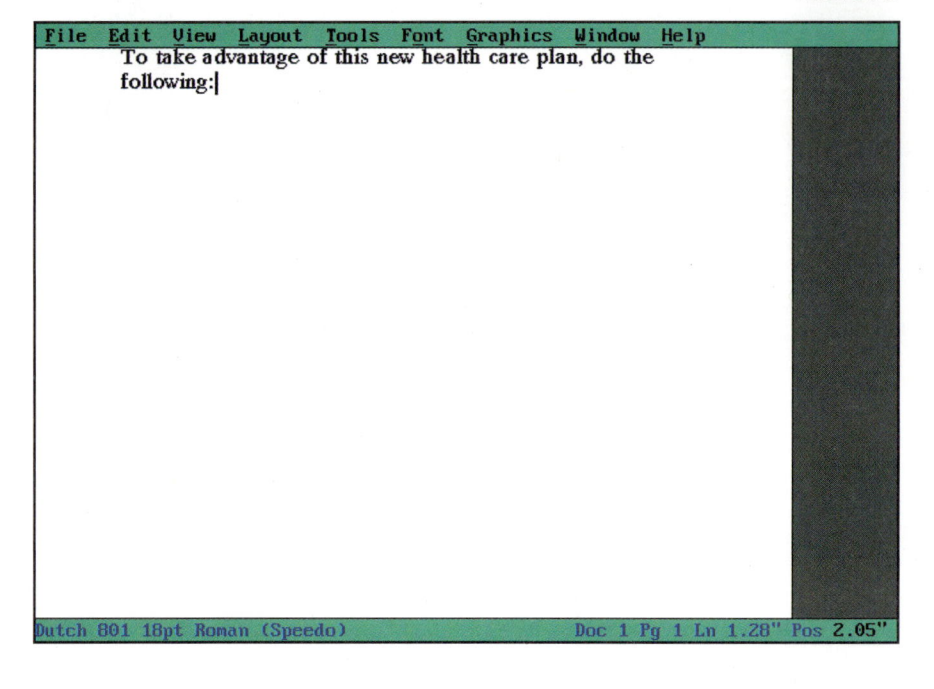

before

> File Edit View Layout Tools Font Graphics Window Help
>
> To take advantage of this new health care plan, do the following:
>
> Dutch 801 18pt Roman (Speedo)   Doc 1 Pg 1 Ln 1.28" Pos 2.05"

Oops!

To undo the change, open the Edit menu (press Alt+E) and select the Undo command (press U).

1. With the cursor at the end of the last line, press **Enter twice**.

   Pressing Enter twice ends the current paragraph and inserts a blank line.

2. Type **1** and then type a period (**.**).

   This step begins a list of numbered steps you want to indent.

3. Press **Alt+L**.

   This step opens the Layout menu. You see a list of Layout commands.

4. Press **A**.

   This step selects the Alignment command. You see a list of alignment choices.

5. Press **I**.

   This step selects the Indent command. Any text you type will be indented from this spot.

6. Type **Attend the enrollment meeting on Friday, November 30 at 10 a.m. in the board room.**

   This sentence is the text for the first point of your numbered list. Notice that as the text you type reaches the end of the line, it wraps to the second line and indents automatically.

Easy WordPerfect for Version 6

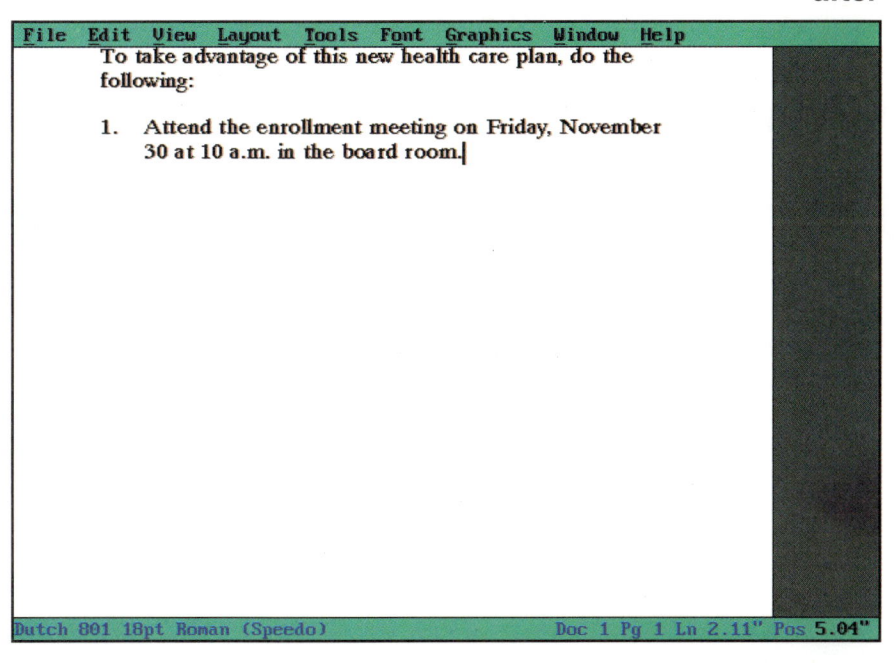

after

1. Press **Alt**+**L** to open the Layout menu.
2. Press **A** to select the Alignment command.
3. Press **I** to select the Indent command.

Reveal Codes

If you don't undo the change immediately, you'll have to delete a hidden code to undo the change. Open the Reveal Codes window (press Alt+F3) and delete the [Lft Indent] code.

REVIEW

To indent text

Try a shortcut

Press F4 to select the Indent command.

Basic Formatting

89

TASK

Create a hanging indent

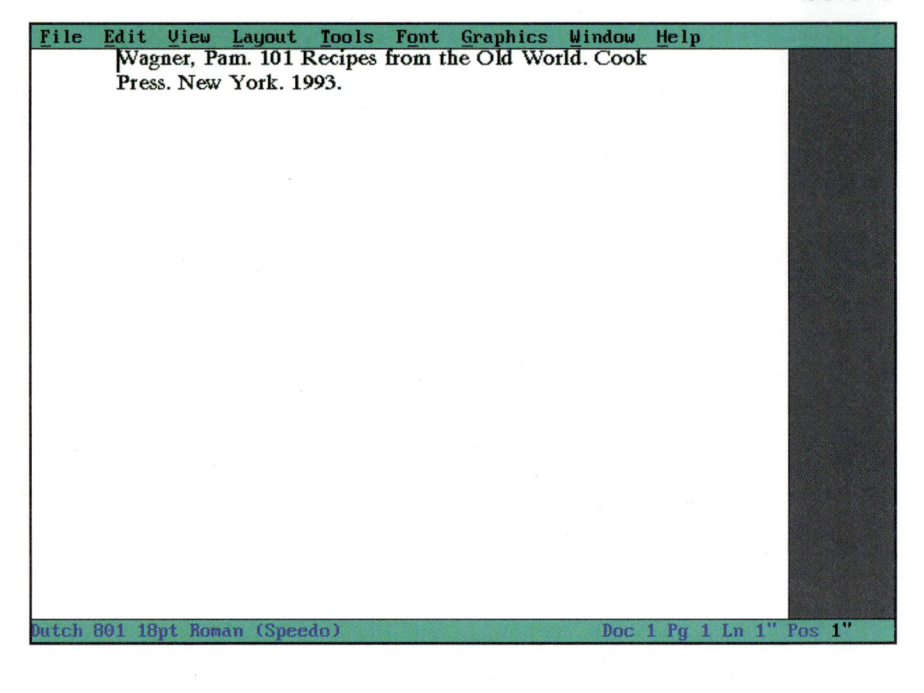

before

> Wagner, Pam. 101 Recipes from the Old World. Cook Press. New York. 1993.

Oops!

To undo the change, open the Edit menu (press Alt+E) and select the Undo command (press U).

1. Move the cursor to the beginning of the first line of text.

   This step moves the cursor to the beginning of the paragraph you want to indent.

2. Press **Alt+L**.

   This step opens the Layout menu. You see a list of Layout commands.

3. Press **A**.

   This step selects the Alignment command. You see a list of alignment choices.

4. Press **H**.

   This step selects the Hanging Indent command. WordPerfect keeps the first line aligned with the left margin and indents the second line.

90

Easy WordPerfect for Version 6

after

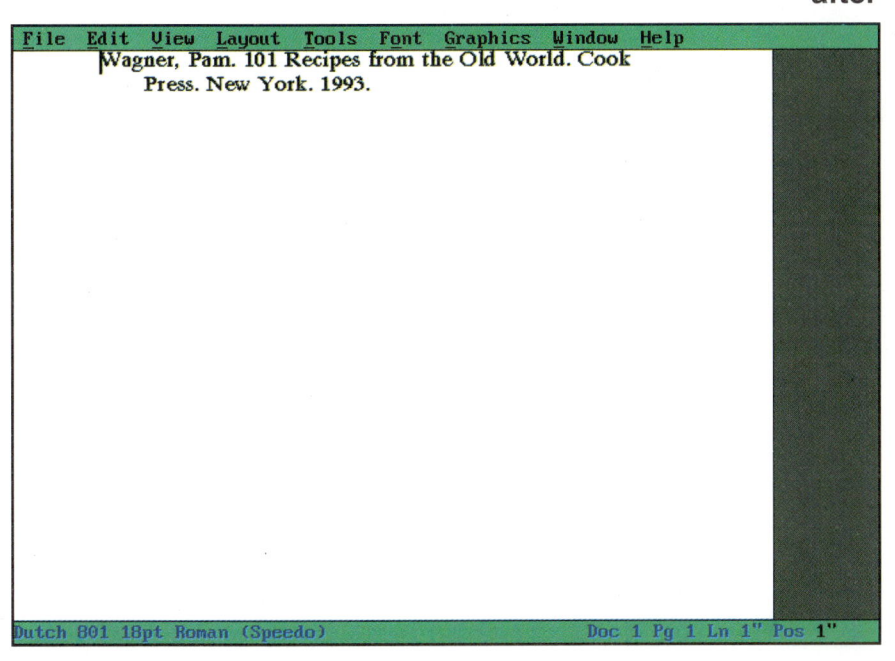

Reveal Codes

If you don't undo the change immediately, you'll have to delete a hidden code to undo the change. Open the Reveal Codes window (press Alt+F3) and delete the `[Lft Indent]` and `[Back Tab]` codes.

REVIEW

To create a hanging indent

1. Move the cursor to the beginning of the paragraph you want to indent.

2. Press **Alt**+**L** to open the Layout menu.

3. Press **A** to select the Alignment command.

4. Press **H** to select the Hanging Indent command.

Basic Formatting

91

TASK

Make text bold

before

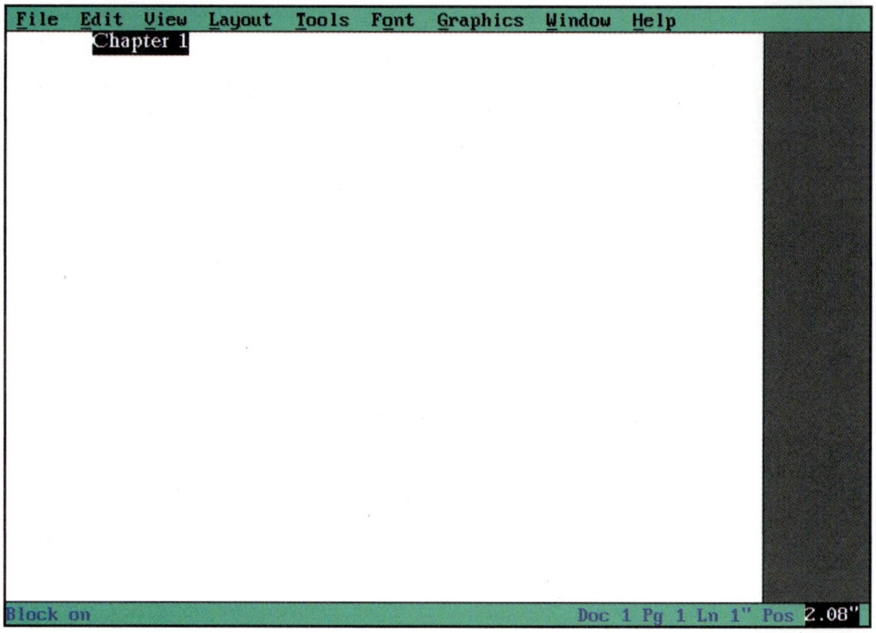

Oops!

To undo the change, open the Edit menu (press Alt+E) and select the Undo command (press U). Or open the Reveal Codes window (press Alt+F3) and delete the `[Bold On]` code.

1. Block the text *Chapter 1.*

   This step selects the text you want to make bold. For help on blocking text, see *TASK: Select a block.*

2. Press **Alt+O**.

   This step opens the Font menu. You see a list of Font commands.

3. Press **B**.

   This step selects the Bold command. If your screen is displayed in Graphics mode, WordPerfect displays the blocked text in bold on-screen, as shown in the After screen.

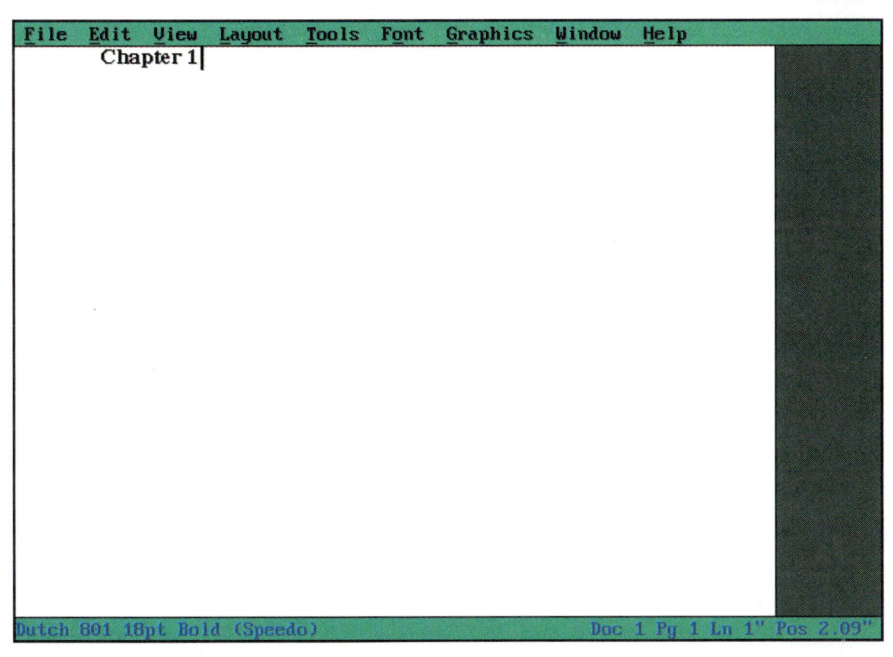

after

1. Block the text you want to make bold.
2. Press **Alt**+**O** to open the Font menu.
3. Press **B** to select the Bold command.

See font changes?

If you can't see the font changes, your screen isn't in Graphics mode. To change to Graphics mode, see TASK: Change to Graphics mode.

REVIEW

To make text bold

Try a shortcut

Press F6 to select the Bold command.

Basic Formatting

TASK

Underline text

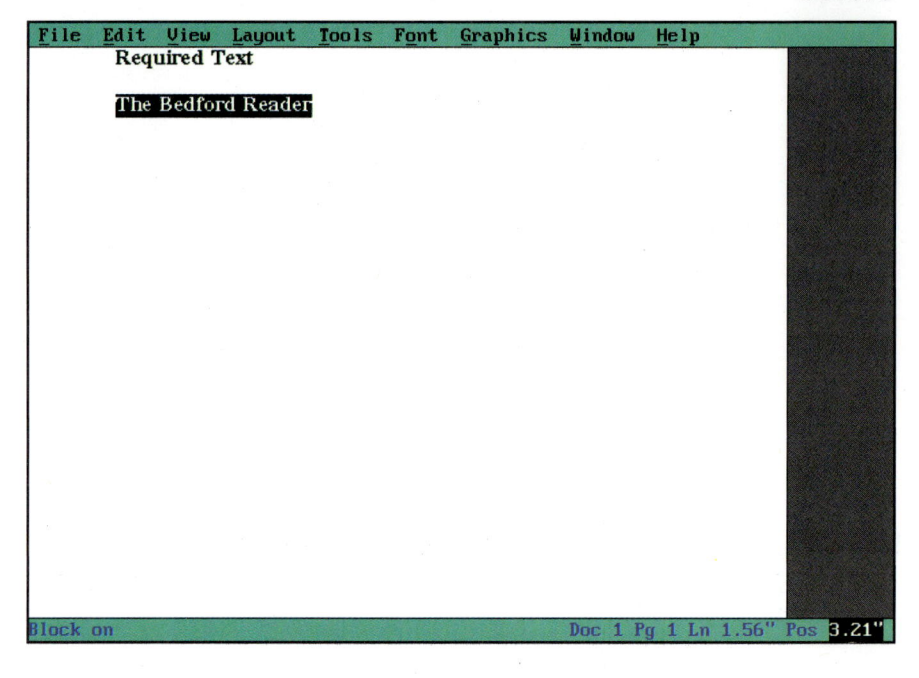

before

```
File  Edit  View  Layout  Tools  Font  Graphics  Window  Help
      Required Text
      The Bedford Reader

Block on                              Doc 1 Pg 1 Ln 1.56" Pos 3.21"
```

Oops!

To undo the change, open the Edit menu (press Alt+E) and select the Undo command (press U). Or open the Reveal Codes window (press Alt+F3) and delete the `[Und On]` code.

1. Block the text *The Bedford Reader.*

   This step selects the text you want to underline. For help on blocking text, see *TASK: Select a block.*

2. Press **Alt**+**O**.

   This step opens the Font menu. You see a list of Font commands.

3. Press **U**.

   This step selects the Underline command. If your screen is displayed in Graphics mode, the blocked text is underlined on-screen, as shown in the After screen.

94

Easy WordPerfect for Version 6

after

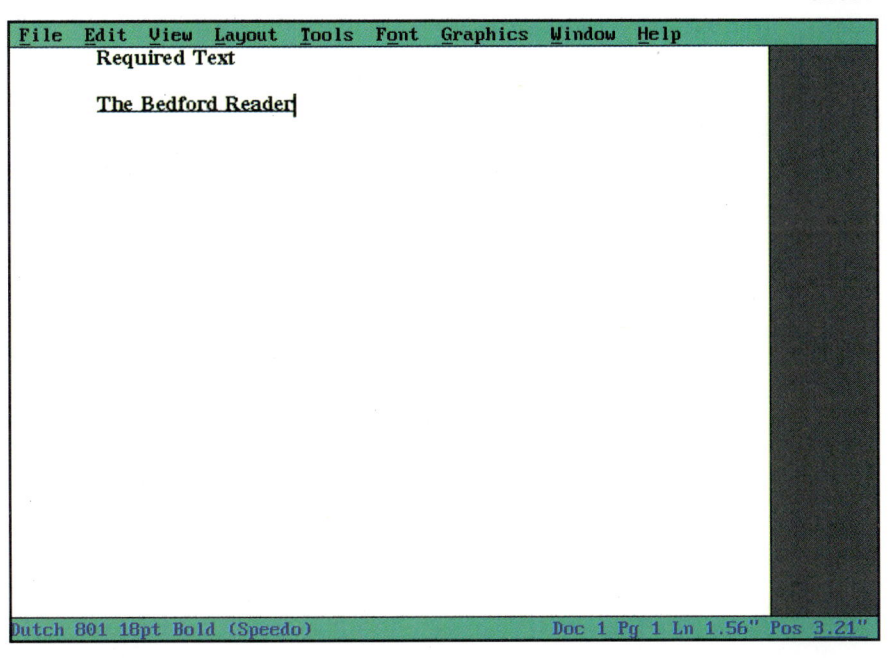

```
File  Edit  View  Layout  Tools  Font  Graphics  Window  Help
        Required Text

        The Bedford Reader
```

Dutch 801 18pt Bold (Speedo)   Doc 1 Pg 1 Ln 1.56" Pos 3.21"

See font changes?
If you can't see the font changes, your screen isn't in Graphics mode. To change to Graphics mode, see TASK: Change to Graphics mode.

REVIEW

To underline text

1. Block the text you want to change.
2. Press **Alt**+**O** to open the Font menu.
3. Press **U** to select the Underline command.

Try a shortcut
Press F8 to select the Underline command.

Basic Formatting

95

TASK

Italicize text

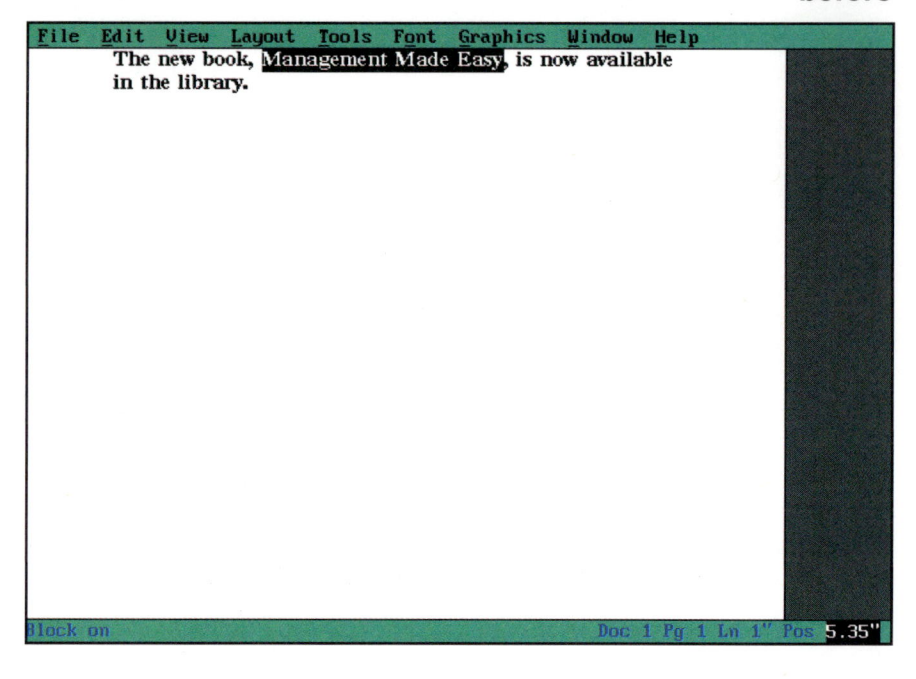

before

```
File  Edit  View  Layout  Tools  Font  Graphics  Window  Help
      The new book, Management Made Easy, is now available
      in the library.




















Block on                                       Doc 1 Pg 1 Ln 1" Pos 5.35"
```

1. Block the text *Management Made Easy*.

   This step selects the text you want to italicize. For help on blocking text, see *TASK: Select a block*.

2. Press **Alt**+**O**.

   This step opens the Font menu. You see a list of Font commands.

3. Press **I**.

   This step selects the Italics command. If your screen is displayed in Graphics mode, WordPerfect displays the blocked text in italics on-screen, as shown in the After screen.

Oops!

To undo the change, open the Edit menu (press Alt+E) and select the Undo command (press U). Or open the Reveal Codes window (press Alt+F3) and delete the `[Italc On]` code.

96 *Easy WordPerfect for Version 6*

after

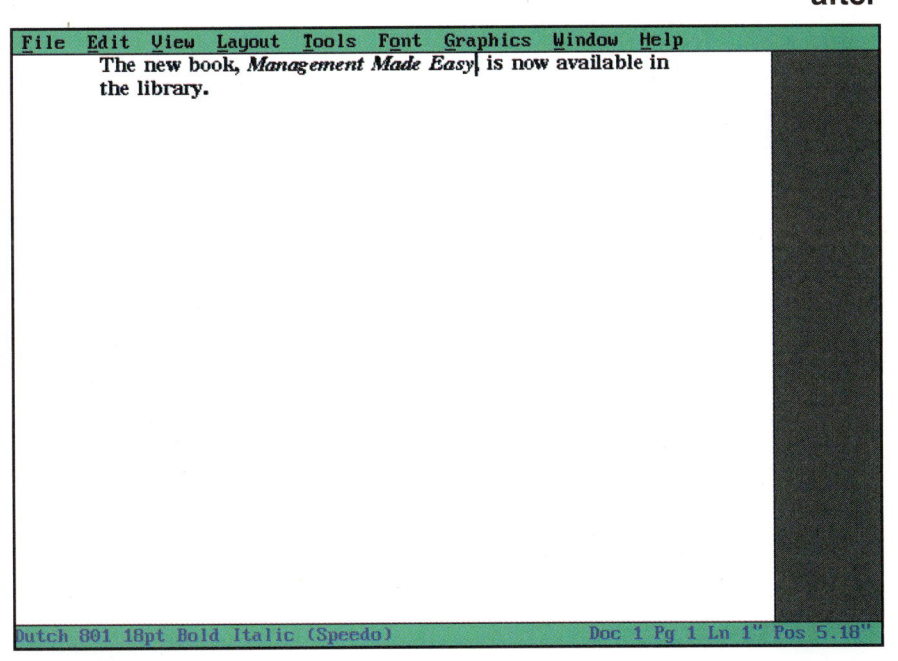

```
File  Edit  View  Layout  Tools  Font  Graphics  Window  Help
The new book, *Management Made Easy* is now available in
the library.




Dutch 801 18pt Bold Italic (Speedo)              Doc 1 Pg 1 Ln 1" Pos 5.18"
```

> **See font changes?**
>
> If you can't see the font changes, your screen isn't in Graphics mode. To change to Graphics mode, see *TASK: Change to Graphics mode*.

REVIEW

To italicize text

1. Block the text you want to change.

2. Press **Alt**+**O** to open the Font menu.

3. Press **I** to select the Italics command.

> **Try a shortcut**
>
> Press Ctrl+I to select the Italics command.

Basic Formatting

97

TASK

Change the font

before

```
File  Edit  View  Layout  Tools  Font  Graphics  Window  Help
      Alana Moore
```
```
Block on                                    Doc 1 Pg 1 Ln 1" Pos 2.42"
```

Oops!

To undo the change, open the Edit menu (press Alt+E) and select the Undo command (press U). Or open the Reveal Codes window (press Alt+F3) and delete the [Font] code.

1. Block the text *Alana Moore*.

   This step selects the text you want to change. For help on blocking text, see *TASK: Select a block*.

2. Press **Alt+O**.

   This step opens the Font menu. You see a list of Font commands.

3. Press **O**.

   This step selects the Font command. You see the Font dialog box.

4. Press **F**.

   This step selects the Font list.

5. Press ↓ until you highlight **Helve-Wp (Type 1)**.

   This step selects the font you want. Your list of fonts might be different. If you don't have this font, select one that you do have.

6. Press **Enter twice**.

   This step confirms the change and returns you to the document. If your screen is displayed in Graphics mode, WordPerfect displays the blocked text in the new font on-screen, as shown in the After screen.

98

Easy WordPerfect for Version 6

after

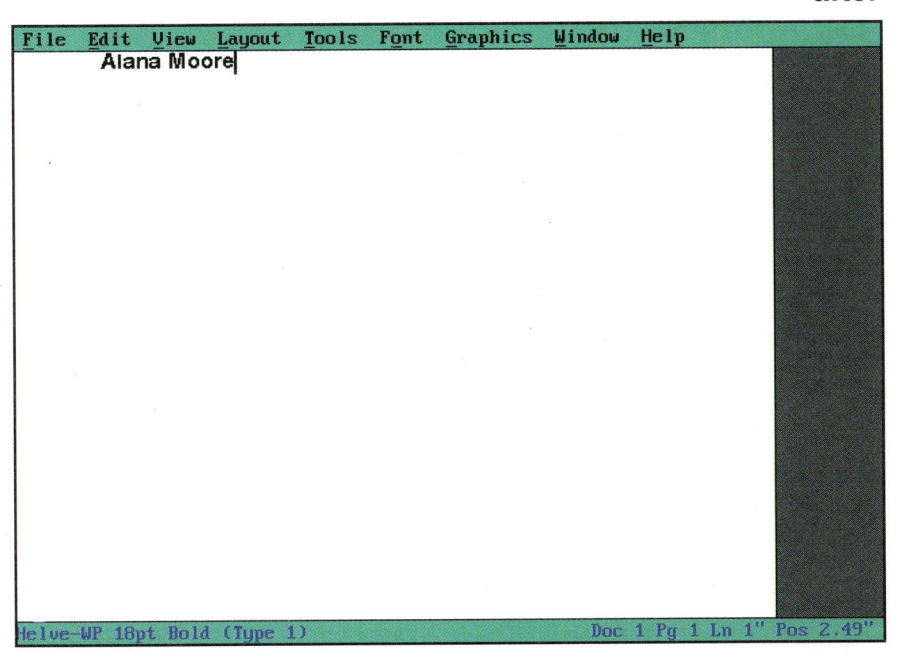

See font changes?

If you can't see the font changes, your screen isn't in Graphics mode. To change to Graphics mode, see *TASK: Change to Graphics mode*.

REVIEW

To change the font

1. Block the text you want to change.

2. Press **Alt+O** to open the Font menu.

3. Press **O** to select the Font command.

4. Press **F** to select the Font list.

5. Use the arrow keys to select the font you want.

6. Press **Enter twice**.

Try a shortcut

Press Ctrl+F8 to display the Font dialog box.

Basic Formatting

TASK

Change the font size

before

[Screenshot showing WordPerfect with "Alana Moore" highlighted, Block on status at bottom]

Oops!

To undo the change, open the Edit menu (press Alt+E) and select the Undo command (press U). Or open the Reveal Codes window (press Alt+F3) and delete the `[Very Large On]` code.

1. Block the text *Alana Moore*.

    This step selects the text you want to change. For help on blocking text, see *TASK: Select a block*.

2. Press **Alt**+**O**.

    This step opens the Font menu. You see a list of Font commands.

3. Press **O**.

    This step selects the Font command. You see the Font dialog box.

4. Press **R**.

    This step selects the Relative Size option and displays other options, which enable you to change the font size.

5. Press **V**.

    This step selects the Very Large option, which makes text very large.

6. Press **Enter**.

    This step confirms the change and returns you to the document. If your screen is displayed in Graphics mode, WordPerfect displays the blocked text in the new font size on-screen, as shown in the After screen.

Easy WordPerfect for Version 6

after

```
File  Edit  View  Layout  Tools  Font  Graphics  Window  Help
    Alana Moore|




















Helve-WP 27pt Bold (Type 1)              Doc 1 Pg 1 Ln 1" Pos 3.24"
```

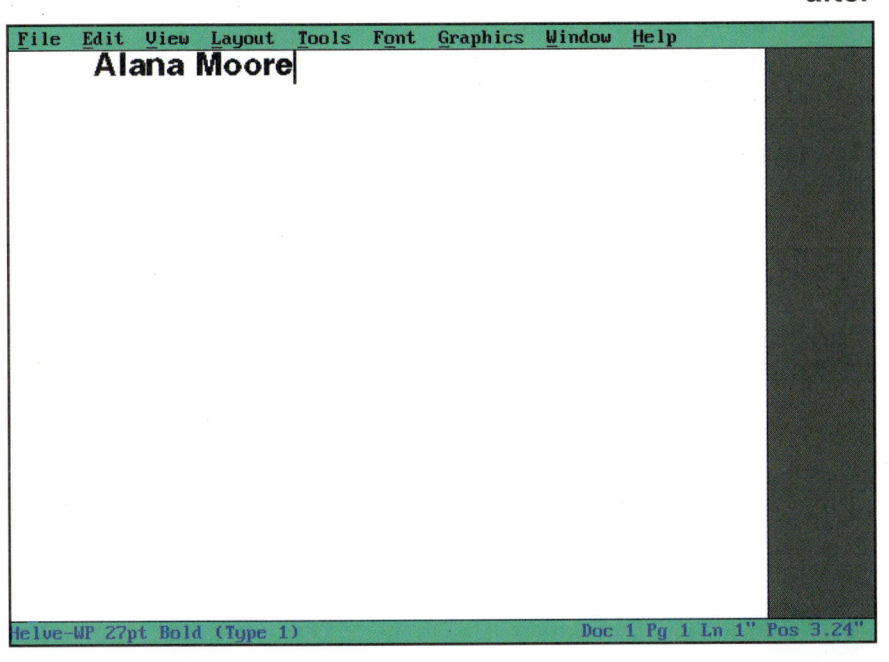

See font changes?

If you can't see the font changes, your screen isn't in Graphics mode. To change to Graphics mode, see *TASK: Change to Graphics mode.*

REVIEW

1. Block the text you want to change.
2. Press **Alt**+**O** to open the Font menu.
3. Press **O** to select the Font command.
4. Press **R** to select Relative Size.
5. Press **F** for Fine, **S** for Small, **L** for Large, **V** for Very Large, or **E** for Extra Large.
6. Press **Enter**.

To change the font size

Try a shortcut

Press Ctrl+F8 to display the Font dialog box.

Basic Formatting

101

TASK

Change the initial font

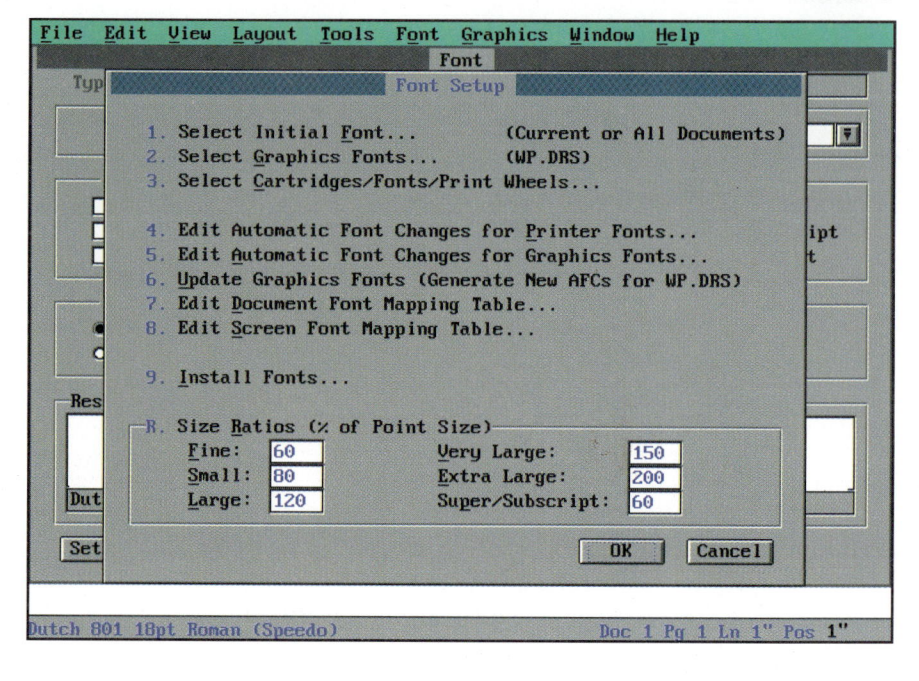

before

[Screenshot of WordPerfect Font Setup dialog box showing options:
1. Select Initial Font... (Current or All Documents)
2. Select Graphics Fonts... (WP.DRS)
3. Select Cartridges/Fonts/Print Wheels...
4. Edit Automatic Font Changes for Printer Fonts...
5. Edit Automatic Font Changes for Graphics Fonts...
6. Update Graphics Fonts (Generate New AFCs for WP.DRS)
7. Edit Document Font Mapping Table...
8. Edit Screen Font Mapping Table...
9. Install Fonts...
R. Size Ratios (% of Point Size)
  Fine: 60   Very Large: 150
  Small: 80   Extra Large: 200
  Large: 120 Super/Subscript: 60]

Oops!
To change to a different font, follow this same procedure.

1. Press **Alt+O**.

   This step opens the Font menu. You see a list of Font commands.

2. Press **O**.

   This step selects the Font command. You see the Font dialog box.

3. Press **Shift+F1**.

   This step displays the Setup options. The Before screen shows this step.

4. Press **F**.

   This step selects the Select Initial Font command. You see a dialog box.

5. Press **F**.

   This step selects the Font list.

6. Press ↑ until you highlight **CG Times**.

   This step selects the font you want. Your list of fonts might be different. If you don't have this font, select one that you do have.

102

Easy WordPerfect for Version 6

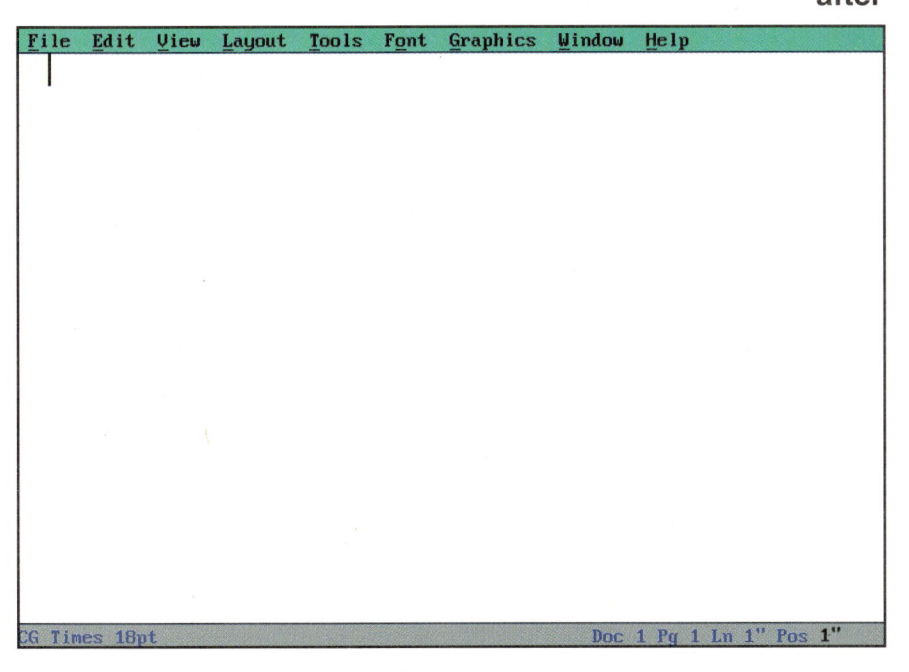

after

```
File  Edit  View  Layout  Tools  Font  Graphics  Window  Help
```

CG Times 18pt   Doc 1 Pg 1 Ln 1" Pos 1"

What's an initial font?

An initial font is the font WordPerfect uses for all new documents.

Caution

Any documents you created before you made this change will not be affected. Only new documents will use this new font.

7. Press **Enter four times**.

   This step confirms the font change and returns you to your document. The font name is displayed in the status line. All new documents will use this font unless you specifically change it. (This book uses Dutch 801 18pt Roman because it's easy to read.)

REVIEW

To change the initial font

1. Press **Alt+O** to open the Font menu.
2. Press **O** to select the Font command.
3. Press **Shift+F1**.
4. Press **F** to select Select Initial Font.
5. Press **F** to select the Font list.
6. Use the arrow keys to select the font you want.
7. Press **Enter four times**.

Basic Formatting

103

More Editing

This section covers the following tasks:

Change the case of a block

Search for text

Search and replace text

Insert the current date

Check spelling

Look up a word in the thesaurus

Display document information

Save a block

Retrieve a block

Sort text

TASK

Change the case of a block

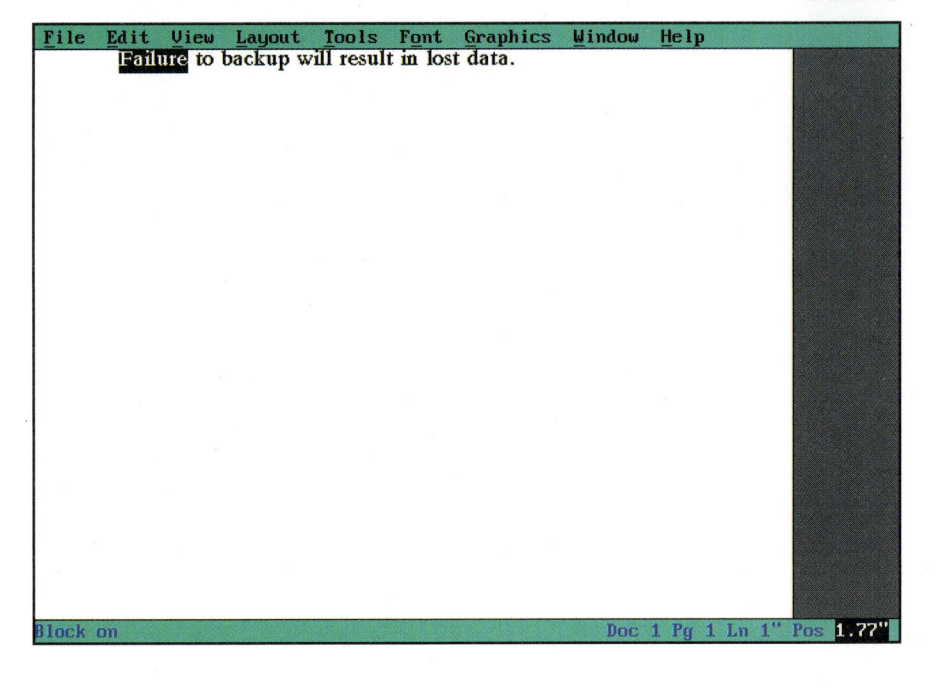

before

[Screenshot of WordPerfect screen showing the word "Failure" highlighted in the sentence "Failure to backup will result in lost data." with "Block on" status at the bottom.]

Oops!

To undo the change, open the Edit menu (press Alt+E) and select the Undo command (press U).

1. Block the word *Failure*.

   This step selects the text you want to change, as shown in the Before screen. For help on blocking text, see *TASK: Select a block*.

2. Press **Alt**+**E**.

   This step opens the Edit menu. You see a list of Edit commands.

3. Press **V**.

   This step selects the Convert Case command. You see a list of choices.

4. Press **U**.

   This step selects the Upper command. WordPerfect converts the blocked text to uppercase.

Easy WordPerfect for Version 6

after

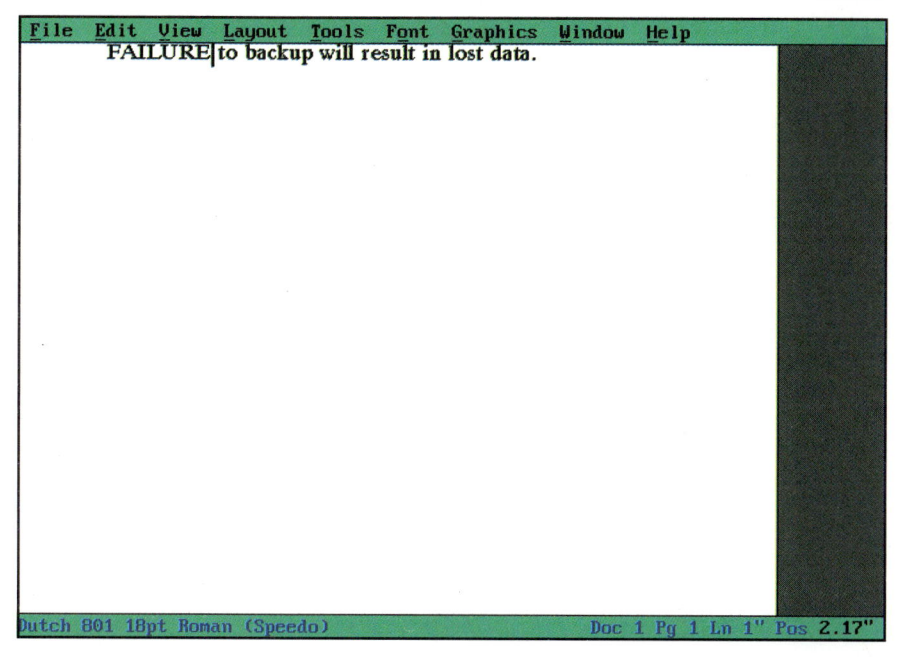

REVIEW

1. Block the text you want to change.
2. Press **Alt**+**E** to open the Edit menu.
3. Press **V** to select the Convert Case command.
4. Press **U** to select Upper.

To change the case of a block

More Editing

107

TASK

Search for text

before

[Screenshot of WordPerfect document showing Chapter 8, Buster Brown's Bride]

Oops!

If WordPerfect cannot find the text, you see the message `Not found`. Press Enter and try again. This time be sure that you type the text correctly.

1. Press **Home**, **Home**, **Home**, **↑** key.

   This step moves the cursor to the top of the document. During a text search, WordPerfect starts from the location of the cursor and moves forward. Moving the cursor to the top of the document ensures that WordPerfect will search every page.

2. Press **Alt+E**.

   This step opens the Edit menu. You see a list of Edit commands.

3. Press **H**.

   This step selects the Search command. You see the Search dialog box.

4. Type **Harry**.

   Harry is the search string, which is the text for which you want to search. If you use only lowercase letters, WordPerfect finds all occurrences of the search string. If you type only uppercase letters, WordPerfect finds only uppercase matches; for example, if you type HARRY, WordPerfect will not find *Harry*.

   WordPerfect also searches for parts of a word. For instance, if you type *the*, WordPerfect stops on *the, other, theater,* and other words that contain the letters *t-h-e*. To search for only the word, insert a space before and after the word in the search string.

Easy WordPerfect for Version 6

after

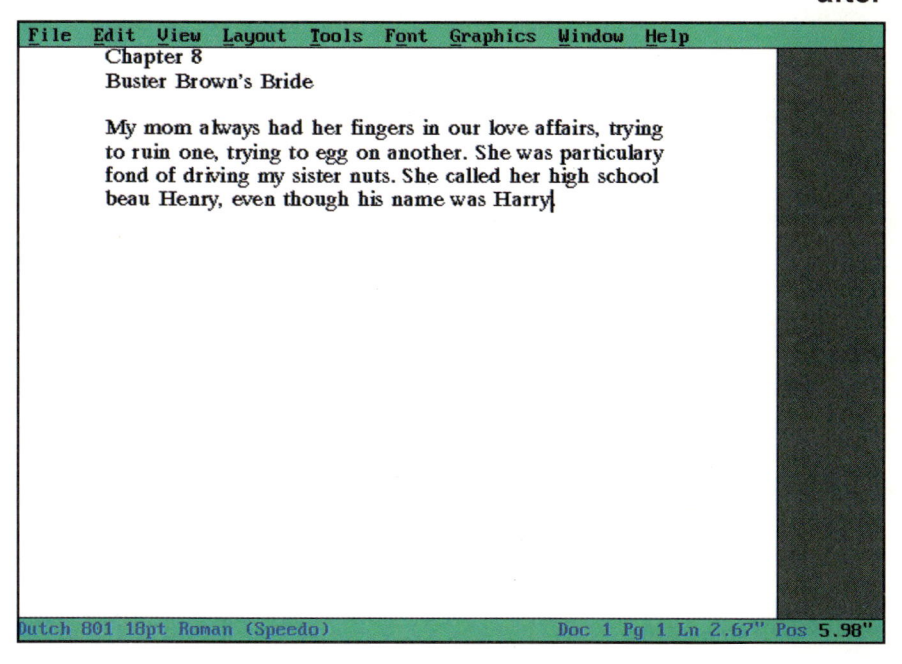

> There are other settings you can change in the Search dialog box; for example, you can do case-sensitive searches, whole-word searches, and backward searches. See Que's *Using WordPerfect 6,* Special Edition, for more information.

5. Press **F2**.

   Pressing the F2 key starts the search and moves the cursor to the right of the first occurrence of the search string.

Repeat a search

You can repeat a search by pressing the F2 key twice.

REVIEW

To search for text

1. Press **Home**, **Home**, **Home**, ↑ key to move the cursor to the beginning of the document.
2. Press **Alt+E** to open the Edit menu.
3. Press **H** to select the Search command.
4. Type the text for which you want to search.
5. Press **F2** to start the search.

Try a shortcut

Press F2 to select the Search command.

More Editing

109

TASK

Search and replace text

before

Oops!
To undo the change, open the Edit menu (press Alt+E) and select the Undo command (press U).

1. Press **Home**, **Home**, **Home**, ↑ key.

   This step moves the cursor to the top of the document, which ensures that WordPerfect will include all text in the search.

2. Press **Alt+E**.

   This step opens the Edit menu. You see a list of Edit commands.

3. Press **L**.

   This step selects the Replace command. You see the Search and Replace dialog box, which has text boxes called Search For and Replace With.

4. Type **FS**.

   FS is the text you want to replace. Type the text exactly as it appears in the document, which means correctly typing the upper- and lowercase letters. You can change the case-sensitive setting and the setting that determines whether WordPerfect looks for whole or partial words. See Que's *Using WordPerfect 6,* Special Edition, for details.

5. Press **Tab**.

   This step moves the cursor to the Replace With text box.

6. Type **First Software**.

   First Software is the text you want WordPerfect to insert in the place of *FS*.

Easy WordPerfect for Version 6

after

```
File  Edit  View  Layout  Tools  Font  Graphics  Window  Help
Press Release
The new version of First Software will include a mailing
label feature. First Software version 2.0 is scheduled for
release in the fall.




Dutch 801 18pt Roman (Speedo)              Doc 1 Pg 1 Ln 1.83" Pos 4.03"
```

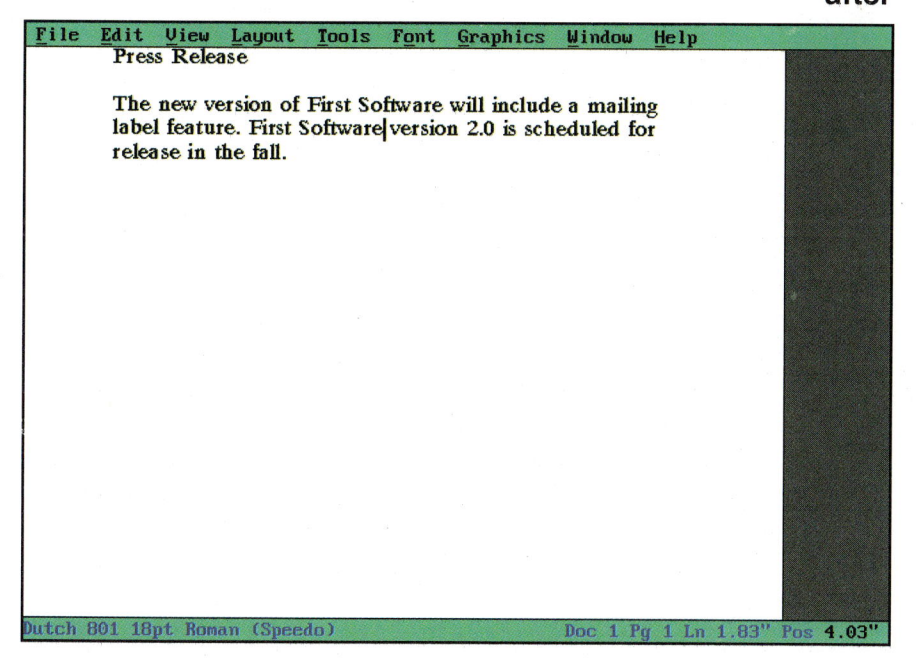

7. Press **F2**.

    Pressing the F2 key starts the replacement. WordPerfect makes all replacements without prompting you for confirmation, and it displays the results in the Search and Replace Results dialog box.

8. Press **Enter**.

    This step closes the Search and Replace Results dialog box.

Other options

You can control how the replacements are made. For instance, you can ask WordPerfect to stop on each replacement and ask for confirmation. For information on all Search and Replace options, see Que's Using WordPerfect 6, Special Edition.

Be careful...

You might want to test your replacement string by confirming the first few changes. That way, if it doesn't work as planned, you can catch any problems before WordPerfect changes the entire document.

REVIEW

To search and replace text

1. Press **Home**, **Home**, **Home**, ↑.
2. Press **Alt**+**E** to open the Edit menu.
3. Press **L** to select the Replace command.
4. Type the search string.
5. Press **Tab**.
6. Type the replacement string.
7. Press **F2**.

More Editing

111

TASK

Insert the current date

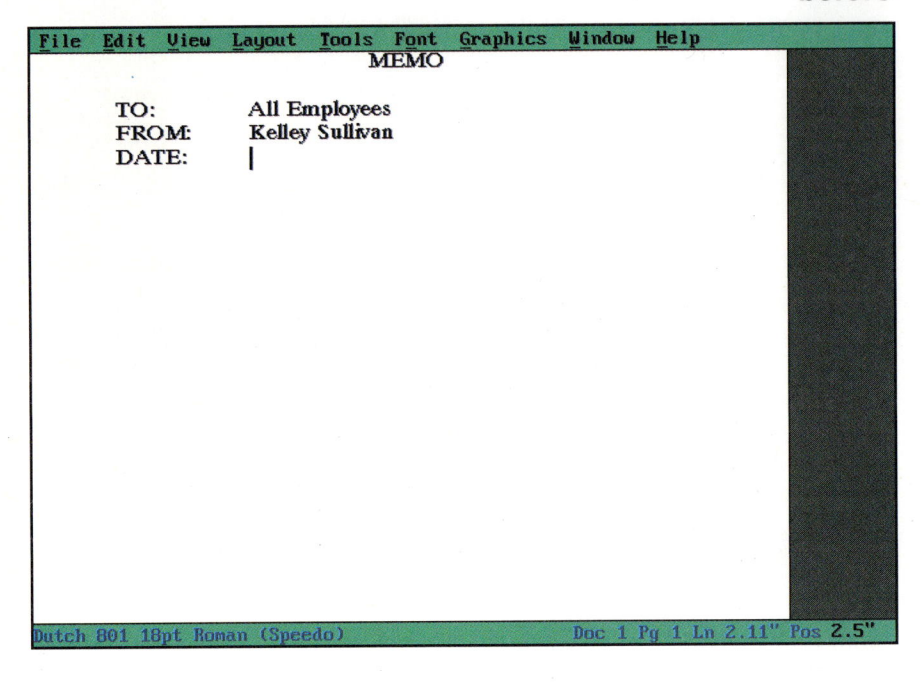

before

```
File  Edit  View  Layout  Tools  Font  Graphics  Window  Help
                         MEMO
        TO:         All Employees
        FROM:       Kelley Sullivan
        DATE:       |




Dutch 801 18pt Roman (Speedo)              Doc 1 Pg 1 Ln 2.11" Pos 2.5"
```

Oops!

To undo the change, open the Edit menu (press Alt+E) and select the Undo command (press U). Or press the Backspace or Del key to delete the date.

1. Position the cursor after the tab that follows the colon in *DATE*.

   The cursor is now at the location where you want to insert today's date.

2. Press **Alt**+**T**.

   This step opens the Tools menu. You see a list of Tools commands.

3. Press **D**.

   This step selects the Date command.

4. Type **T**.

   This step selects Text from the list of choices. This option inserts the current date into the document.

112

Easy WordPerfect for Version 6

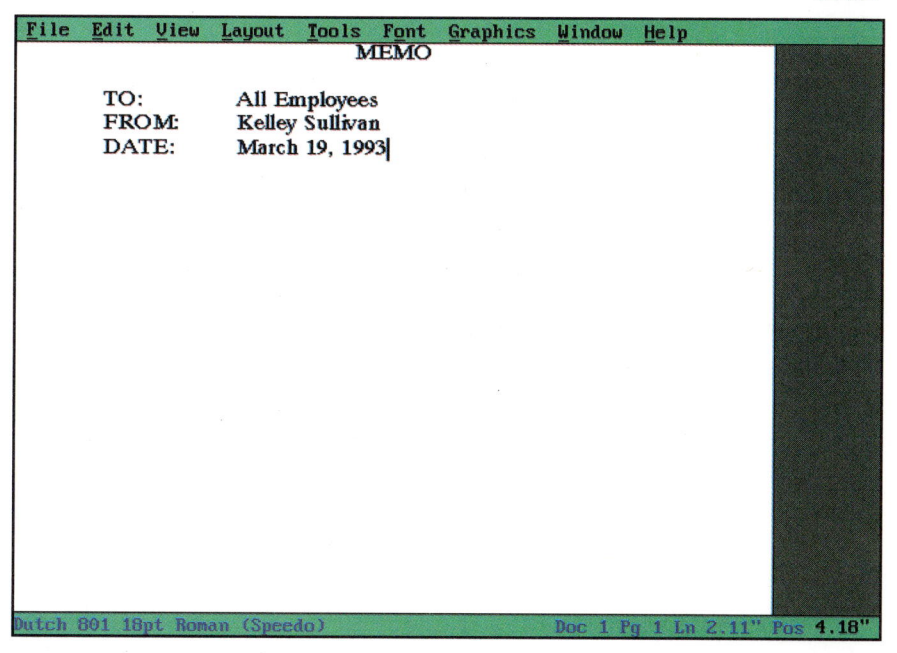

after

To insert the current date

1. Move the cursor to the location where you want to insert the date.

2. Press **Alt**+**T** to open the Tools menu.

3. Press **D** to select Date.

4. Press **T** to select Text.

Update the date

To enter a date code, which updates the date automatically, press C (select Code) instead of T in step 4.

TASK

Check spelling

before

[Screenshot of WordPerfect document showing a MEMO with TO: All Employees, FROM: Kelley Sullivan, DATE: March 19, 1993, and the text "Our committment is to quality."]

Oops!
If you want to stop a spelling check in progress, press the Esc key.

1. Press **Alt**+**T**.

   This step opens the Tools menu and displays a list of Tools commands.

2. Press **W**.

   This step selects the Writing Tools command. You see additional choices listed.

3. Press **S**.

   This step selects the Speller command. You see the Speller dialog box.

4. Press **D**.

   This step selects the Document command. WordPerfect begins the spelling check and stops on words that aren't in its dictionary. WordPerfect stops on the word *Kelley.* You see the Word Not Found dialog box.

5. Press **S**.

   This step selects Skip in this Document and tells WordPerfect to ignore all occurrences of this word. WordPerfect continues the spelling check. Press S until WordPerfect stops on the word *committment;* you see alternative spellings in the dialog box.

6. Press **R**.

   This step selects the Replace Word command and replaces the misspelling with the correction, *commitment.* You see a message saying that the spelling check is complete.

Easy WordPerfect for Version

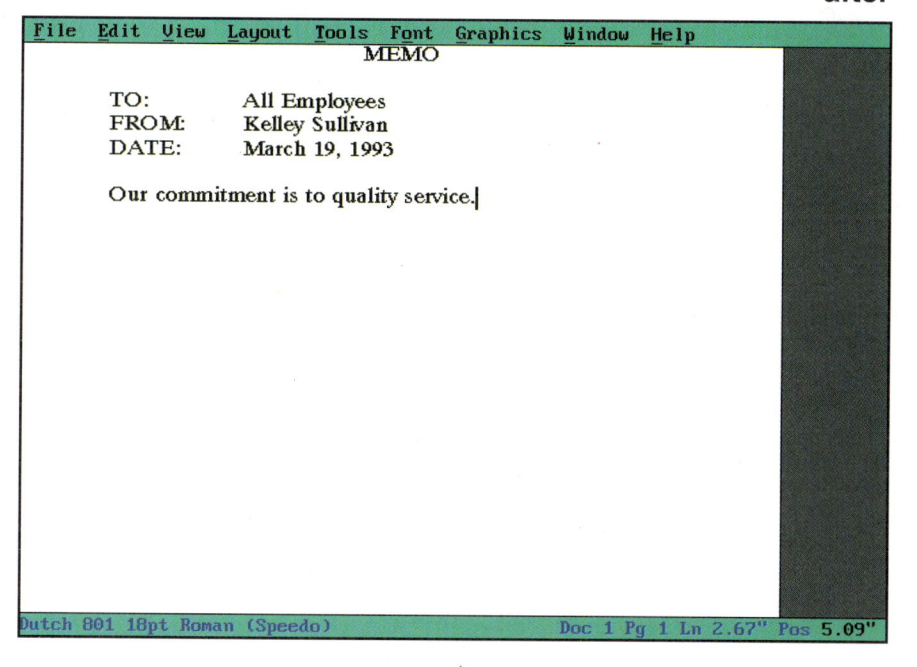

after

```
File  Edit  View  Layout  Tools  Font  Graphics  Window  Help
                         MEMO
        TO:        All Employees
        FROM:      Kelley Sullivan
        DATE:      March 19, 1993

        Our commitment is to quality service.|




Dutch 801 18pt Roman (Speedo)              Doc 1 Pg 1 Ln 2.67" Pos 5.09"
```

WordPerfect's dictionary

WordPerfect compares the words in your document to the words in its dictionary. The words that WordPerfect stops on aren't necessarily misspelled; they just might not be in its dictionary.

7. Press **Enter**.

   This step clears the message.

REVIEW

1. Press **Alt**+**T** to open the Tools menu.
2. Press **W** to select the Writing Tools command.
3. Press **S** to select Speller.
4. Press **D** to select Document.
5. Each time WordPerfect stops on a word, select one of these options:
   - Select an alternative spelling from those displayed. Then press **R**.
   - Press **O** to skip the word once, or **S** to skip the word throughout the document.
   - Press **T** to add the word to the dictionary.
   - Press **W** to edit the word.
   - If WordPerfect stops on a double word, press **S** to skip the double word or **D** to delete it.
6. Press **Enter** when the spelling check is complete.

To check spelling

Try a shortcut

Press Ctrl+F2 to select the Spell Check command.

More Editing

115

TASK

Look up a word in the thesaurus

before

```
File  Edit  View  Layout  Tools  Font  Graphics  Window  Help
                         REVIEW
    June 18, 1993
    For Pam Wagner
    Given by Barb Paynter

    Pam is a diligent worker.
```

Dutch 801 18pt Roman (Speedo)   Doc 1 Pg 1 Ln 2.67" Pos 2.82"

Oops!
To undo the change, open the Edit menu (press Alt+E) and select the Undo command (press U).

1. Use the arrow keys to move to the word *diligent*.

   The cursor is on the word you want to look up in the thesaurus.

2. Press **Alt**+**T**.

   This step opens the Tools menu and displays a list of Tools commands.

3. Press **W**.

   This step selects the Writing Tools command. You see additional choices listed.

4. Press **T**.

   This step selects the Thesaurus command. You see a list of synonyms for the word.

5. Press the ↓ key until you highlight **hard-working**.

   This step selects the word you want to use instead of the original word.

6. Press **R**.

   This step selects the Replace option and replaces the original word with the word from the synonym list.

Easy WordPerfect for Version 6

after

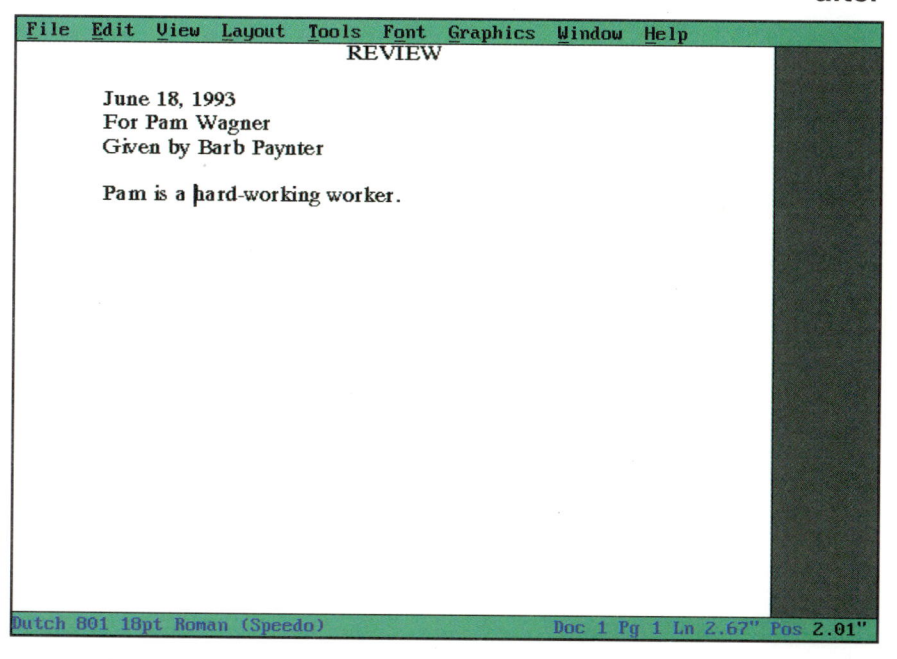

> **Use other thesaurus options**
>
> The Thesaurus feature offers many choices, such as displaying synonyms of the listed synonyms. See Que's Using WordPerfect 6, Special Edition.

REVIEW

To look up a word in the thesaurus

1. Move the cursor to the word you want to look up in the thesaurus.
2. Press **Alt**+**T** to open the Tools menu.
3. Press **W** to select Writing Tools.
4. Press **T** to select Thesaurus.
5. Select the new word you want.
6. Press **R** to replace the original word.

TASK

Display document information

before

[Screenshot of WordPerfect document showing "Chapter 1 — The Marriage Trefecta"]

Oops!
To close the dialog box, press Enter.

1. Press **Alt**+**T**.

   This step opens the Tools menu and displays a list of Tools commands.

2. Press **W**.

   This step selects the Writing Tools command. You see additional choices listed.

3. Press **D**.

   This step selects the Document Info option and displays the Document Information dialog box, which shows the number of characters, words, lines, sentences, paragraphs, and pages in your document. Other statistics about the document are displayed as well. The After screen shows this step.

4. Press **Enter**.

   This step closes the Document Information dialog box.

118

Easy WordPerfect for Version 6

after

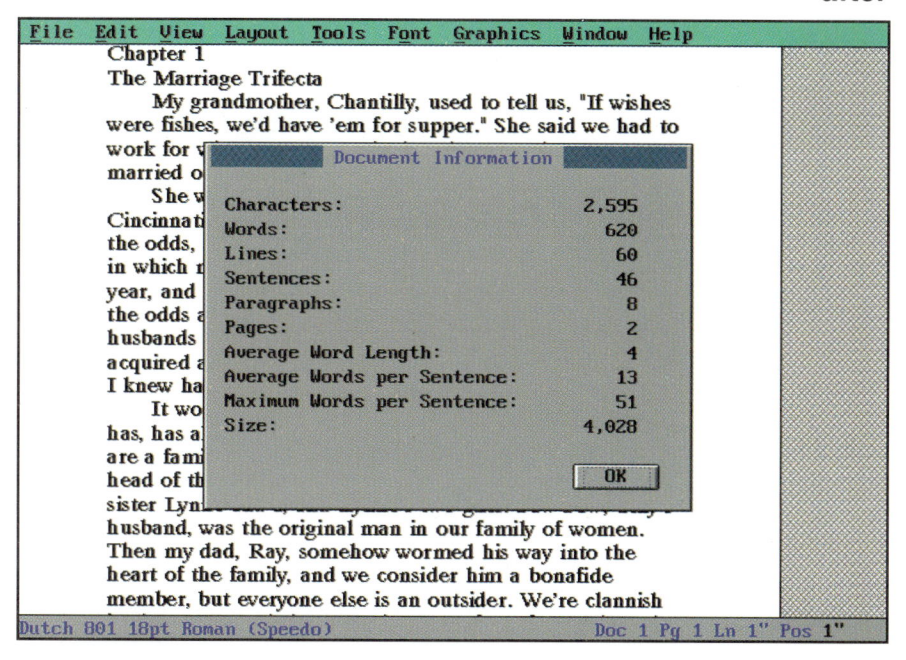

REVIEW

To display document information

1. Press **Alt**+**T** to open the Tools menu.

2. Press **W** to select the Writing Tools command.

3. Press **D** to select the Document Info option.

4. Press **Enter** to close the dialog box.

More Editing

119

TASK

Save a block

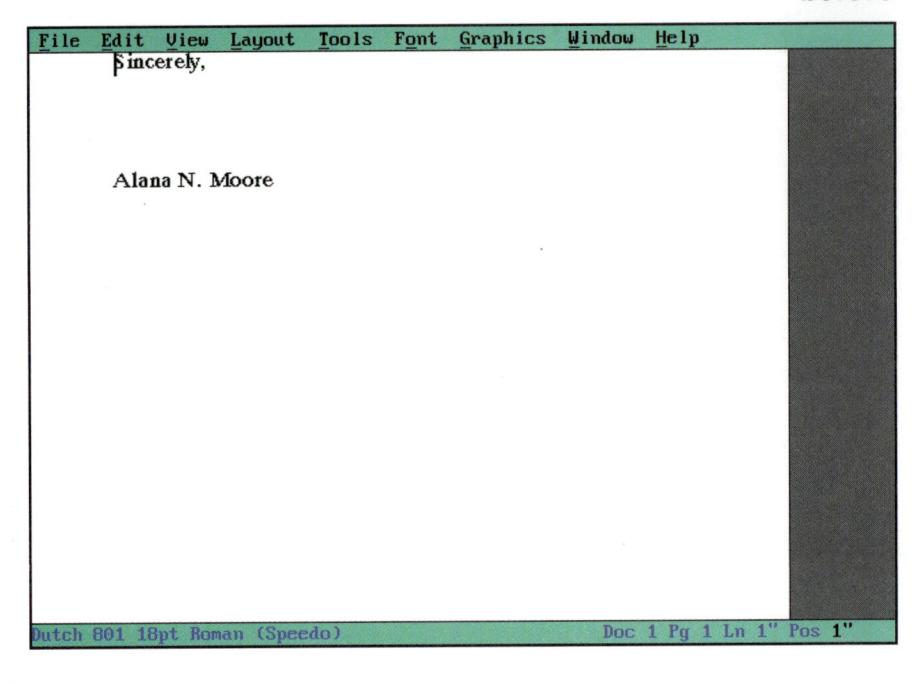

before

[screen showing WordPerfect with "Sincerely," and "Alana N. Moore" visible, menu bar: File Edit View Layout Tools Font Graphics Window Help; status bar: Dutch 801 18pt Roman (Speedo)   Doc 1 Pg 1 Ln 1" Pos 1"]

Oops!

If you highlight the wrong block, press the Esc key and start over.

1. Block the line that starts with *Sincerely*, and block the name.

   This step selects the text you want to save. For help on blocking text, see *TASK: Select a block*.

2. Press **Alt**+**F**.

   This step opens the File menu and displays a list of File commands.

3. Press **A**.

   This step selects the Save As command. You see the Save Block dialog box.

4. Type **CLOSE**.

   This step specifies that you want to save the block to a file named *CLOSE*.

5. Press **Enter**.

   Pressing Enter completes the operation. The text remains in the document and is saved to disk under the file name you assigned.

Easy WordPerfect for Version 6

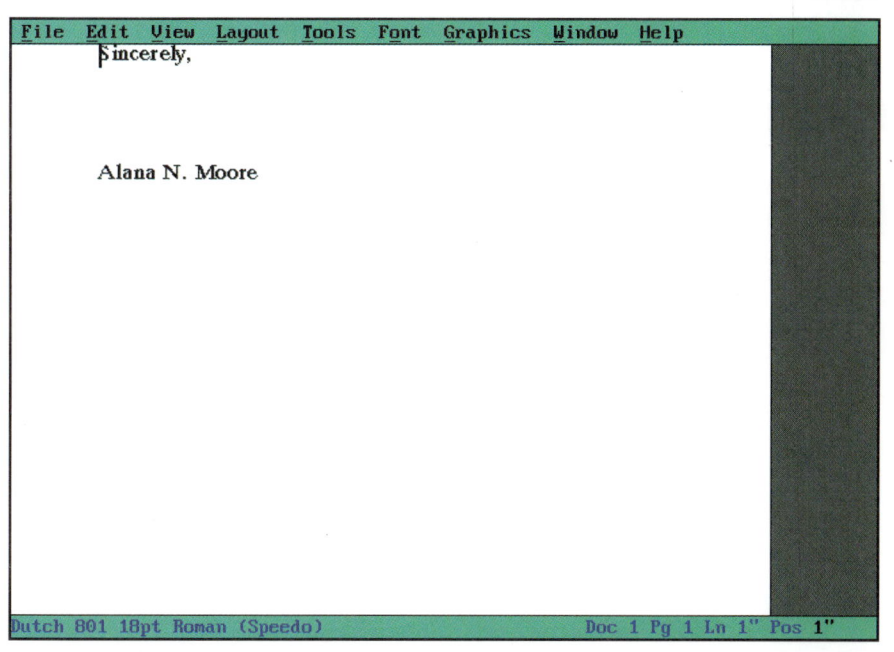

after

1. Block the text you want to save.
2. Press **Alt**+**F** to open the File menu.
3. Press **A** to select the Save As command.
4. Type a file name for the block of text.
5. Press **Enter**.

Retrieve a saved block

To retrieve a block you have saved, see TASK: Retrieve a block.

REVIEW

To save a block

More Editing

121

TASK

Retrieve a block

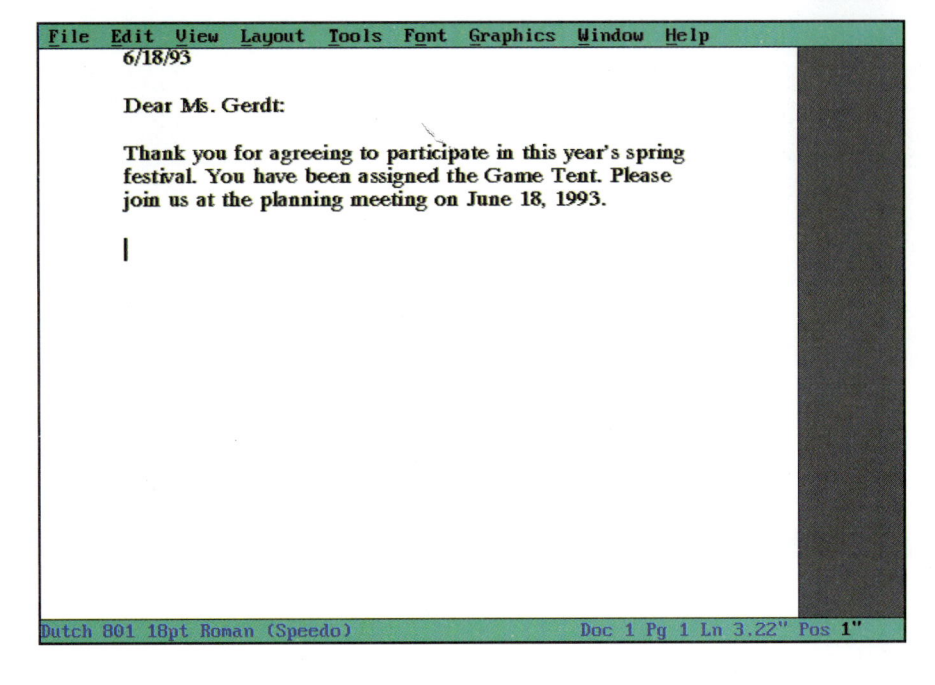

before

Oops!
To cancel a retrieval before you press Enter, press the Esc key. If you have already pressed Enter (and WordPerfect has inserted the text), you must delete the text manually.

1. Press **Enter** to move the cursor to the second line below the end of the text.

   This step positions the cursor on the spot where you want to insert the block of text you saved in *TASK: Save a block*.

2. Press **Alt**+**F**.

   This step opens the File menu and displays a list of File commands.

3. Press **R**.

   This step selects the Retrieve command. You see the Retrieve dialog box.

4. Type **CLOSE**.

   This step specifies that you want to retrieve a file called *CLOSE*.

5. Press **Enter**.

   Pressing Enter completes the operation. WordPerfect inserts the block into the document.

Easy WordPerfect for Version 6

after

REVIEW

To retrieve a block

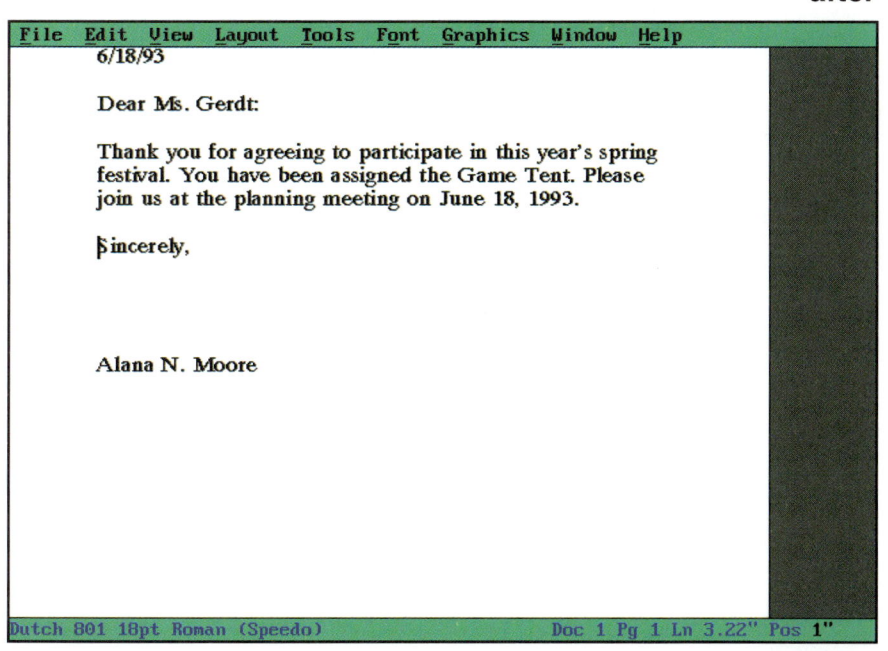

Save a block

To retrieve a block, you must first have saved it. See *TASK: Save a block*.

1. Move the cursor to the location where you want to insert a saved block of text.

2. Press **Alt**+**F** to open the File menu.

3. Press **R** to select the Retrieve command.

4. Type the name of the file you want to retrieve.

5. Press **Enter**.

More Editing

123

TASK

Sort text

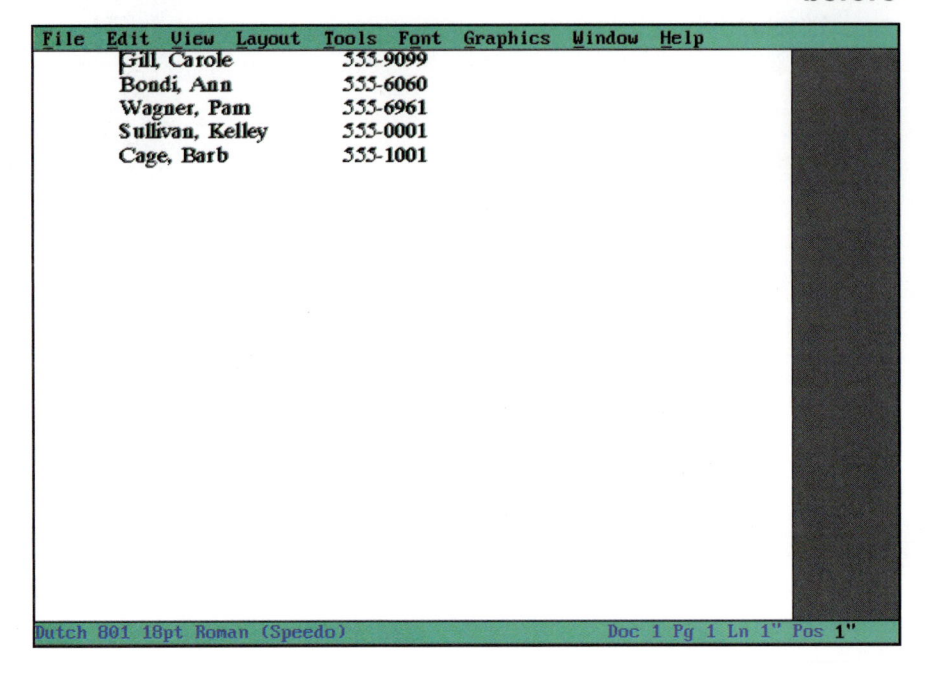

before

```
File  Edit  View  Layout  Tools  Font  Graphics  Window  Help
   Gill, Carole          555-9099
   Bondi, Ann            555-6060
   Wagner, Pam           555-6961
   Sullivan, Kelley      555-0001
   Cage, Barb            555-1001




Dutch 801 18pt Roman (Speedo)              Doc 1 Pg 1 Ln 1" Pos 1"
```

Oops!

To undo the change, open the Edit menu (press Alt+E) and select the Undo command (press U).

1. Block the phone list.

   This step selects the text you want to sort. For help on blocking text, see *TASK: Select a block*.

2. Press **Alt+T**.

   This step opens the Tools menu and displays a list of Tools commands.

3. Press **R**.

   This step selects the Sort command. You see the Sort dialog box. The options in this box control how WordPerfect will perform the sort. The default options are sufficient for this task.

4. Press **Enter**.

   Pressing Enter tells WordPerfect to sort the text. WordPerfect sorts the list alphabetically by the first word on each line.

Easy WordPerfect for Version 6

after

```
 File   Edit   View   Layout   Tools   Font   Graphics   Window   Help
       Bondi, Ann          555-6060
       Cage, Barb          555-1001
       Gill, Carole        555-9099
       Sullivan, Kelley    555-0001
       Wagner, Pam         555-6961




















 Dutch 801 18pt Roman (Speedo)              Doc 1 Pg 1 Ln 1" Pos 1"
```

Use other options

You can enter more complex sort criteria, such as a paragraph sort or a sort on more than the first word. See Que's *Using WordPerfect 6,* Special Edition.

REVIEW

To sort text

1. Block the text you want to sort.
2. Press **Alt+T** to open the Tools menu.
3. Press **R** to select the Sort command.
4. Press **Enter**.

More Editing

125

More Formatting

This section covers the following tasks:

- Set left tabs
- Align numbers at the decimal point
- Double space a document
- Add a paragraph border
- Shade a paragraph
- Center text on a page
- Number pages
- Add a page border
- Set margins
- Change to Page mode
- Create a header
- Edit a header
- Create a footer
- Edit a footer
- Insert a special character
- Draw a horizontal line
- Insert a graphic
- Insert a table
- Enter text into a table
- Add a row to a table
- Delete a row from a table
- Create a two-column document
- Type text in the second column

TASK

Set left tabs

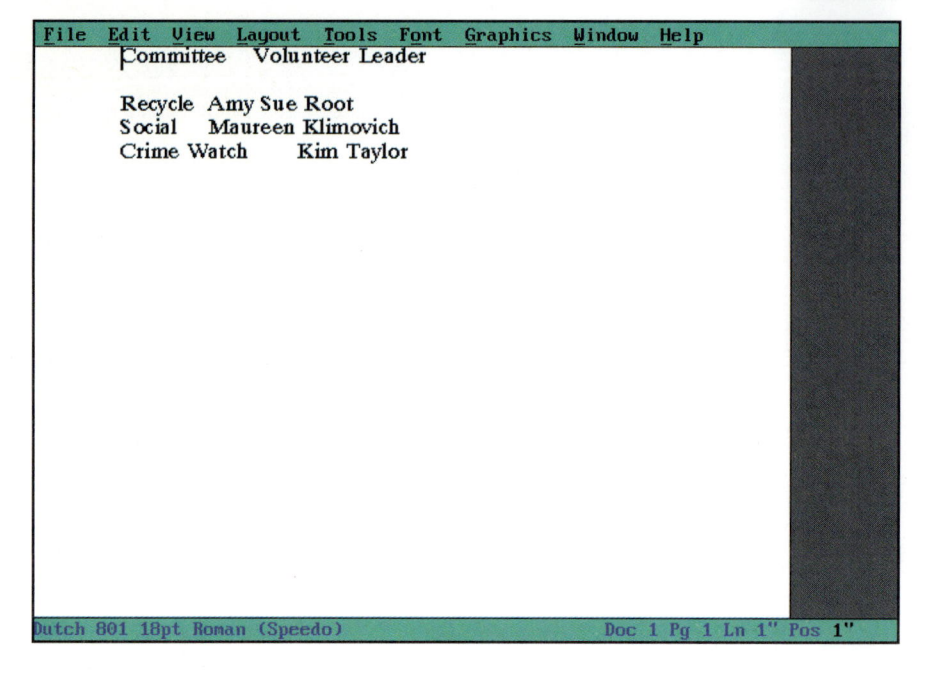

before

```
 File   Edit  View  Layout  Tools  Font  Graphics  Window  Help
      Committee    Volunteer Leader

      Recycle    Amy Sue Root
      Social     Maureen Klimovich
      Crime Watch    Kim Taylor




 Dutch 801 18pt Roman (Speedo)              Doc 1 Pg 1 Ln 1" Pos 1"
```

Oops!
To undo the change, open the Edit menu (press Alt+E) and select the Undo command (press U).

1. Press **Home**, **Home**, **Home**, ↑ key.

   This step moves the cursor to the top of the document. Moving the cursor here ensures that your tab changes will affect the entire document.

2. Press **Alt+L**.

   This step opens the Layout menu and displays a list of Layout commands.

3. Press **B**.

   This step selects the Tab Set command. You see the Tab Set dialog box. The ruler at the top displays the current tab settings.

4. Press **A**.

   This step selects the Clear All option. All existing tabs are cleared.

5. Use the arrow keys to move the cursor under the 3-inch mark on the ruler.

   This spot is the location for the tab stop, 3 inches from the edge of the paper.

128

Easy WordPerfect for Version 6

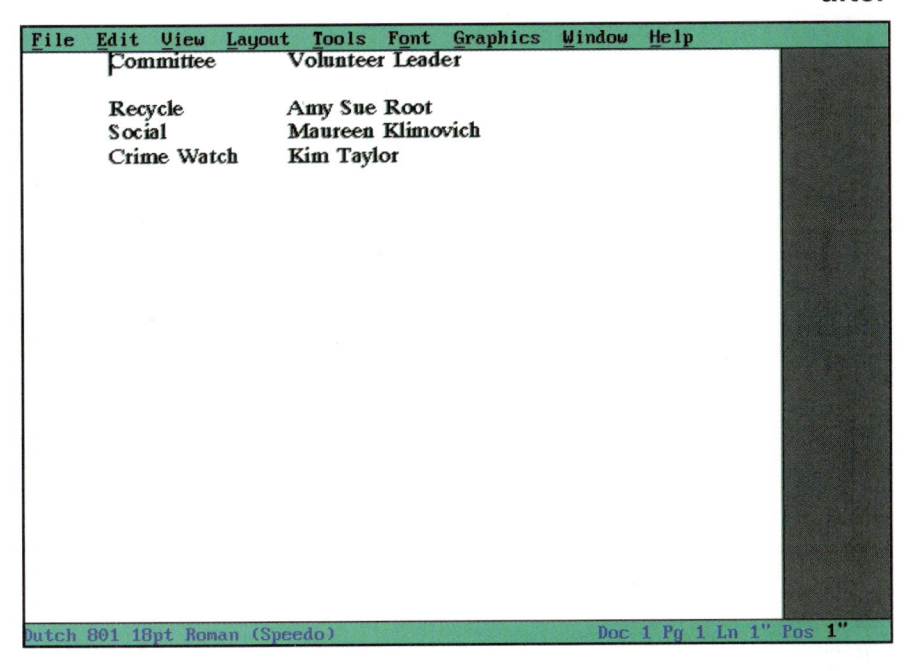

after

```
 File   Edit   View   Layout   Tools   Font   Graphics   Window   Help
       Committee           Volunteer Leader

          Recycle          Amy Sue Root
          Social           Maureen Klimovich
          Crime Watch      Kim Taylor











Dutch 801 18pt Roman (Speedo)                Doc 1 Pg 1 Ln 1" Pos 1"
```

Reveal Codes

If you don't undo the tab change immediately, you can delete a hidden code to return to the normal tab settings. Display the Reveal Codes window (press Alt+F3) and delete the [Tab Set] code.

6. Press **L**.

   This step tells WordPerfect to add a left tab stop for the entire document.

7. Press **Tab** until you move to the OK button; then press **Enter**.

   This step confirms the settings, closes the Tab Set dialog box, and returns you to the document.

REVIEW

To set left tabs

1. Press **Home**, **Home**, **Home**, ↑ key to move to the top of the document.

2. Press **Alt**+**L** to open the Layout menu.

3. Press **B** to select the Tab Set command.

4. Press **A** to select the Clear All option.

5. Use the arrow keys to position the cursor where you want a tab. Then Press **L**.

6. Press **Tab** to move to OK; then press **Enter**.

Set different tabs

You also can set right, decimal, and center tab stops and insert a dot leader before a tab stop. See Que's Using WordPerfect 6, Special Edition.

More Formatting

129

TASK

Align numbers at the decimal point

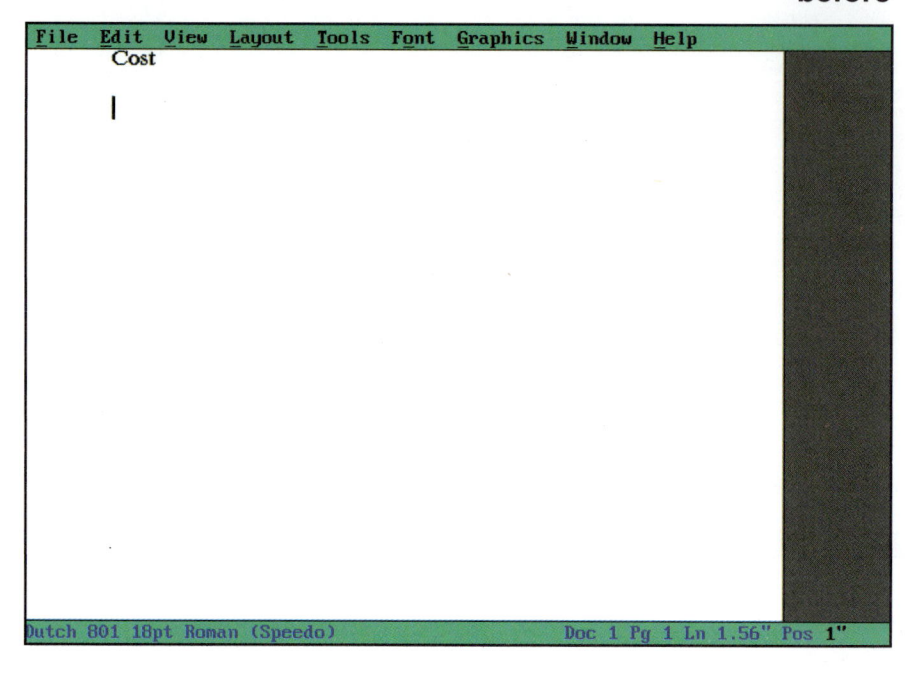

before

```
File  Edit  View  Layout  Tools  Font  Graphics  Window  Help
      Cost
      |
```
Dutch 801 18pt Roman (Speedo)   Doc 1 Pg 1 Ln 1.56" Pos 1"

Oops!

To undo the change, open the Edit menu (press Alt+E) and select the Undo command (press U).

1. Press **Alt+L**.

   This step opens the Layout menu and displays a list of Layout commands.

2. Press **A**.

   This step selects the Alignment command. You see a list of alignment options.

3. Press **D**.

   This step selects the Decimal Tab option.

4. Type **110.25**.

   As you type, text moves left until you type a decimal point (a period). Then the text moves right.

5. Press **Enter**.

   Pressing Enter ends this line and moves the cursor to the beginning of the next line.

6. Repeat steps 1–3.

   This step selects the Decimal Tab option.

7. Type **55.35** and press **Enter**.

   Notice how both numbers align at the decimal point.

130   *Easy WordPerfect for Version 6*

after

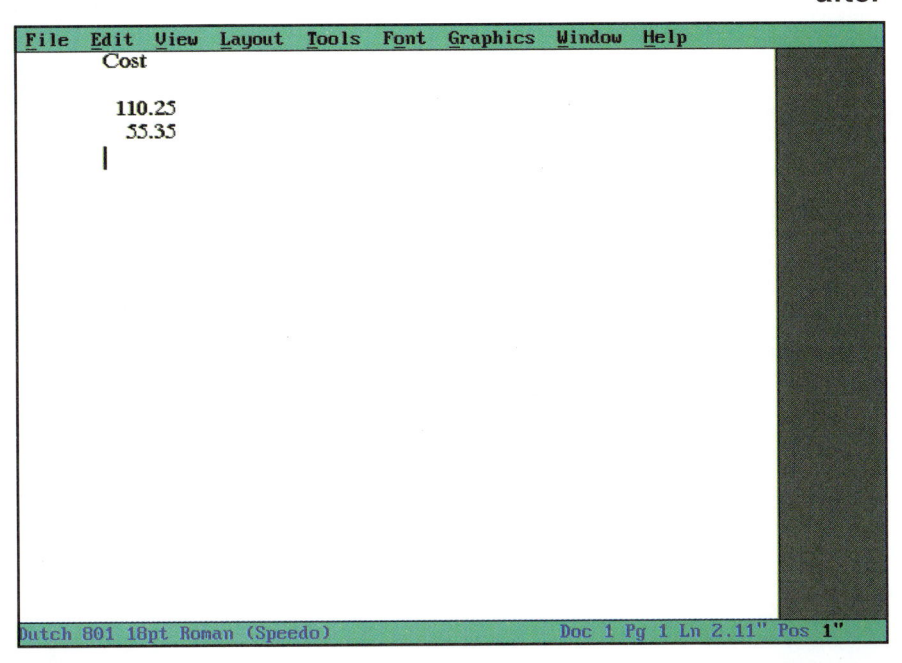

```
File  Edit  View  Layout  Tools  Font  Graphics  Window  Help
      Cost
         110.25
          55.35
         |




Dutch 801 18pt Roman (Speedo)              Doc 1 Pg 1 Ln 2.11" Pos 1"
```

Set different tabs

You also can set left, right, and center tab stops and insert a dot leader before a tab stop. See *TASK: Set left tabs* and Que's *Using WordPerfect 6,* Special Edition.

REVIEW

1. Move the cursor to the place where you want to start typing text.

2. Press **Alt**+**L** to open the Layout menu.

3. Press **A** to select the Alignment command.

4. Press **D** to select Decimal Tab.

5. Type a number and press **Enter**.

To align numbers at the decimal point

Try a shortcut

To select the Decimal Tab command, press Ctrl+F6.

More Formatting

131

TASK

Double-space a document

before

```
File  Edit  View  Layout  Tools  Font  Graphics  Window  Help
Chapter 1
The Marriage Trifecta
     My grandmother, Chantilly, used to tell us, "If wishes
were fishes, we'd have 'em for supper." She said we had to
work for what we want, and what she wanted was to get me
married off.
     She went on a Senior Citizen Trip to the racetrack in
Cincinnati, met this old guy who taught her how to figure
the odds, and set up the Marriage Trifecta, a sort of raffle
in which my family and friends tried to guess the month,
year, and groom of my wedding. Like a bookie, she'd figure
the odds and pay-off for any number of combinations of
husbands and wedding dates. She'd update the chart as I
acquired and discarded new prospects. Practically everyone
I knew had a stake in the Marriage Trifecta.
     It wouldn't have been such a big deal, but my family
has, has always had, this incredible influence over me. We
are a family of women: there's Tilly, my grandmother and
head of the family; Mom and her sister Aunt Kay; my
sister Lynne and I; and Lynne's two girls. Paw Paw, Tilly's
husband, was the original man in our family of women.
Then my dad, Ray, somehow wormed his way into the
heart of the family, and we consider him a bonafide
member, but everyone else is an outsider. We're clannish
Dutch 801 18pt Roman (Speedo)                Doc 1 Pg 1 Ln 1" Pos 1"
```

Oops!
To undo the change, open the Edit menu (press Alt+E) and select the Undo command (press U).

1. Press **Home**, **Home**, **Home**, ↑ key.

   This step moves the cursor to the top of the document. Moving the cursor here ensures that the spacing change affects the entire document.

2. Press **Alt+L**.

   This step opens the Layout menu and displays a list of Layout commands.

3. Press **L**.

   This step selects the Line command and displays the Line Format dialog box.

4. Press **S**.

   This step selects the Line Spacing option.

5. Type **2**.

   This step tells WordPerfect to double-space the document.

6. Press **Enter twice**.

   This step confirms the new spacing increment and returns you to the document. WordPerfect double-spaces the text.

132

Easy WordPerfect for Version 6

after

```
File  Edit  View  Layout  Tools  Font  Graphics  Window  Help
Chapter 1
The Marriage Trifecta
    My grandmother, Chantilly, used to tell us, "If wishes
were fishes, we'd have 'em for supper." She said we had to
work for what we want, and what she wanted was to get me
married off.
    She went on a Senior Citizen Trip to the racetrack in
Cincinnati, met this old guy who taught her how to figure
the odds, and set up the Marriage Trifecta, a sort of raffle
in which my family and friends tried to guess the month,
year, and groom of my wedding. Like a bookie, she'd figure
the odds and pay-off for any number of combinations of
Dutch 801 18pt Roman (Speedo)              Doc 1 Pg 1 Ln 1" Pos 1"
```

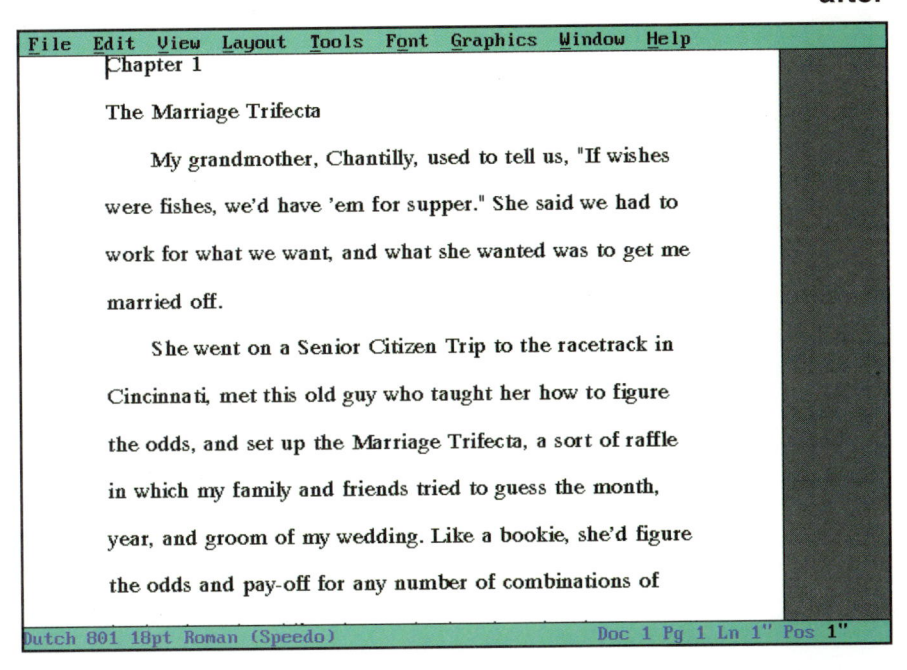

Reveal Codes

If you don't undo the change immediately, you have to use a different method. Display the Reveal Codes window (press Alt+F3) and delete the `[Ln Spacing]` code.

REVIEW

To double-space a document

1. Press **Home**, **Home**, **Home**, ↑ key to go to the top of the document.

2. Press **Alt+L** to open the Layout menu.

3. Press **L** to select the Line command.

4. Press **S** to select Line Spacing.

5. Type **2** to indicate that you want to double-space the text.

6. Press **Enter twice**.

Use other spacing increments

You can use other spacing increments by typing the appropriate number in step 5.

More Formatting

133

TASK

Add a paragraph border

before

Oops!

To undo the change, open the Edit menu (press Alt+E) and select the Undo command (press U).

1. Block the first paragraph.

   This step selects the paragraph to which you want to add a border. For help with blocking text, see *TASK: Select a block*.

2. Press **Alt**+**L**.

   This step opens the Layout menu and displays a list of Layout commands.

3. Press **L**.

   This step selects the Line command and displays the Line Format dialog box.

4. Press **B**.

   This step selects the Paragraph Borders option. You see the Create Paragraph Border dialog box, from which you can select the type of border you want. WordPerfect's default settings are sufficient for this task.

5. Press **Enter twice**.

   This step confirms the paragraph borders setting and returns you to your document. To see the border, you need to change to Graphics mode. The After screen shows the document in this mode. See *TASK: Change to Graphics mode*.

134   *Easy WordPerfect for Version 6*

after

1. Block the paragraph(s) to which you want to add borders.

2. Press **Alt+L** to open the Layout menu.

3. Press **L** to select the Line command.

4. Press **B** to select Paragraph Borders.

5. Press **Enter twice**.

REVIEW

To add a paragraph border

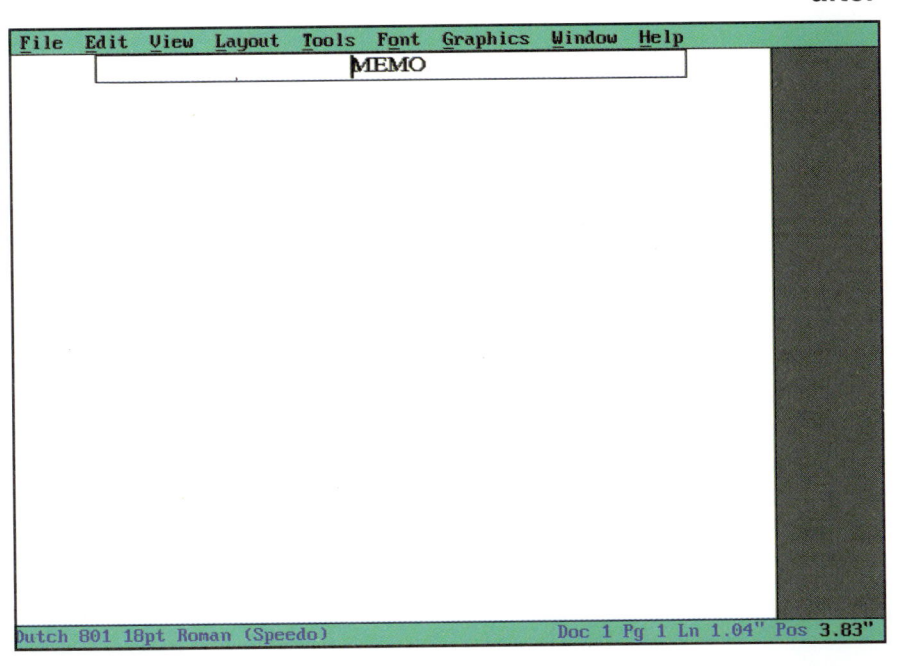

Reveal Codes

If you don't undo the change immediately, you have to use a different method. Display the Reveal Codes window (press Alt+F3) and delete the `[+Para Border]` code.

More information

For more information on paragraph borders, see Que's *Using WordPerfect 6,* Special Edition.

More Formatting

135

TASK

Shade a paragraph

before

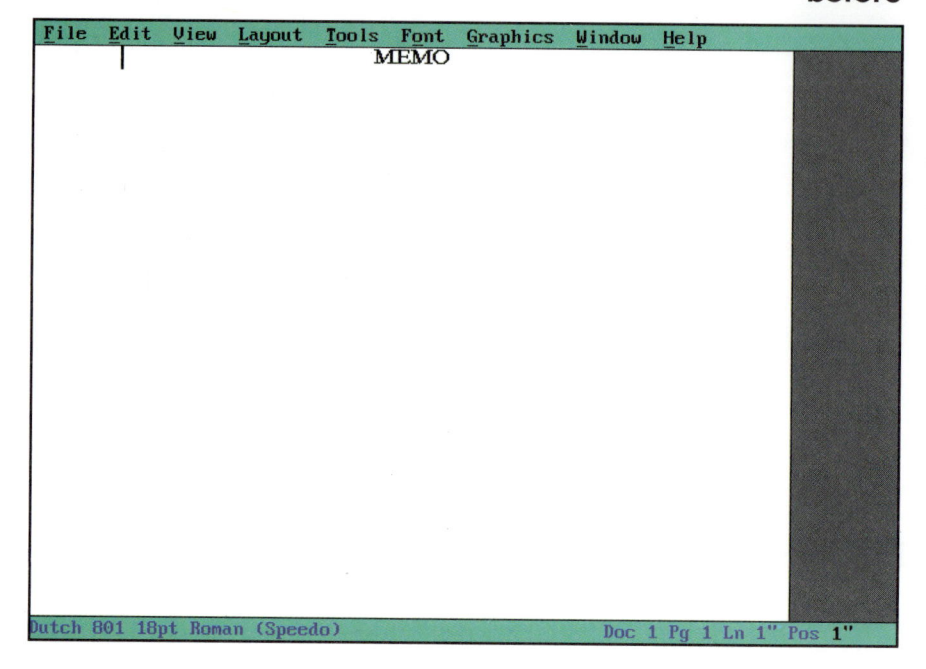

```
File  Edit  View  Layout  Tools  Font  Graphics  Window  Help
                        MEMO




















Dutch 801 18pt Roman (Speedo)              Doc 1 Pg 1 Ln 1" Pos 1"
```

Oops!
To undo the change, open the Edit menu (press Alt+E) and select the Undo command (press U).

1. Block the first paragraph.

   This step selects the paragraph to which you want to add shading with a border. For help with blocking text, see *TASK: Select a block*.

2. Press **Alt+L**.

   This step opens the Layout menu and displays a list of Layout commands.

3. Press **L**.

   This step selects the Line command and displays the Line Format dialog box.

4. Press **B**.

   This step selects the Paragraph Borders option.

5. Press **F**.

   This step selects the Fill Style option. You see a list of fill styles.

6. Press ↓ until you highlight **10% Shaded Fill**.

   This step selects the fill (shading) style you want.

136   *Easy WordPerfect for Version 6*

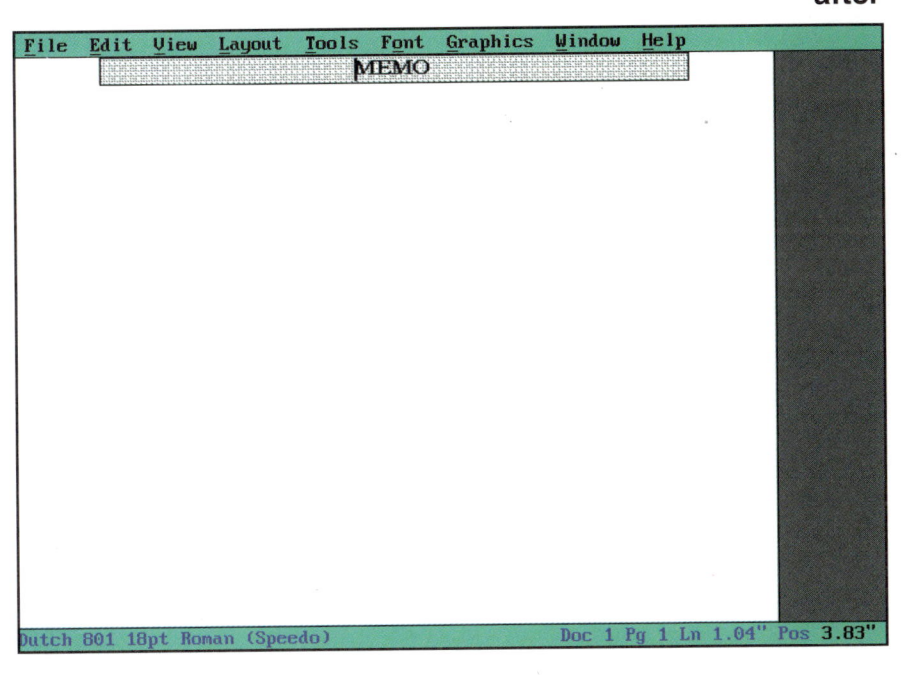

after

7. Press **Enter three times**.

    This step confirms the shading changes and returns you to the document. To see the shading, you need to change to Graphics mode. The After screen shows the document in this mode. See *TASK: Change to Graphics mode*.

REVIEW

To shade a paragraph

1. Block the paragraph(s) you want to shade.
2. Press **Alt**+**L** to open the Layout menu.
3. Press **L** to select the Line command.
4. Press **B** to select Paragraph Borders.
5. Press **F** to select Fill Style.
6. Select the fill style you want.
7. Press **Enter three times**.

Reveal Codes

If you don't undo the change immediately, you have to use a different method. Display the Reveal Codes window (press Alt+F3) and delete the `[+Para Border]` code.

More information

For more information on shading paragraphs, see Que's *Using WordPerfect 6,* Special Edition.

More Formatting

137

TASK

Center text on a page

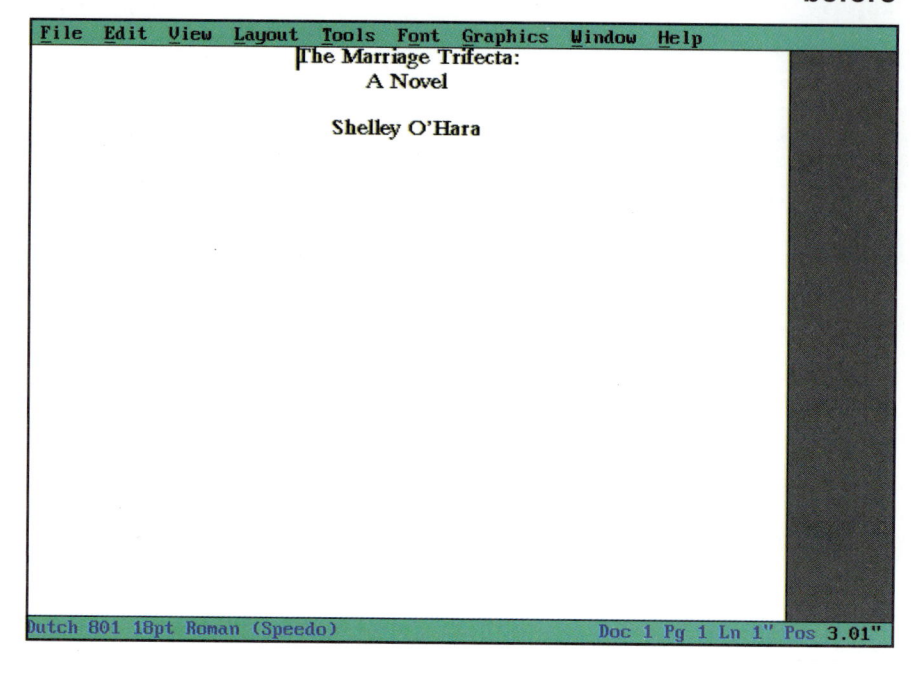

before

```
File   Edit   View   Layout   Tools   Font   Graphics   Window   Help
       The Marriage Trifecta:
              A Novel

            Shelley O'Hara
```

Dutch 801 18pt Roman (Speedo)   Doc 1 Pg 1 Ln 1" Pos 3.01"

Oops!

To undo the change, immediately select Edit Undo. Or display the Reveal Codes window (press Alt+F3) and delete the [Cntr Cur Pg] code.

1. Press **Home**, **Home**, **Home**, ↑ key.

   This step moves the cursor to the top of the document.

2. Press **Alt**+**L**.

   This step opens the Layout menu and displays a list of Layout commands.

3. Press **P**.

   This step selects the Page command and displays a list of Page options.

4. Press **C**.

   This step selects the Center Current Page command. This command centers text vertically on the page, between the top and bottom margins.

5. Press **Enter**.

   You cannot see the change on-screen. To see the change, preview your document. See *TASK: Preview a document.* The After screen shows a full-page preview.

138   *Easy WordPerfect for Version 6*

after

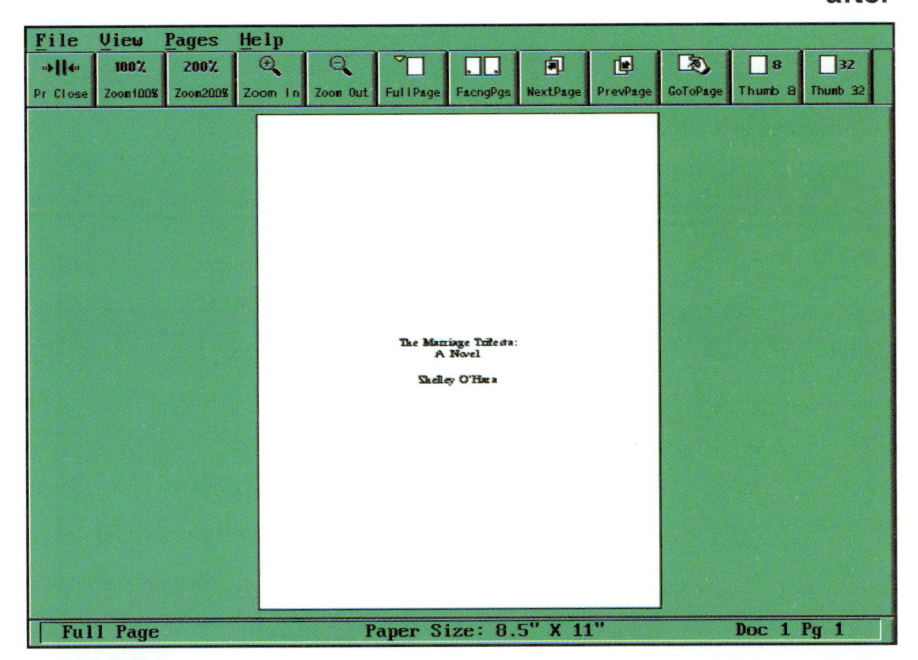

Use when...

This feature is useful for title pages and for one-page letters.

REVIEW

To center text on a page

1. Press **Home**, **Home**, **Home**, ↑.
2. Press **Alt**+**L** to open the Layout menu.
3. Press **P** to select the Page command.
4. Press **C** to select the Center Current Page command.
5. Press **Enter**.

TASK

Number pages

before

[Screenshot of WordPerfect showing Chapter 1 "The Marriage Trifecta" document]

Oops!

To undo the change, open the Edit menu (press Alt+E) and select the Undo command (press U). Or display the Reveal Codes window (press Alt+F3) and delete the `[Pg Num Pos]` code.

1. Press **Home**, **Home**, **Home**, **↑** key.

    This step moves the cursor to the top of the document. Moving the cursor here ensures that WordPerfect will number every page in the document.

2. Press **Alt**+**L**.

    This step opens the Layout menu and displays a list of Layout commands.

3. Press **P**.

    This step selects the Page command and displays the Page Format dialog box.

4. Press **N**.

    This step selects Page Numbering and displays the Page Numbering dialog box.

5. Press **P**.

    This step selects Page Number Position. WordPerfect displays the various page-number positions on-screen.

6. Press **C**.

    This step tells WordPerfect to place the page number at the bottom center of the page.

Easy WordPerfect for Version 6

after

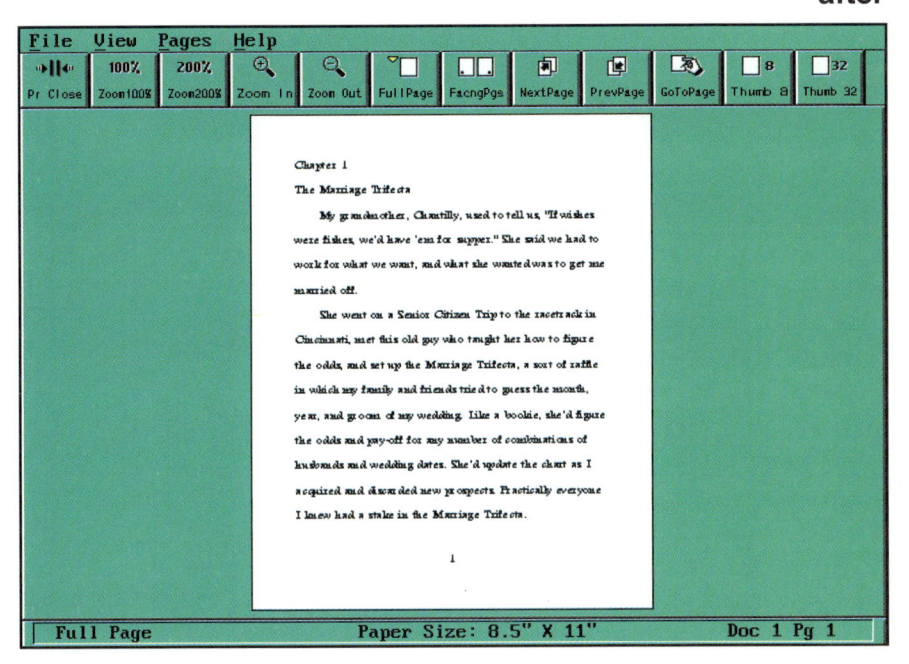

Use other numbering options

If you want to place the numbers in a different position—other than the bottom center—select that position in step 6.

7. Press **Enter three times**.

   This step returns you to your document. You cannot see the page number on the document screen. To see the number, you must preview the document. See *TASK: Preview a document*. The After screen shows a full-page preview.

REVIEW

To number pages

1. Press **Home**, **Home**, **Home**, ↑ key to move the cursor to the top of the document.

2. Press **Alt+L** to open the Layout menu.

3. Press **P** to select the Page command.

4. Press **N** to select the Page Numbering command.

5. Press **P** to select the Page Number Position command.

6. Select the page-number position you want.

7. Press **Enter three times**.

More information

For information on all page numbering options, see Que's *Using WordPerfect 6, Special Edition*.

More Formatting   141

TASK

Add a page border

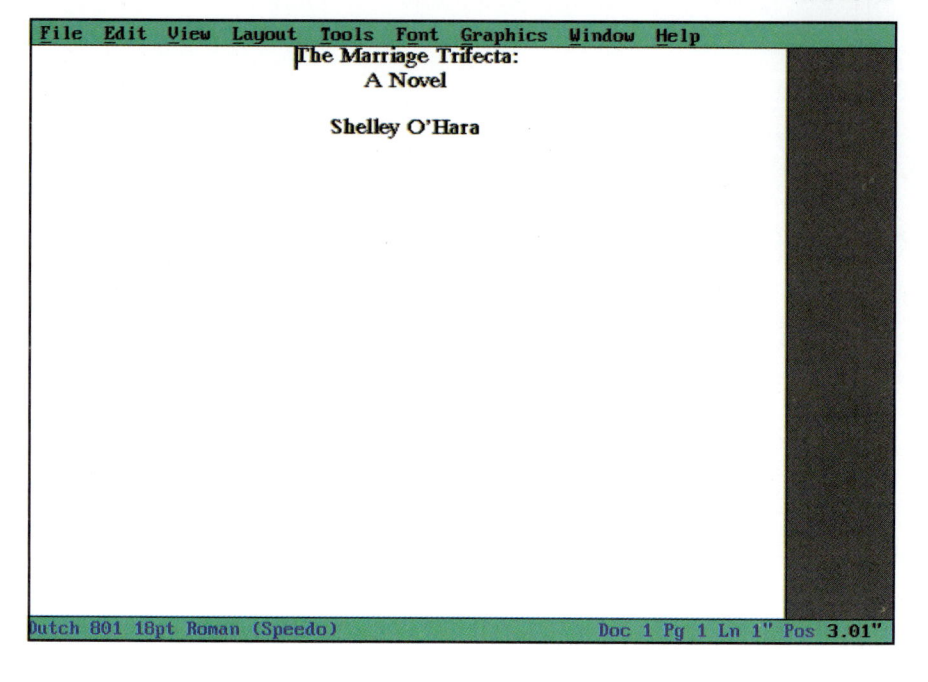

before

Oops!
To undo the change, open the Edit menu (press Alt+E) and select the Undo command (press U).

1. Select the first page of text.

   This step selects the page to which you want to add a page border.

2. Press **Alt+L**.

   This step opens the Layout menu and displays a list of Layout commands.

3. Press **P**.

   This step selects the Page command and displays the Page Format dialog box.

4. Press **B**.

   This step selects the Page Borders option and displays the Create Page Border dialog box, from which you can select the type of border you want. WordPerfect's default settings are sufficient for this task.

5. Press **Enter twice**.

   This step confirms the page border setting and returns you to the document. To see the border, you need to change to Graphics mode. The After screen shows the document in this mode. See *TASK: Change to Graphics mode*.

after

1. Select the text on the page to which you want to add a border.
2. Press **Alt**+**L** to open the Layout menu.
3. Press **P** to select the Page command.
4. Press **B** to select Page Borders.
5. Press **Enter twice**.

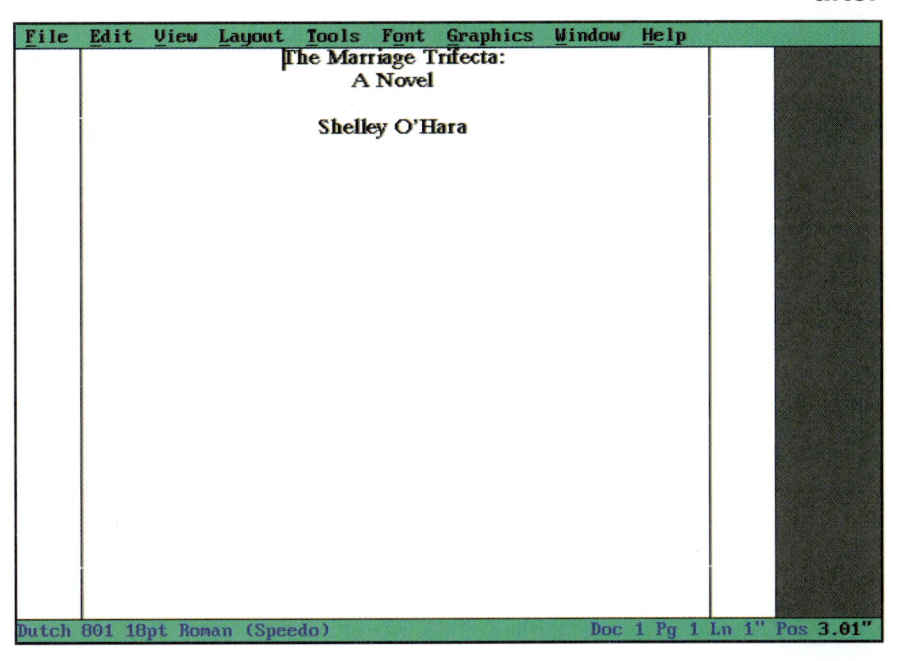

Reveal Codes

If you don't undo the change immediately, you have to use a different method. Display the Reveal Codes window (press Alt+F3) and delete the [Pg Border] code.

REVIEW

To add a page border

More information

For more information on borders, see Que's Using WordPerfect 6, Special Edition.

TASK

Set margins

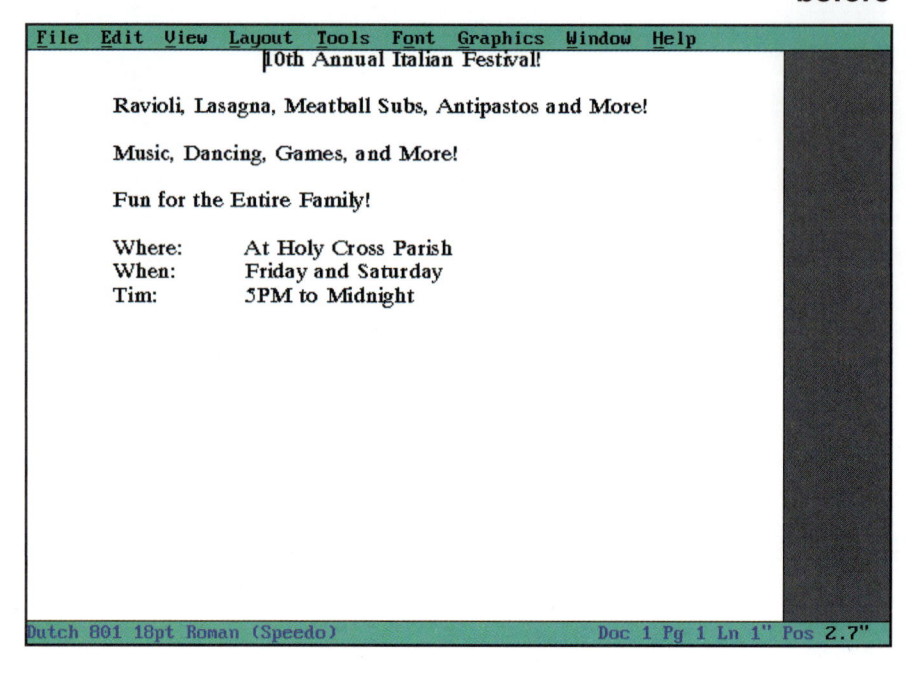

before

```
File  Edit  View  Layout  Tools  Font  Graphics  Window  Help
            10th Annual Italian Festival!
       Ravioli, Lasagna, Meatball Subs, Antipastos and More!
       Music, Dancing, Games, and More!
       Fun for the Entire Family!
       Where:      At Holy Cross Parish
       When:       Friday and Saturday
       Tim:        5PM to Midnight




Dutch 801 18pt Roman (Speedo)              Doc 1 Pg 1 Ln 1" Pos 2.7"
```

Oops!
To undo the change, open the Edit menu (press Alt+E) and select the Undo command (press U).

1. Press **Home**, **Home**, **Home**, **↑** key.

   This step moves the cursor to the top of the document. Moving the cursor here ensures that the margin changes affect the entire document.

2. Press **Alt+L**.

   This step opens the Layout menu and displays a list of Layout commands.

3. Press **M**.

   This step selects the Margins command. You see the Margin Format dialog box, where you set the left, right, top, and bottom margins.

4. Press **L** and type **2**.

   This step selects Left Margin and sets a 2-inch margin.

5. Press **Tab** and type **2**.

   This step moves the cursor to the right margin entry and sets a 2-inch margin.

6. Repeat step 5 **twice**.

   This step moves the cursor to the top and bottom margin entries and sets 2-inch margins.

144   *Easy WordPerfect for Version 6*

after

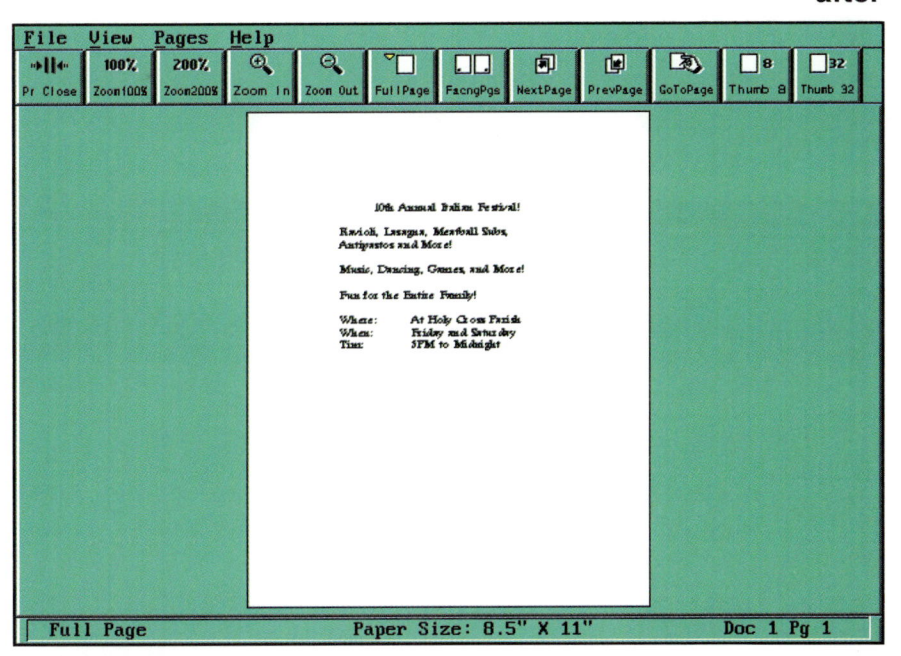

7. Press **Enter twice**.

   Pressing Enter confirms the margin settings.

   You see the effects of left and right margin changes, but not top and bottom. To see the total effect, switch to Page mode (see *TASK: Change to Page mode*) or preview the document (see *TASK: Preview a document*). The After screen shows a full-page preview.

More information

For more information on margin settings, see Que's *Using WordPerfect 6,* Special Edition.

REVIEW

To set margins

1. Press **Home**, **Home**, **Home**, ↑ key to go to the top of the document.

2. Press **Alt**+**L** to open the Layout menu.

3. Press **M** to select Margins.

4. Press **L** to select Left Margin; then type a new margin.

5. Press **Tab** to move to the next margin entry, and type a new margin setting.

6. Repeat step 5 until you make all the margin changes you want.

7. Press **Enter twice**.

More Formatting

145

TASK

Change to Page mode

before

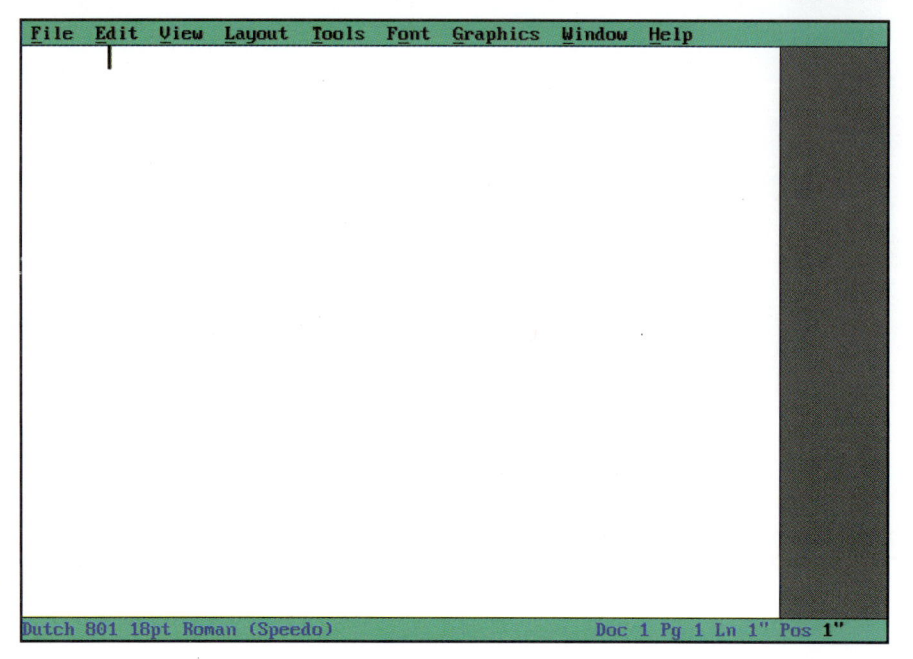

Oops!

To return to Graphics mode, press Alt+V to open the View menu. Then press G to select Graphics Mode.

1. Press **Alt+V**.

   This step opens the View menu. You see a list of View commands.

2. Press **A**.

   This step selects the Page Mode command and switches your screen to Page mode. In Page mode, you can see margin changes.

Easy WordPerfect for Version 6

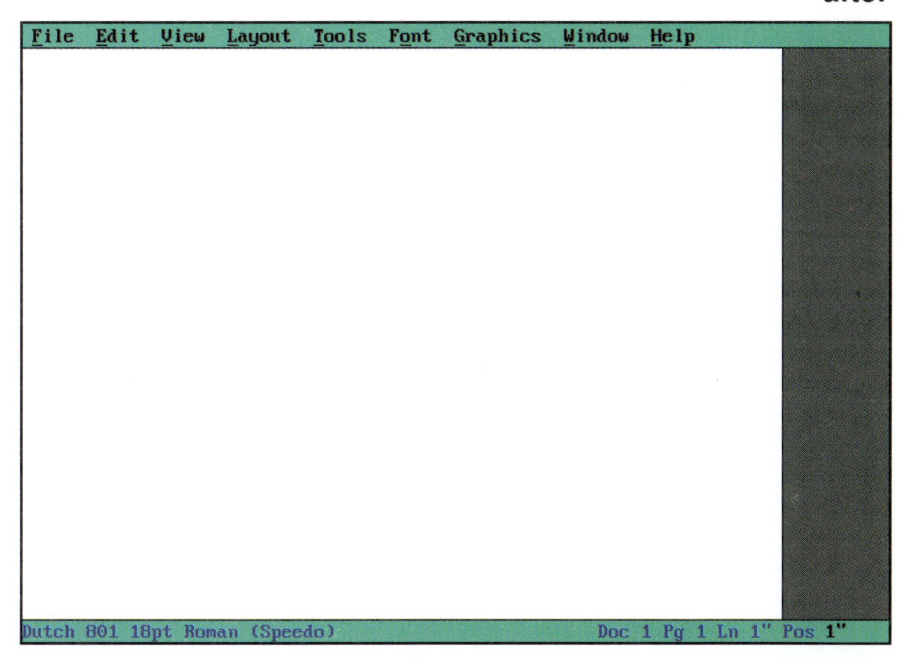

after

1. Press **Alt**+**V** to open the View menu.
2. Press **A** to select the Page Mode command.

REVIEW

To change to Page mode

More Formatting

147

TASK

Create a header

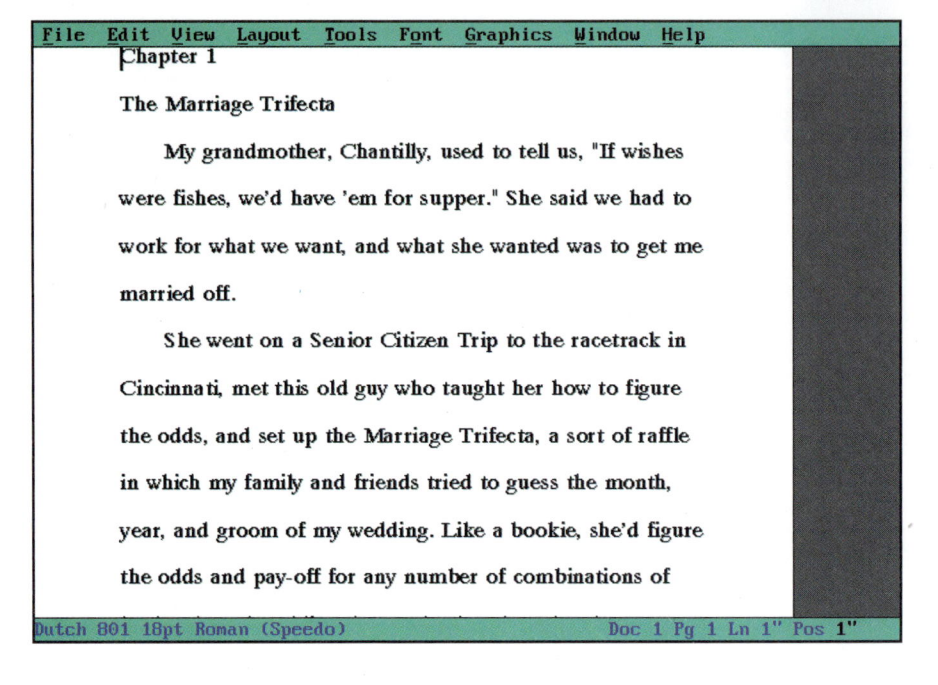

before

> File Edit View Layout Tools Font Graphics Window Help
>
> Chapter 1
>
> The Marriage Trifecta
>
>   My grandmother, Chantilly, used to tell us, "If wishes were fishes, we'd have 'em for supper." She said we had to work for what we want, and what she wanted was to get me married off.
>
>   She went on a Senior Citizen Trip to the racetrack in Cincinnati, met this old guy who taught her how to figure the odds, and set up the Marriage Trifecta, a sort of raffle in which my family and friends tried to guess the month, year, and groom of my wedding. Like a bookie, she'd figure the odds and pay-off for any number of combinations of
>
> Dutch 801 18pt Roman (Speedo)　　　　　Doc 1 Pg 1 Ln 1" Pos 1"

Oops!

To undo the change, open the Edit menu (press Alt+E) and select the Undo command (press U). If you need to edit the header, see *TASK: Edit a header.*

1. Press **Home**, **Home**, **Home**, ↑ key.

   This step moves the cursor to the top of the document.

2. Press **Alt+L**.

   This step opens the Layout menu and displays a list of Layout commands.

3. Press **H**.

   This step selects the Header/Footer/Watermark command and displays the dialog box for this command.

4. Press **H**.

   This step selects Headers and prompts you to select which header you want to create, A or B.

5. Press **A**.

   This step selects Header A. You can select the pages on which you want the header to appear. WordPerfect's default setting (All Pages) is sufficient for this task.

6. Press **C**.

   This step selects Create and tells WordPerfect to create the header. The Header Editing screen appears.

148　　　　　　　　　　　　　　　　　　　　　　　*Easy WordPerfect for Version 6*

after

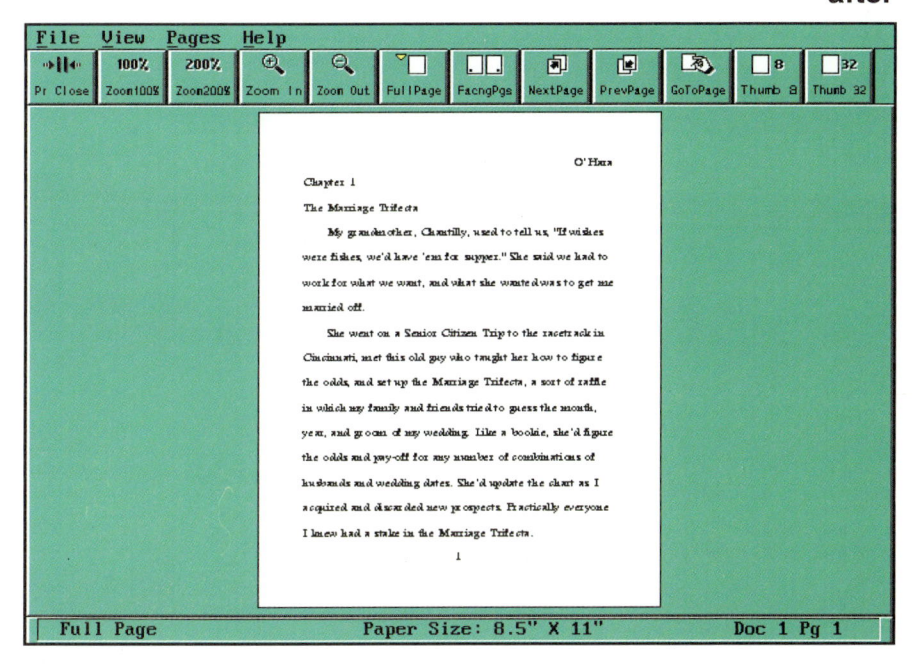

7. Press **Alt+F6** and then type **O'Hara**.

   Pressing Alt+F6 specifies that you want to right-align the header. *O'Hara* is the text you want in the header.

8. Press **F7** and then **Enter**.

   This step confirms the header and returns you to your document. You don't see the header text on the document screen. To see the header, you must preview the document. See *TASK: Preview a document.* The After screen shows a full-page preview.

Reveal Codes

If you don't undo the change immediately, you have to use a different method. Display the Reveal Codes window (press Alt+F3) and delete the [Header] code.

REVIEW

To create a header

1. Press **Alt+L** to open the Layout menu.
2. Press **H** to select Header/Footer/Watermark.
3. Press **H** to select Headers.
4. Press **A** to create Header A, or **B** to create Header B.
5. Press **C** to create the header on every page.
6. Type the header.
7. Press **F7** and then **Enter**.

More information

For more information on header options, see Que's *Using WordPerfect 6,* Special Edition.

TASK

Edit a header

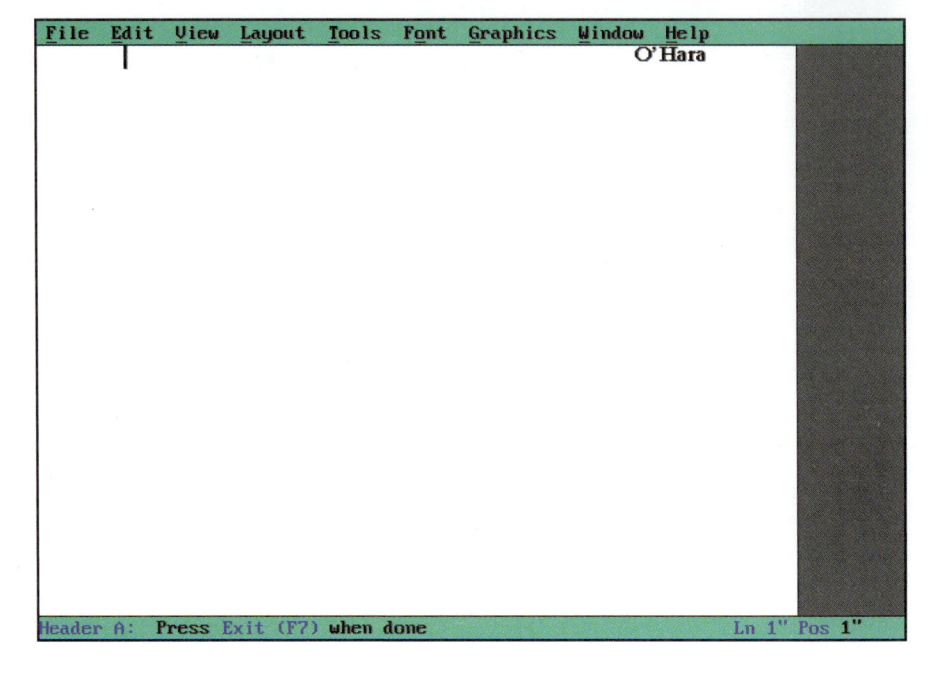

before

[Screenshot of WordPerfect header editing screen showing menu bar with File, Edit, View, Layout, Tools, Font, Graphics, Window, Help, with "O'Hara" displayed, and status line "Header A: Press Exit (F7) when done   Ln 1" Pos 1""]

Oops!

If you change your mind about the edited header, press the Esc key to return to the document, with the original header intact.

1. Press **Alt+L**.

    This step opens the Layout menu and displays a list of Layout commands.

2. Press **H**.

    This step selects the Header/Footer/Watermark command and displays the dialog box for this command.

3. Press **H**.

    This step selects Headers and prompts you to select which header you want to edit, A or B.

4. Press **A**.

    This step selects Header A and displays the Header A dialog box.

5. Press **E**.

    This step selects Edit. The Header Editing screen appears, as shown in the Before screen.

6. Press the → key.

    This step moves the cursor to the beginning of the header text.

7. Type **S.** and press the **space bar**.

    This step inserts the text you want to add and inserts a space.

150

Easy WordPerfect for Version 6

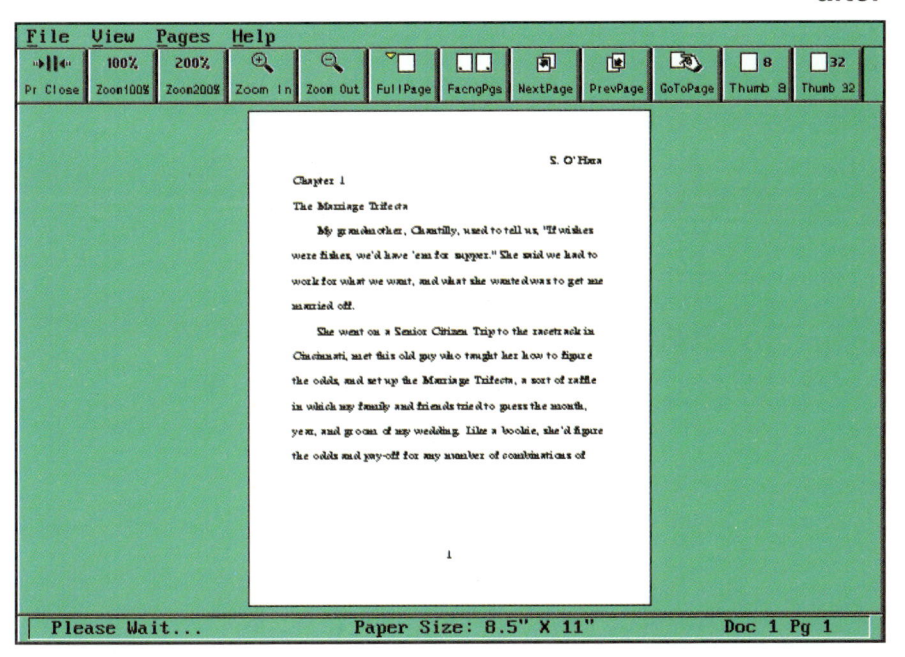

after

More information

For more information on header options, see Que's *Using WordPerfect 6,* Special Edition.

8. Press **F7** and then **Enter**.

   This step returns you to the document. You cannot see the header on the document screen. You must preview the document to see the header. See *TASK: Preview a document.* The After screen shows a full-page preview.

REVIEW

To edit a header

1. Press **Alt**+**L** to open the Layout menu.
2. Press **H** to select Header/Footer/Watermark.
3. Press **H** to select Headers.
4. Press **A** to edit Header A, or **B** to edit Header B.
5. Press **E** to select Edit.
6. Make your changes to the header text.
7. Press **F7** and then **Enter**.

TASK

Create a footer

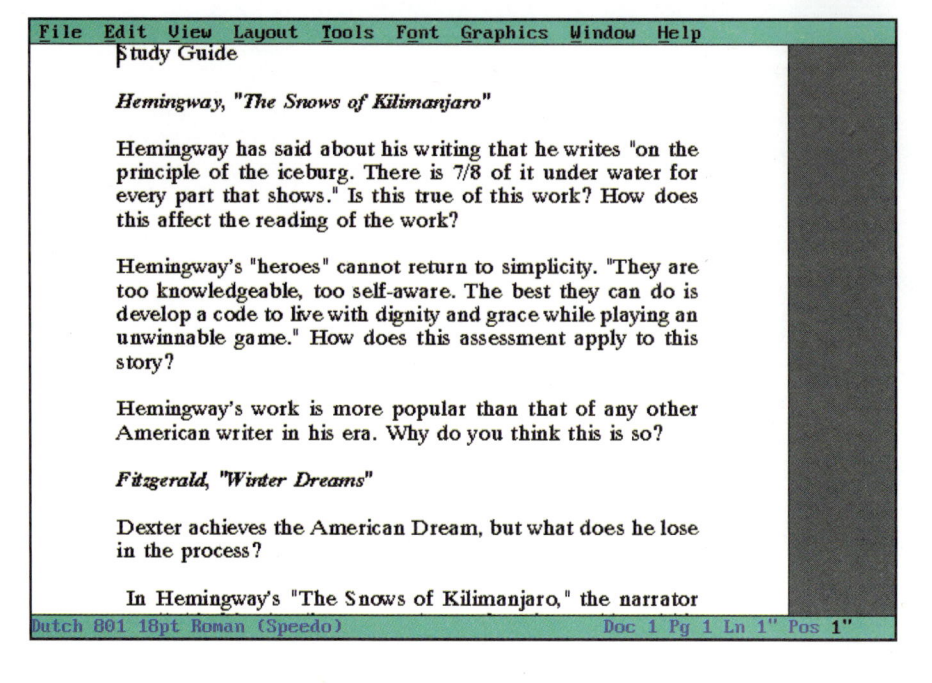

before

Oops!

To undo the change, open the Edit menu (press Alt+E) and select the Undo command (press U). If you need to edit the footer, see *TASK: Edit a footer*.

1. Press **Home**, **Home**, **Home**, ↑ key.

   This step moves the cursor to the top of the document.

2. Press **Alt+L**.

   This step opens the Layout menu and displays a list of Layout commands.

3. Press **H**.

   This step selects the Header/Footer/Watermark command and displays the dialog box for this command.

4. Press **F**.

   This step selects Footers and prompts you to select which footer you want to create, A or B.

5. Press **A**.

   This step selects Footer A. You can select the pages on which you want the footer to appear. WordPerfect's default setting (All Pages) is sufficient for this task.

6. Press **C**.

   This step selects Create and tells WordPerfect to create the footer. The Footer Editing screen appears.

152

Easy WordPerfect for Version 6

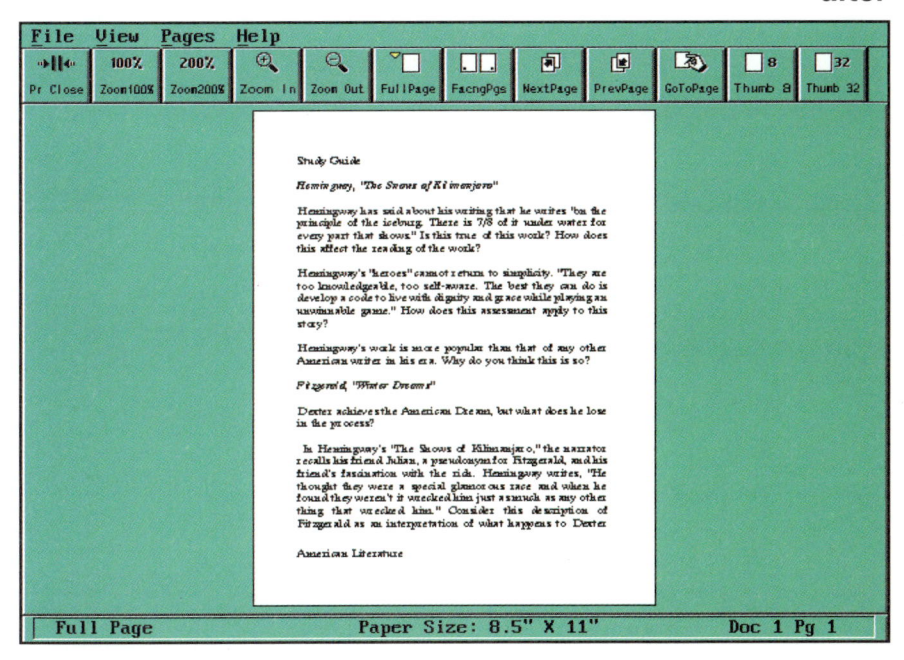

after

Reveal Codes

If you don't undo the change immediately, you have to use a different method. Display the Reveal Codes window (press Alt+F3) and delete the [Footer] code.

7. Type **American Literature**.

   This step inserts the text for the footer.

8. Press **F7** and then **Enter**.

   This step confirms the footer and returns you to your document. You don't see the footer text on the document screen. To see the footer, you must preview the document. See *TASK: Preview a document.* The After screen shows a full-page preview.

REVIEW

To create a footer

1. Press **Alt+L** to open the Layout menu.
2. Press **H** to select Header/Footer/Watermark.
3. Press **F** to select Footers.
4. Press **A** to create footer A, or **B** to create footer B.
5. Press **C** to create the footer on every page.
6. Type the footer.
7. Press **F7** and then **Enter**.

More information

For more information on footer options, see Que's *Using WordPerfect 6,* Special Edition.

TASK

Edit a footer

before

Oops!
If you change your mind about the edited footer, press the Esc key to return to the document, with the original footer intact.

1. Press **Alt+L**.

   This step opens the Layout menu and displays a list of Layout commands.

2. Press **H**.

   This step selects the Header/Footer/Watermark command and displays the dialog box for this command.

3. Press **F**.

   This step selects Footers and prompts you to select which footer you want to edit, A or B.

4. Press **A**.

   This step selects Footer A and displays the Footer A dialog box.

5. Press **E**.

   This step selects Edit. The Footer Editing screen appears, as shown in the Before screen.

6. Press **End** and then **Alt+F6**.

   This step moves the cursor to the end of the line and specifies that you want to right-align the text you add to the footer.

7. Type **Fall 1993**.

   This step inserts the text you want to add to the footer.

154   *Easy WordPerfect for Version 6*

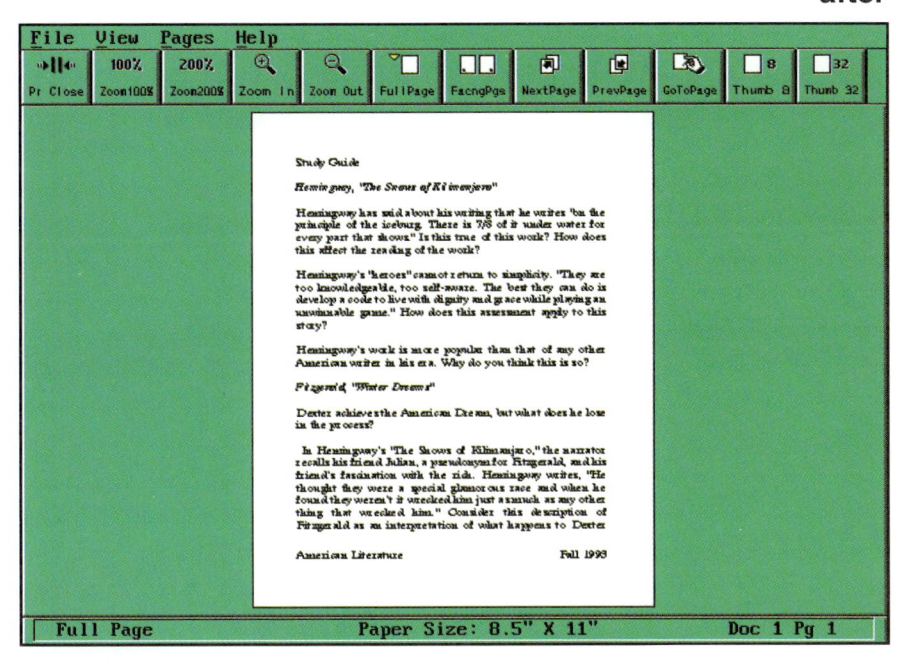

after

More information

For more information on footer options, see Que's *Using WordPerfect 6, Special Edition*.

8. Press **F7** and then **Enter**.

    This step returns you to the document. You cannot see the footer on the document screen. You must preview the document to see the footer. See *TASK: Preview a document*. The After screen shows a full-page preview.

REVIEW

To edit a footer

1. Press **Alt+L** to open the Layout menu.
2. Press **H** to select Header/Footer/Watermark.
3. Press **F** to select Footers.
4. Press **A** to edit Footer A, or **B** to edit Footer B.
5. Press **E** to select Edit.
6. Make your changes to the footer text.
7. Press **F7** and then **Enter**.

More Formatting

TASK

Insert a special character

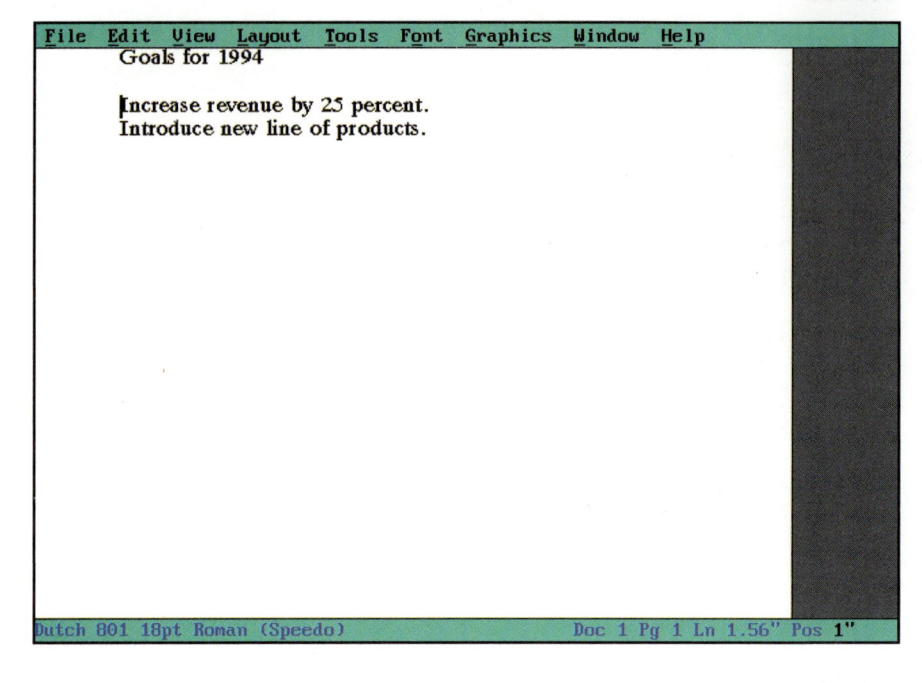

before

```
File  Edit  View  Layout  Tools  Font  Graphics  Window  Help
      Goals for 1994

      Increase revenue by 25 percent.
      Introduce new line of products.




















Dutch 801 18pt Roman (Speedo)                Doc 1 Pg 1 Ln 1.56" Pos 1"
```

Oops!

If you don't want to insert the character, press the Esc key to close the dialog box.

1. Move the cursor before the *I* in *Increase*.

   This step places the cursor where you want the special character to appear.

2. Press **Alt**+**O**.

   This step opens the Font menu, which lists the Font commands.

3. Press **W**.

   This step selects the WP Characters command and displays the WordPerfect Characters dialog box. WordPerfect has several character sets. This box shows you the selected set, displays the characters within that set, and lists the number of the selected character.

4. Press the ↓ key.

   This step selects the Set option.

5. Press **Enter**.

   This step displays a list of character sets.

6. Press **T**.

   This step selects the Typographical set. The first, selected character—the bullet—is the one you want.

156   *Easy WordPerfect for Version 6*

after

Delete the character

Delete the special character as you would any other character: press the Del or Backspace key.

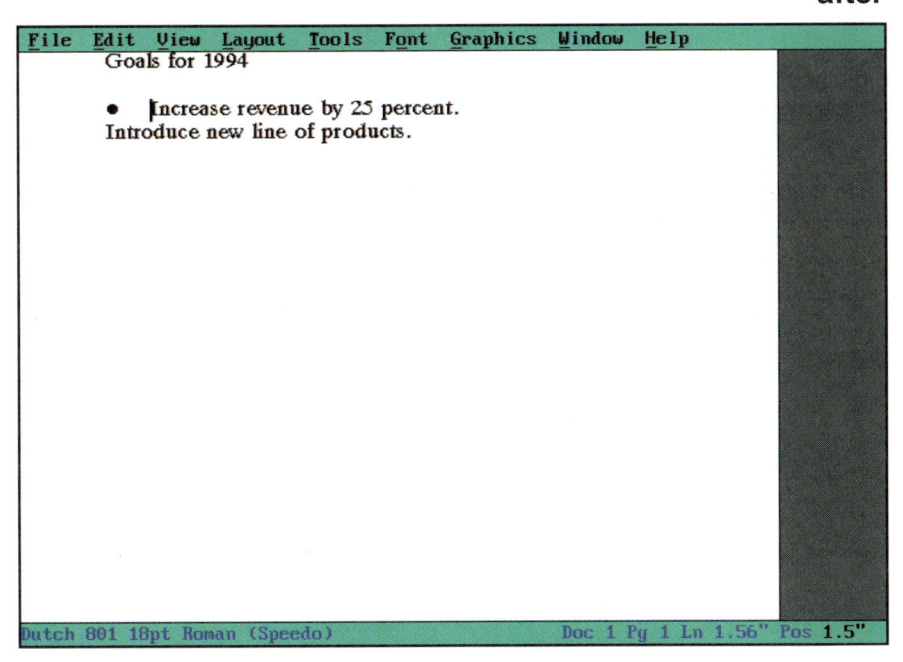

7. Press **I**.

   This step selects the Insert button, closes the dialog box, and inserts the symbol.

8. Press **Tab**.

   This step inserts a tab.

REVIEW

To insert a special character

1. Press **Alt+O** to open the Font menu.
2. Press **W** to select the WP Characters command.
3. Press **↓** and then **Enter** to display a list of character sets.
4. Select the character set you want.
5. Select the character you want to insert.
6. Press **I** to select Insert.

Try a shortcut

To select the Characters command, press Ctrl+W.

More Formatting

157

TASK

Draw a horizontal line

before

```
File  Edit  View  Layout  Tools  Font  Graphics  Window  Help
Broad Ripple News




















Dutch 801 18pt Roman (Speedo)                    Doc 1 Pg 1 Ln 1" Pos 1"
```

Oops!
To undo the change, open the Edit menu (press Alt+E) and select the Undo command (press U).

1. Move the cursor before the *B* in *Broad*.

   This step positions the cursor where you want to draw the line.

2. Press **Alt+G**.

   This step opens the Graphics menu and displays a list of Graphics commands.

3. Press **L**.

   This step selects the Graphics Lines command. You see another set of choices.

4. Press **C**.

   This step selects Create. You see the Create Graphics Line dialog box that lists the options you can use to draw the line. WordPerfect's default settings are sufficient for this task.

5. Press **Enter**.

   This step accepts the default settings for a horizontal line. You are returned to the document screen. To see the line, you must change to Graphics mode or preview the document. See *TASK: Change to Graphics mode* or *TASK: Preview the document*. The After screen shows the document in Graphics mode.

after

1. Move the cursor to the spot where you want to insert the line.

2. Press **Alt**+**G** to open the Graphics menu.

3. Press **L** to select Graphics Lines.

4. Press **C** to select Create.

5. Press **Enter**.

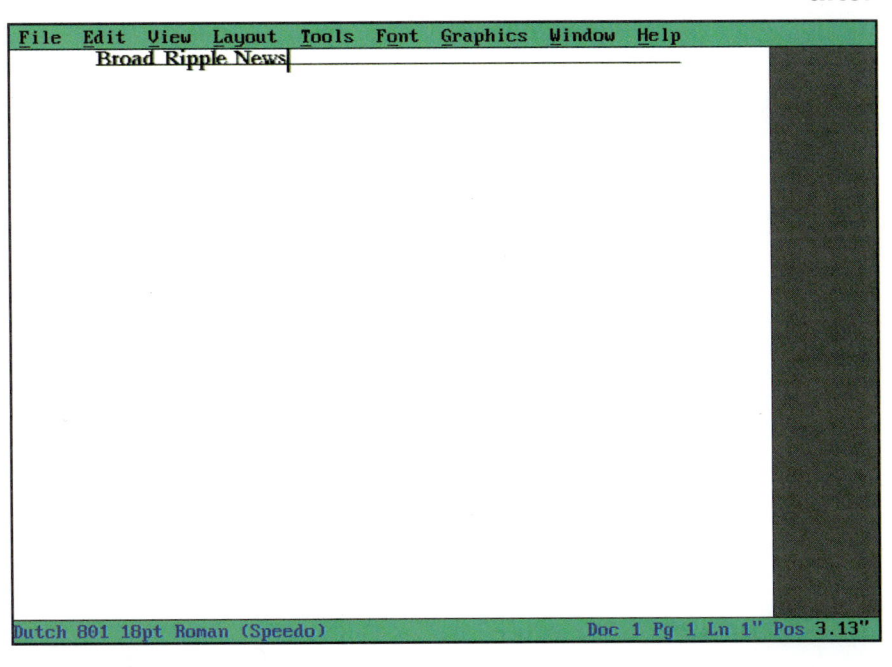

Reveal Codes

If you don't undo the change immediately, you have to use a different method. Display the Reveal Codes window (press Alt+F3) and delete the `[Graphic Line]` code.

REVIEW

To draw a horizontal line

More information

For more information on adding graphics lines, see Que's Using WordPerfect 6, Special Edition.

More Formatting

159

TASK

Insert a graphic

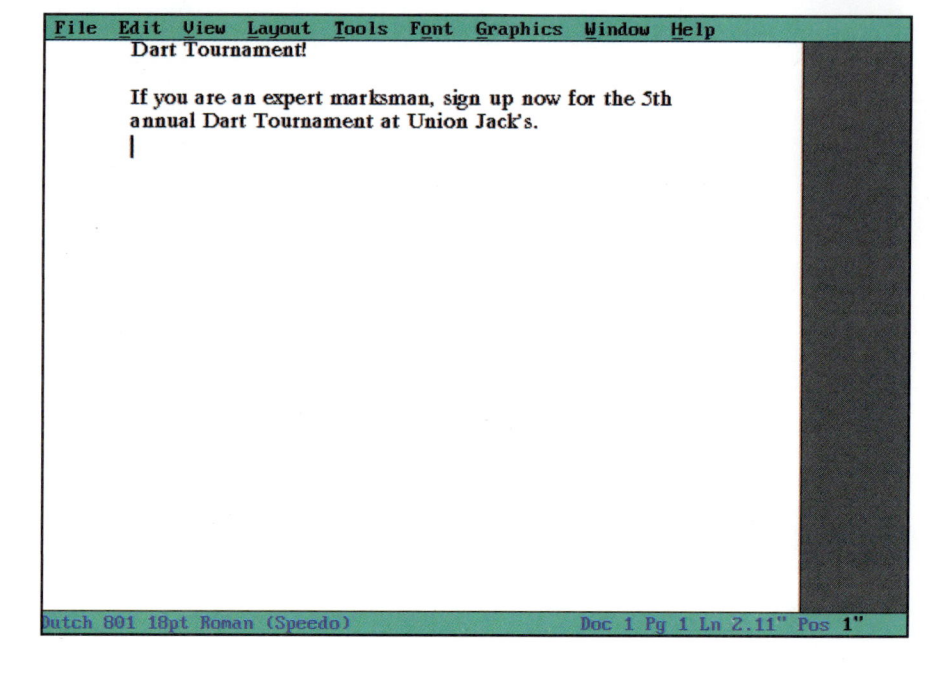

before

[Screenshot of WordPerfect screen showing:]

```
File  Edit  View  Layout  Tools  Font  Graphics  Window  Help
Dart Tournament!

If you are an expert marksman, sign up now for the 5th
annual Dart Tournament at Union Jack's.

Dutch 801 18pt Roman (Speedo)              Doc 1 Pg 1 Ln 2.11" Pos 1"
```

1. Position the cursor after the last paragraph.

2. Press **Alt+G**.

   This step opens the Graphics menu and displays a list of Graphics commands.

3. Press **R**.

   This step selects the Retrieve Image command. You see the Retrieve Image File dialog box.

4. Press **F5** and then **Enter**.

   This step displays a list of files.

5. Use the arrow keys to highlight **ARCHERY.WPG**.

   This step selects the graphics image you want to insert.

6. Press **Enter**.

   The image is inserted on-screen. To see the image, you must change to Graphics mode or preview the document. See *TASK: Change to Graphics mode* or *TASK: Preview the document*. The After screen shows the document in Graphics mode.

Oops!

To undo the change, open the Edit menu (press Alt+E) and select the Undo command (press U).

160   *Easy WordPerfect for Version 6*

after

```
File  Edit  View  Layout  Tools  Font  Graphics  Window  Help
Dart Tournament!
If you are an expert marksman, sign up now for the 5th
annual Dart Tournament at Union Jack's.
```

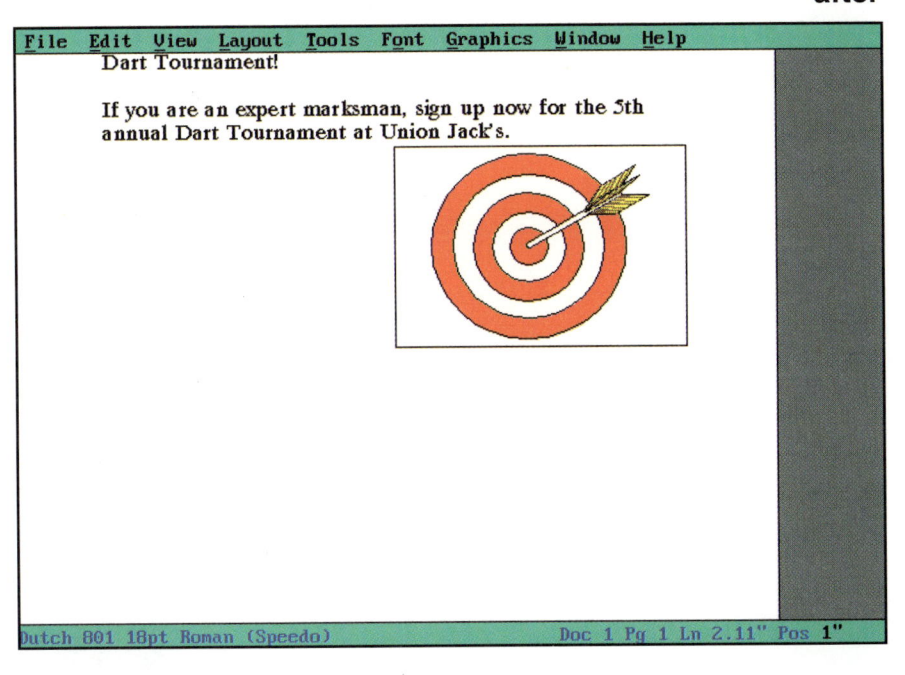

Dutch 801 18pt Roman (Speedo)   Doc 1 Pg 1 Ln 2.11" Pos 1"

Reveal Codes

If you don't undo the change immediately, you have to use a different method. Display the Reveal Codes window (press Alt+F3) and delete the `[Para Box;FigureBox]` code.

REVIEW

To insert a graphic

1. Move the cursor to the spot where you want to insert the graphic.

2. Press **Alt+G** to open the Graphics menu.

3. Press **R** to select Retrieve Image.

4. Press **F5** and then **Enter** to display a list of files.

5. Select the graphics file you want.

6. Press **Enter**.

More information

For more information on adding and moving graphics, see Que's *Using WordPerfect 6, Special Edition.*

More Formatting

161

TASK

Insert a table

before

Oops!

To undo the table, select the Edit Undo command immediately. Or display the Reveal Codes window (press Alt+F3) and delete the [Tbl Def] code.

1. Press **Alt+L**.

   This step opens the Layout menu and displays a list of Layout commands.

2. Press **T**.

   This step selects the Tables command.

3. Press **C**.

   This step selects the Create command and displays the Create Table dialog box, which enables you to specify the number of columns and rows in the table.

4. Press **Tab**.

   Pressing Tab accepts the default number of columns (3) and moves to the Rows text box.

5. Type **3** and press **Enter**.

   This step tells WordPerfect to create a table with 3 rows.

6. Press **Enter**.

   This step confirms the table definition and inserts a table with 3 columns and 3 rows on-screen. You can adjust the column widths if you want.

Easy WordPerfect for Version 6

after

7. Press **Esc**.

   This step selects the default column widths.

REVIEW

To insert a table

1. Press **Alt**+**L** to open the Layout menu.
2. Press **T** to select the Tables command.
3. Press **C** to select the Create command.
4. Type the number of columns you want and press **Tab**.
5. Type the number of rows you want and press **Enter twice**.
6. Adjust the column widths if necessary.
7. Press **Esc**.

More information

For more information on the Table feature, see Que's *Using WordPerfect 6,* Special Edition.

More Formatting

163

TASK

Enter text into a table

before

[screenshot of WordPerfect window with "Committee Assignments" table containing 3 columns and 3 rows, empty]

Oops!

To edit text in a cell, use any of the editing techniques and keystrokes you would use in a regular document.

1. Type **Project** and press **Tab**.

   This step enters information into the first cell in the table and moves the insertion point to the next column in that row. A cell is the intersection of a row and column. To create a table, see *TASK: Insert a table*.

2. Type **Team Leader** and press **Tab**.

   This step enters information into that cell and moves the insertion point to the next column.

3. Type **Goal** and press **Tab**.

   This step completes the headings for the table. Follow the same steps to enter information into the other cells.

4. Type **Crime Watch** and press **Tab**.

5. Type **Michael O'Hara** and press **Tab**.

6. Type **Set up Crime Watch program** and press **Tab**.

7. Type **Recycle** and press **Tab**.

8. Type **Alana Moore** and press **Tab**.

9. Type **Involve more neighbors in the recycling program**.

   This step completes the text for the table.

Easy WordPerfect for Version 6

after

```
File  Edit  View  Layout  Tools  Font  Graphics  Window  Help
```

Committe Assignments		
Project	Team Leader	Goal
Crime Watch	Michael O'Hara	Set up Crime Watch program
Recycle	Alana Moore	Involve more neighbors in the recycling program

Dutch 801 18pt Roman (Speedo)   Cell C3 Doc 1 Pg 1 Ln 2.98" Pos 7.35"

1. Type the text in the first cell and press **Tab**.

2. Continue typing text and pressing **Tab** until you complete all cells.

Caution

Don't press Enter in a cell unless you want to insert a line break. Pressing Enter does not move you to the next row. Press Tab instead. (Note, however, that pressing Tab while in the last cell adds a new row of cells. See *TASK: Delete a row from a table* if that isn't what you wanted.)

REVIEW

To enter text into a table

More Formatting

165

TASK

Add a row to a table

before

```
File   Edit   View   Layout   Tools   Font   Graphics   Window   Help
```

Committe Assignments		
Project	Team Leader	Goal
Crime Watch	Michael O'Hara	Set up Crime Watch program
Recycle	Alana Moore	Involve more neighbors in the recycling program

Dutch 801 18pt Roman (Speedo)   Cell A3 Doc 1 Pg 1 Ln 2.43" Pos **1.08"**

Oops!

To undo the change, open the Edit menu (press Alt+E) and select the Undo command (press U).

1. Put the cursor in the last row of the table.

   To access the Table commands, the cursor must be within the table. Make sure that you put the cursor in the row below where you want WordPerfect to add the row.

2. Press **Alt**+**L**.

   This step opens the Layout menu and displays a list of Layout commands.

3. Press **T**.

   This step selects the Tables command.

4. Press **I**.

   This step selects the Insert Row command. WordPerfect inserts a row into the table.

Easy WordPerfect for Version 6

after

> **Delete a row**
>
> To delete a row, see *TASK: Delete a row from a table.*

REVIEW

To add a row to a table

1. Put the cursor in a row in the table. WordPerfect will insert the new row above this row.

2. Press **Alt**+**L** to open the Layout menu.

3. Press **T** to select the Tables command.

4. Press **I** to select the Insert Row command.

> **Try a shortcut**
>
> Press Ctrl+Ins to select the Insert Row command.

More Formatting

167

TASK

Delete a row from a table

before

```
File  Edit  View  Layout  Tools  Font  Graphics  Window  Help
```

Committe Assignments		
Project	Team Leader	Goal
Crime Watch	Michael O'Hara	Set up Crime Watch program
Festival	Stephanie Lynne	Plan annual festival
Recycle	Alana Moore	Involve more neighbors in the recycling program

Dutch 801 18pt Roman (Speedo)   Cell A3 Doc 1 Pg 1 Ln 2.43" Pos **1.08"**

Oops!
To undo the change, open the Edit menu (press Alt+E) and select the Undo command (press U).

1. Put the cursor in the row that begins with the word *Festival*.

   This is the row you want to delete.

2. Press **Alt**+**L**.

   This step opens the Layout menu and displays a list of Layout commands.

3. Press **T**.

   This step selects the Tables command.

4. Press **D**.

   This step selects the Delete Row command, and WordPerfect deletes the row.

168   *Easy WordPerfect for Version 6*

after

```
File  Edit  View  Layout  Tools  Font  Graphics  Window  Help
```

Committe Assignments		
Project	Team Leader	Goal
Crime Watch	Michael O'Hara	Set up Crime Watch program
Recycle	Alana Moore	Involve more neighbors in the recycling program

Dutch 801 18pt Roman (Speedo)   Cell A3 Doc 1 Pg 1 Ln 2.43" Pos **1.08"**

1. Put the cursor in the row you want to delete.
2. Press **Alt**+**L** to open the Layout menu.
3. Press **T** to select the Tables command.
4. Press **D** to select the Delete Row command.

Try a shortcut

Press Ctrl+Del to select the Delete Row command.

REVIEW

To delete a row from a table

More information

For more information on working with tables, see Que's *Using WordPerfect 6,* Special Edition.

More Formatting

169

TASK

Create a two-column document

before

```
File  Edit  View  Layout  Tools  Font  Graphics  Window  Help
```

Dutch 801 18pt Roman (Speedo)   Doc 1 Pg 1 Ln 1" Pos 1"

Oops!

To change the document back to a single column, select the Edit Undo command immediately. Or display the Reveal Codes window (press Alt+F3) and delete the `[Col Def]` code.

1. Press **Alt**+**L**.

   This step opens the Layout menu and displays a list of Layout commands.

2. Press **C**.

   This step selects the Columns command. You see the Text Columns dialog box.

3. Press **N**.

   This step selects the Number of Columns option.

4. Type **2**.

   This step tells WordPerfect to make two columns.

5. Press **Enter twice**.

   Pressing Enter accepts the defaults for the other settings and returns you to the document. The only noticeable change is in the status bar, where you now see the `Col` indicator.

Easy WordPerfect for Version 6

after

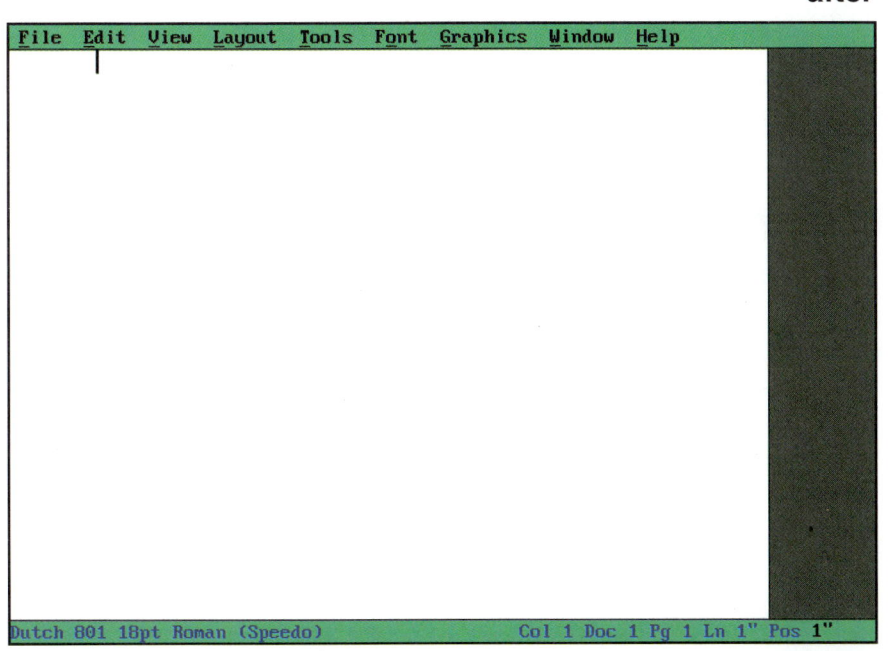

> **More information**
>
> For more information on working with columns, see Que's *Using WordPerfect 6,* Special Edition.

REVIEW

To create a two-column document

1. Press **Alt**+**L** to open the Layout menu.
2. Press **C** to select the Columns command.
3. Press **N** to select the Number of Columns option.
4. Type the number of columns you want.
5. Press **Enter twice**.

More Formatting

TASK

Type text in the second column

before

[Screenshot of WordPerfect showing first column with text:]

New Businesses

Three new businesses opened this summer in Broad Ripple. Millie's Attic offers dolls, quilts, teddy bears, and other craft items. The Jelly Roll is a coffee shop and bakery. And Rebels is a clothing store for young women and men.

Oops!
Edit the text the same way you would in a one-column document. All editing and formatting features work the same.

---

1. **Position the cursor at the end of the second paragraph.**

   This step places the cursor where you want to insert a column break so that you can type text in the second column. Normally WordPerfect automatically wraps text to the second column after the first column fills up, but you want to type text in the second column *before* filling up the first column.

2. **Press Ctrl+Enter.**

   This step enters a column break and moves the cursor to the next column.

3. **Type the text shown in the After screen.**

   This step enters text into the second column.

Easy WordPerfect for Version 6

after

1. Type text as you would in a normal document.

2. Press **Ctrl+Enter** to move the cursor to the second column.

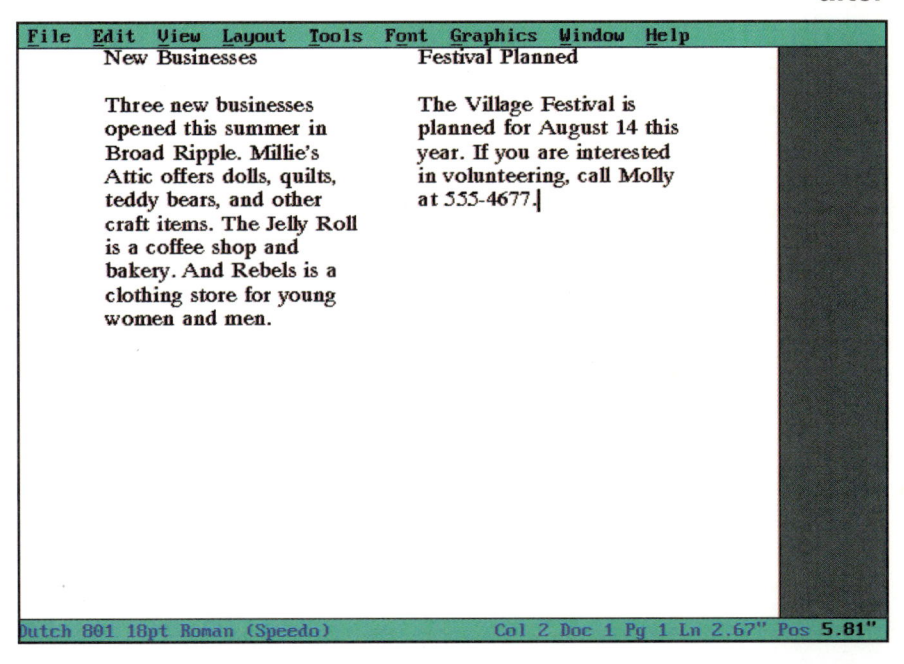

3. Type the text you want in the second column.

REVIEW

To type text in the second column

More Formatting

173

Printing

This section covers the following tasks:

Preview a document

Print a document

Print a block

TASK

Preview a document

before

> File Edit View Layout Tools Font Graphics Window Help
>
> Chapter 1
> The Marriage Trifecta
>
> My grandmother, Chantilly, used to tell us, "If wishes were fishes, we'd have 'em for supper." She said we had to work for what we want, and what she wanted was to get me married off.
>
> She went on a Senior Citizen Trip to the racetrack in Cincinnati, met this old guy who taught her how to figure the odds, and set up the Marriage Trifecta, a sort of raffle in which my family and friends tried to guess the month, year, and groom of my wedding. Like a bookie, she'd figure the odds and pay-off for any number of combinations of
>
> Dutch 801 18pt Roman (Speedo)   Doc 1 Pg 1 Ln 1" Pos 3.71"

Oops!
Press the Esc key to exit Preview mode.

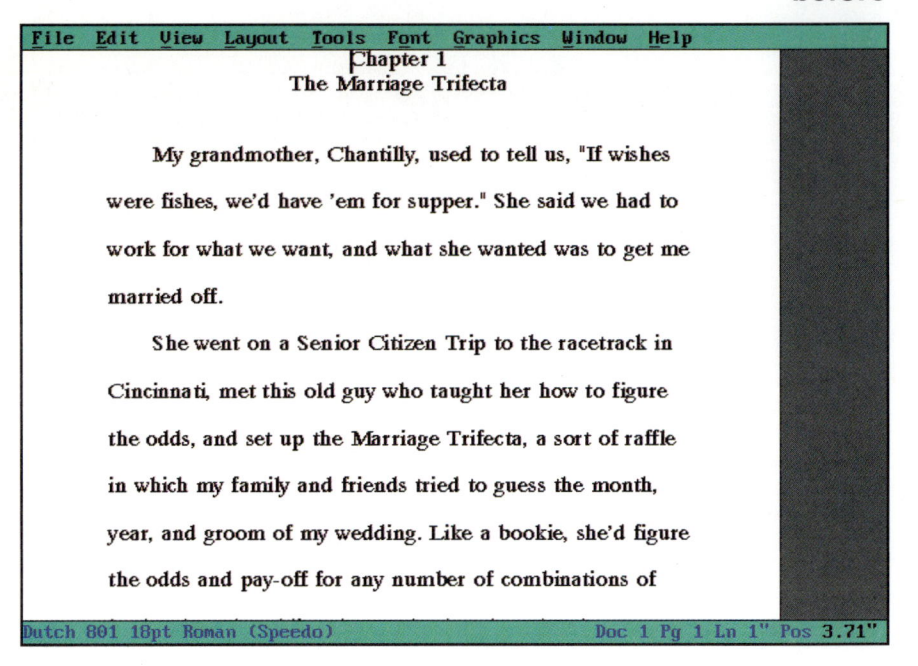

1. Press **Alt**+**F**.

   This step opens the File menu and displays a list of File commands.

2. Press **V**.

   This step selects the Print Preview command. You see a graphical representation of how the document will look when you print it.

3. Press **Esc**.

   Pressing Esc returns you to the document.

176

Easy WordPerfect for Version 6

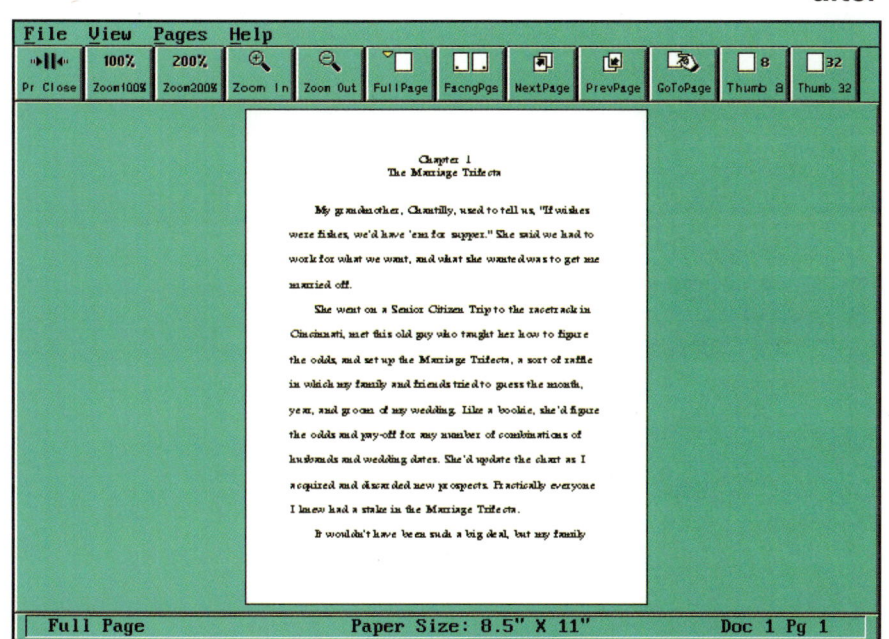

after

1. Press **Alt**+**F** to open the File menu.
2. Press **V** to select Print Preview.
3. Press **Esc** to return to the document.

Zoom and other options

For more information on other print preview options, see Que's Using WordPerfect 6, Special Edition.

REVIEW

To preview a document

TASK

Print a document

before

```
File  Edit  View  Layout  Tools  Font  Graphics  Window  Help
                         Chapter 1
                    The Marriage Trifecta

        My grandmother, Chantilly, used to tell us, "If wishes
        were fishes, we'd have 'em for supper." She said we had to
        work for what we want, and what she wanted was to get me
        married off.
            She went on a Senior Citizen Trip to the racetrack in
        Cincinnati, met this old guy who taught her how to figure
        the odds, and set up the Marriage Trifecta, a sort of raffle
        in which my family and friends tried to guess the month,
        year, and groom of my wedding. Like a bookie, she'd figure
        the odds and pay-off for any number of combinations of

Dutch 801 18pt Roman (Speedo)          Doc 1 Pg 1 Ln 1" Pos 3.71"
```

Oops!

If you don't want to print the document, press Esc instead of Enter in step 3.

1. Press **Alt+F**.

   This step opens the File menu and displays a list of File commands.

2. Press **P**.

   This step selects the Print/Fax command and displays the Print/Fax dialog box. This dialog box is where you control what is printed, how it is printed, how many copies are printed, and other options. The After screen shows this dialog box.

3. Press **Enter**.

   This step accepts WordPerfect's default settings. Your document begins printing immediately.

Easy WordPerfect for Version 6

after

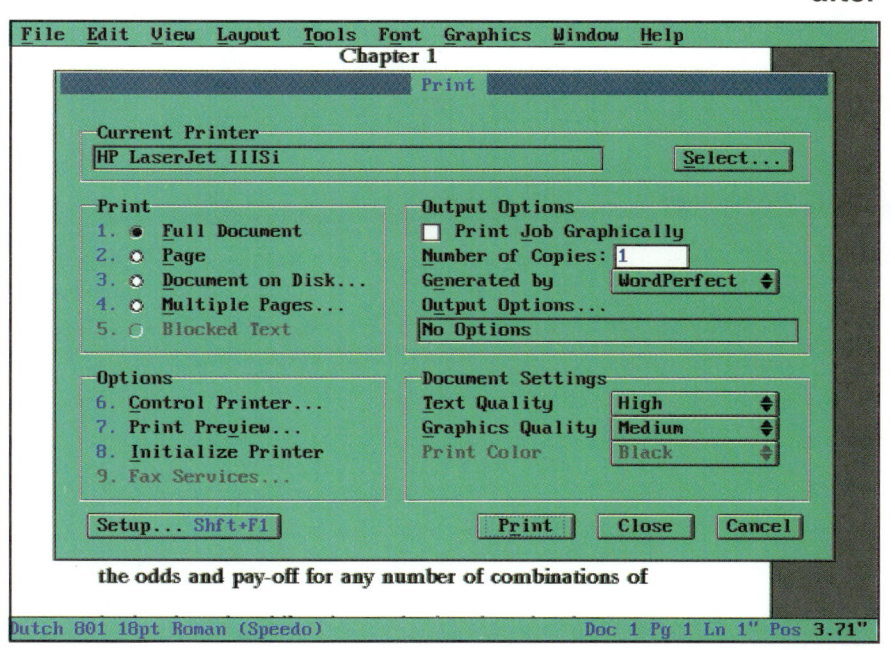

Use printing options

You can specify various printing options, such as the number of copies and the text quality. See Que's Using WordPerfect 6, Special Edition.

REVIEW

To print a document

1. Press **Alt**+**F** to open the File menu.
2. Press **P** to select the Print/Fax command.
3. Press **Enter**.

Try a shortcut

Press Shift+F7 to display the Print dialog box.

Printing

179

TASK

Print a block

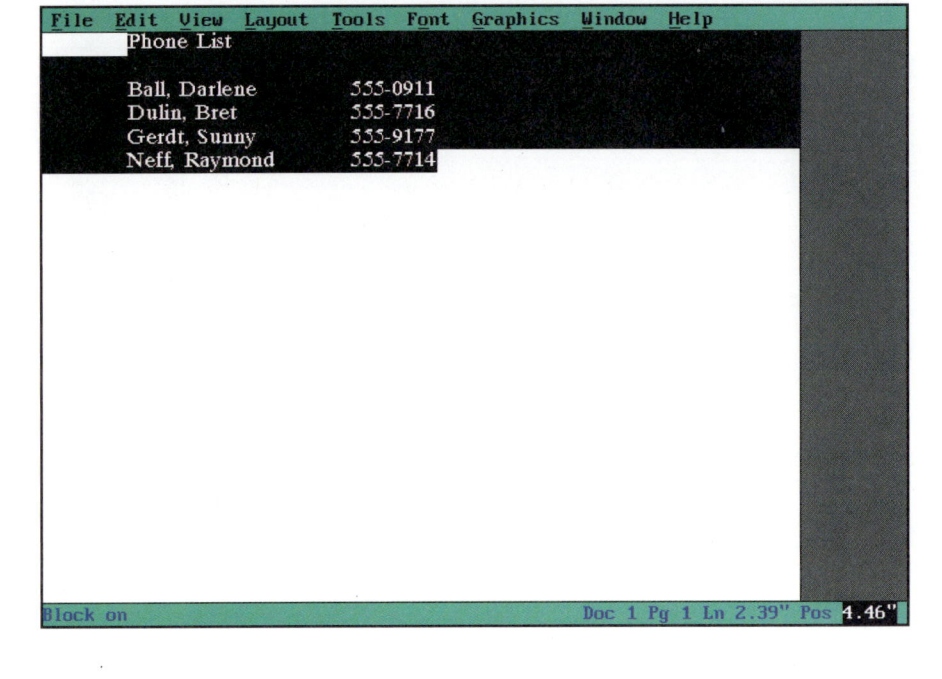

before

```
File  Edit  View  Layout  Tools  Font  Graphics  Window  Help
Phone List

Ball, Darlene      555-0911
Dulin, Bret        555-7716
Gerdt, Sunny       555-9177
Neff, Raymond      555-7714
```

Block on   Doc 1 Pg 1 Ln 2.39" Pos 4.46"

Oops!

If you highlight the wrong block, press the Esc key and start over.

1. Block the phone list.

   This step blocks the text you want to print. For help on blocking text, see *TASK: Select a block*.

2. Press **Alt+F**.

   This step opens the File menu and displays a list of File commands.

3. Press **P**.

   This step selects the Print/Fax command. WordPerfect automatically selects Blocked Text as the Print option. The After screen shows this step.

4. Press **Enter**.

   WordPerfect prints the blocked text.

Easy WordPerfect for Version 6

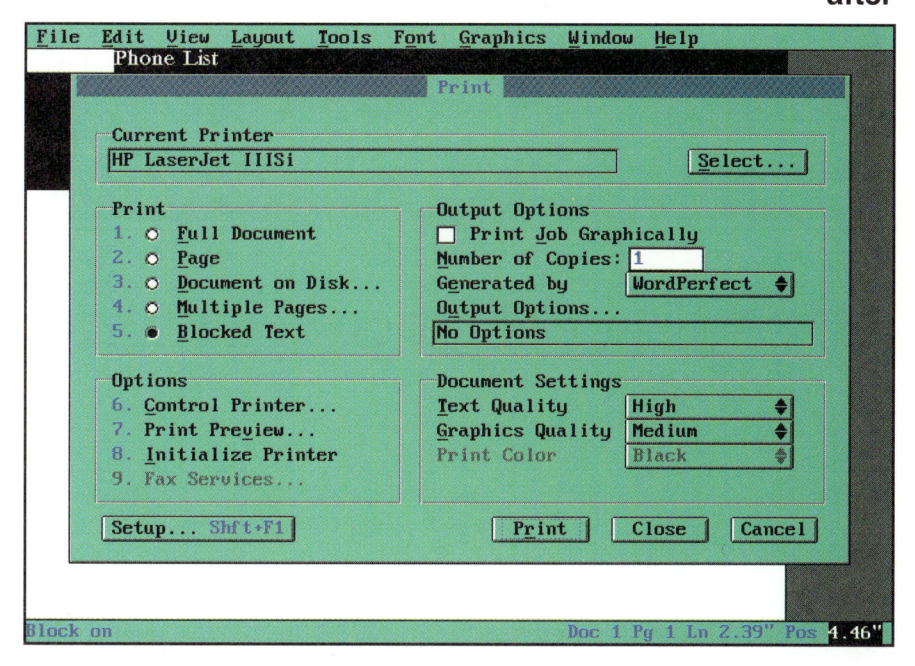

after

1. Block the text you want to print.
2. Press **Alt**+**F** to open the File menu.
3. Press **P** to select the Print/Fax command.
4. Press **Enter**.

REVIEW

To print a block

Printing

181

More Files

This section covers the following tasks:

Start the File Manager

Use the File Manager to open a file

Create a directory

Display a different directory

Change the default directory

Copy a file

Rename a file

Delete a file

Find a file

TASK

Start the File Manager

before

Oops!
To close the File Manager, press the Esc key.

1. Press **Alt+F**.

   This step opens the File menu and displays a list of File commands.

2. Press **F**.

   This step selects the File Manager command. You are asked to specify a directory.

3. Press **Enter**.

   This step accepts the default directory (the current directory). You see the File Manager on-screen. On the left is a list of files, and on the right is a list of menu options.

Easy WordPerfect for Version 6

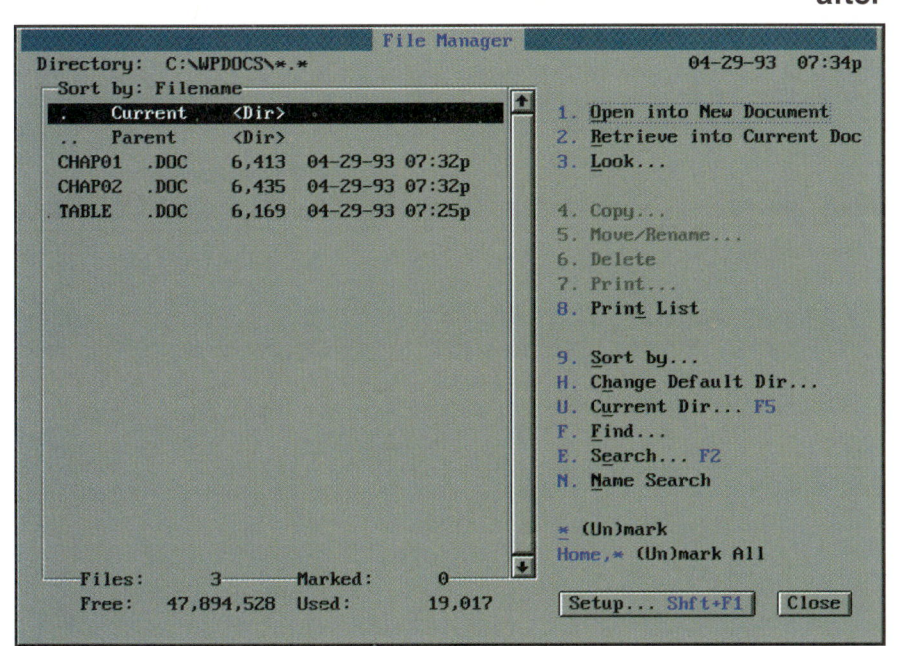

after

![File Manager screenshot]

1. Press **Alt+F** to open the File menu.
2. Press **F** to select the File Manager command.
3. Press **Enter**.

More information

For complete information on all File Manager options, see Que's Using WordPerfect 6, Special Edition.

REVIEW

To start the File Manager

Try a shortcut

Press F5 to select the File Manager command.

More Files

185

TASK

Use the File Manager to open a file

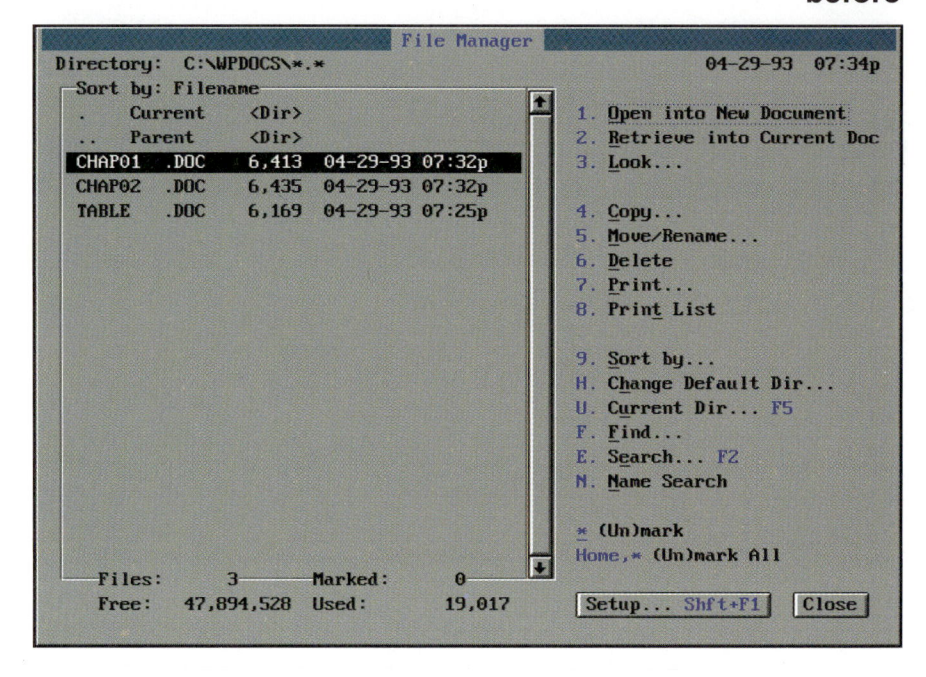

before

```
                           File Manager
Directory:  C:\WPDOCS\*.*                        04-29-93  07:34p
Sort by: Filename
 .       Current    <Dir>              1. Open into New Document
 ..      Parent     <Dir>              2. Retrieve into Current Doc
CHAP01   .DOC    6,413  04-29-93 07:32p  3. Look...
CHAP02   .DOC    6,435  04-29-93 07:32p
TABLE    .DOC    6,169  04-29-93 07:25p  4. Copy...
                                         5. Move/Rename...
                                         6. Delete
                                         7. Print...
                                         8. Print List

                                         9. Sort by...
                                         H. Change Default Dir...
                                         U. Current Dir... F5
                                         F. Find...
                                         E. Search... F2
                                         N. Name Search

                                         * (Un)mark
                                         Home,* (Un)mark All

Files:      3       Marked:      0
Free:  47,894,528   Used:   19,017    [Setup... Shft+F1]  [Close]
```

Oops!

If this isn't the file you want, close it. See *TASK: Save and clear a document.*

1. Start the File Manager.

   For help with this step, see *TASK: Start the File Manager.*

2. Use the arrow keys to highlight the file **CHAP01.DOC**.

   This step selects the file you want to open. If you don't have this file, select one that you do have. The Before screen shows this step.

3. Press **Enter**.

   WordPerfect displays the CHAP01.DOC file on-screen.

Easy WordPerfect for Version 6

after

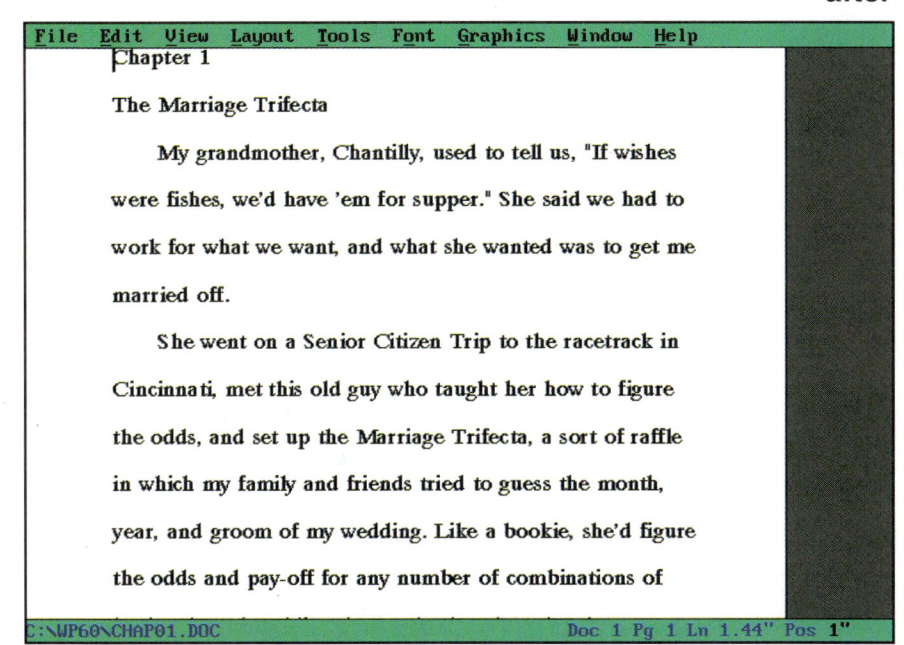

```
File  Edit  View  Layout  Tools  Font  Graphics  Window  Help
Chapter 1
The Marriage Trifecta
    My grandmother, Chantilly, used to tell us, "If wishes
were fishes, we'd have 'em for supper." She said we had to
work for what we want, and what she wanted was to get me
married off.
    She went on a Senior Citizen Trip to the racetrack in
Cincinnati, met this old guy who taught her how to figure
the odds, and set up the Marriage Trifecta, a sort of raffle
in which my family and friends tried to guess the month,
year, and groom of my wedding. Like a bookie, she'd figure
the odds and pay-off for any number of combinations of
C:\WP60\CHAP01.DOC                    Doc 1 Pg 1 Ln 1.44" Pos 1"
```

Can't find file?

If you don't see the file in the list, you might need to display a different directory. See *TASK: Display a different directory*.

1. Start the File Manager.
2. Highlight the file you want to open.
3. Press **Enter**.

REVIEW

To use the File Manager to open a file

More Files

187

TASK

Create a directory

before

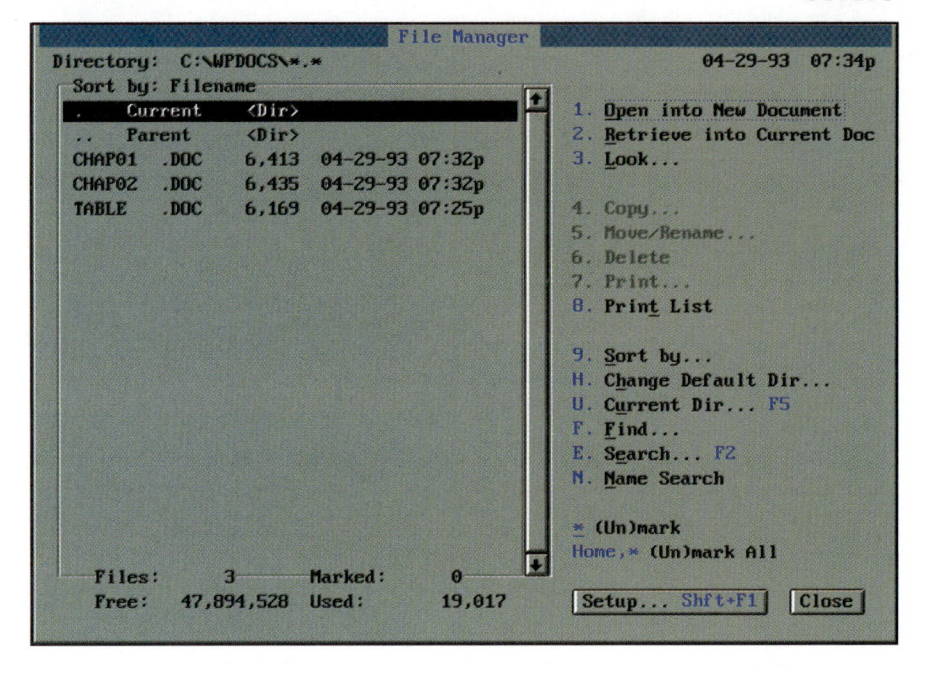

```
                        File Manager
Directory: C:\WPDOCS\*.*                      04-29-93  07:34p
Sort by: Filename
.       Current     <Dir>            1. Open into New Document
..      Parent      <Dir>            2. Retrieve into Current Doc
CHAP01  .DOC        6,413  04-29-93 07:32p    3. Look...
CHAP02  .DOC        6,435  04-29-93 07:32p
TABLE   .DOC        6,169  04-29-93 07:25p    4. Copy...
                                              5. Move/Rename...
                                              6. Delete
                                              7. Print...
                                              8. Print List

                                              9. Sort by...
                                              H. Change Default Dir...
                                              U. Current Dir...  F5
                                              F. Find...
                                              E. Search...       F2
                                              N. Name Search

                                              * (Un)mark
                                              Home,* (Un)mark All

Files:      3      Marked:     0
Free: 47,894,528   Used:  19,017   Setup... Shft+F1   Close
```

Oops!

If you don't want to create a directory, press N to select No in step 5.

1. Start the File Manager.

   For help with this step, see *TASK: Start the File Manager.*

2. Press **H**.

   This step selects the Change Default Dir command and displays the Change Default Directory dialog box.

3. Type **C:\WPDOCS\BOOK**.

   This step enters the name of the directory you want to create—BOOK—and creates it within the C:\WPDOCS directory.

4. Press **Enter**.

   You see a prompt that asks whether you want to create this directory.

5. Type **Y**.

   This step confirms the directory name, and WordPerfect creates the directory.

188   *Easy WordPerfect for Version 6*

after

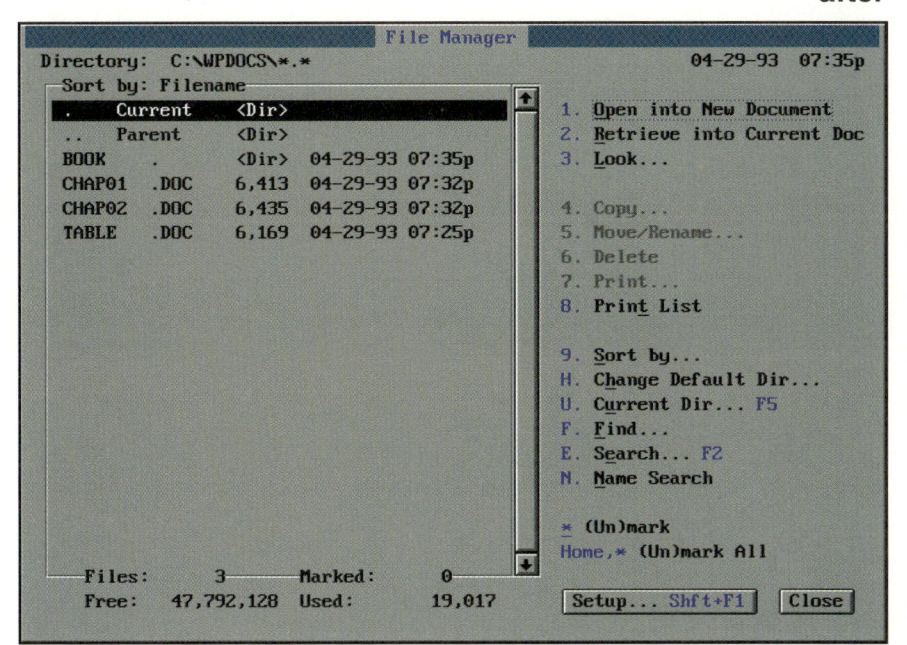

```
                          File Manager
Directory:  C:\WPDOCS\*.*                      04-29-93  07:35p
 Sort by: Filename
       Current     <Dir>                1. Open into New Document
  ..   Parent      <Dir>                2. Retrieve into Current Doc
  BOOK     .       <Dir>  04-29-93 07:35p  3. Look...
  CHAP01  .DOC     6,413  04-29-93 07:32p
  CHAP02  .DOC     6,435  04-29-93 07:32p  4. Copy...
  TABLE   .DOC     6,169  04-29-93 07:25p  5. Move/Rename...
                                        6. Delete
                                        7. Print...
                                        8. Print List

                                        9. Sort by...
                                        H. Change Default Dir...
                                        U. Current Dir... F5
                                        F. Find...
                                        E. Search... F2
                                        N. Name Search

                                        * (Un)mark
                                        Home,* (Un)mark All
  Files:      3      Marked:      0
  Free: 47,792,128  Used:    19,017   Setup... Shft+F1   Close
```

Change directories

This task does not change the current or default directories. To display a different directory, see *TASK: Display a different directory*. To change the default directory, see *TASK: Change the default directory*.

---

1. Start the File Manager.
2. Press **H** to select the Change Default Dir command.
3. Type the name of the new directory.
4. Press **Enter**.
5. Press **Y** to select Yes.

REVIEW

To create a directory

More Files   189

TASK

Display a different directory

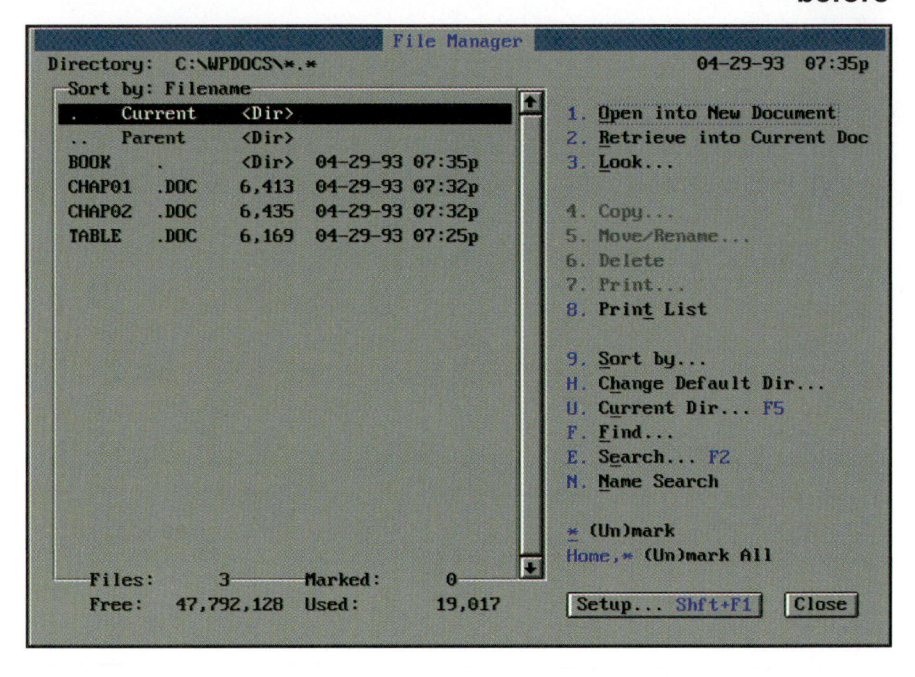

before

```
┌─ File Manager ──────────────────────────────────┐
Directory:  C:\WPDOCS\*.*              04-29-93  07:35p
┌─Sort by: Filename──────────────┐
│ .      Current    <Dir>        │  1. Open into New Document
│ ..     Parent     <Dir>        │  2. Retrieve into Current Doc
│ BOOK   .          <Dir>  04-29-93 07:35p │  3. Look...
│ CHAP01 .DOC       6,413  04-29-93 07:32p │
│ CHAP02 .DOC       6,435  04-29-93 07:32p │  4. Copy...
│ TABLE  .DOC       6,169  04-29-93 07:25p │  5. Move/Rename...
│                                │  6. Delete
│                                │  7. Print...
│                                │  8. Print List
│                                │
│                                │  9. Sort by...
│                                │  H. Change Default Dir...
│                                │  U. Current Dir... F5
│                                │  F. Find...
│                                │  E. Search... F2
│                                │  N. Name Search
│                                │
│                                │  * (Un)mark
│                                │  Home,* (Un)mark All
└─Files:    3    Marked:    0 ───┘
  Free:  47,792,128  Used:  19,017    [Setup... Shft+F1] [Close]
```

Oops!
To return to the original directory, select the Parent <Dir> directory and press Enter.

1. Start the File Manager.

   For help with this step, see *TASK: Start the File Manager.*

2. Use the arrow keys to highlight the directory **BOOK**.

   This selects the parent directory. The directories are listed along with files in the list on the left. Directories are indicated with <Dir> next to their names and are listed before file names. If you don't have this directory, select one that you do have.

3. Press **Enter**.

   This step displays the BOOK directory, which doesn't contain any files.

Easy WordPerfect for Version 6

after

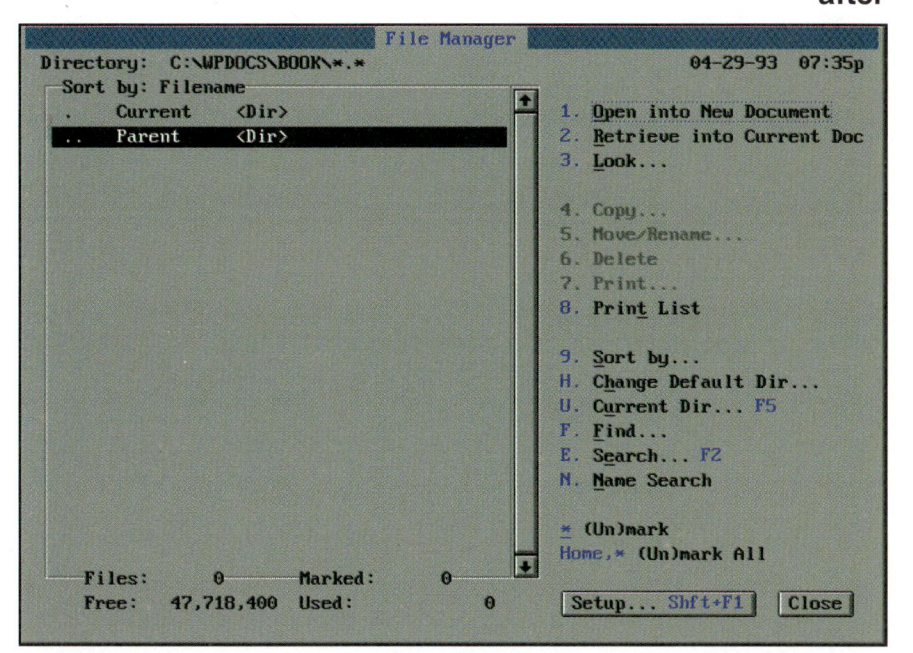

```
┌──────────────────── File Manager ────────────────────┐
│ Directory:  C:\WPDOCS\BOOK\*.*              04-29-93  07:35p │
│ ┌Sort by: Filename──────────┐                                │
│ │ .     Current   <Dir>     │    1. Open into New Document   │
│ │ ..    Parent    <Dir>     │    2. Retrieve into Current Doc│
│ │                           │    3. Look...                  │
│ │                           │                                │
│ │                           │    4. Copy...                  │
│ │                           │    5. Move/Rename...           │
│ │                           │    6. Delete                   │
│ │                           │    7. Print...                 │
│ │                           │    8. Print List               │
│ │                           │                                │
│ │                           │    9. Sort by...               │
│ │                           │    H. Change Default Dir...    │
│ │                           │    U. Current Dir...   F5      │
│ │                           │    F. Find...                  │
│ │                           │    E. Search...        F2      │
│ │                           │    N. Name Search              │
│ │                           │                                │
│ │                           │    * (Un)mark                  │
│ │                           │    Home,* (Un)mark All         │
│ ├Files:     0    Marked:    0 ┤                              │
│  Free: 47,718,400 Used:       0    [Setup... Shft+F1] [Close]│
└──────────────────────────────────────────────────────────────┘
```

Try another method

If you know the name of the directory you want, you can specify the directory name before you start the File Manager. Press Alt+F, press F, type the name of the directory, and then press Enter.

REVIEW

To display a different directory

1. Start the File Manager.
2. Highlight the directory you want.
3. Press **Enter**.

Close the File Manager

Press Esc at any time to return to the document screen.

More Files

191

TASK

Change the default directory

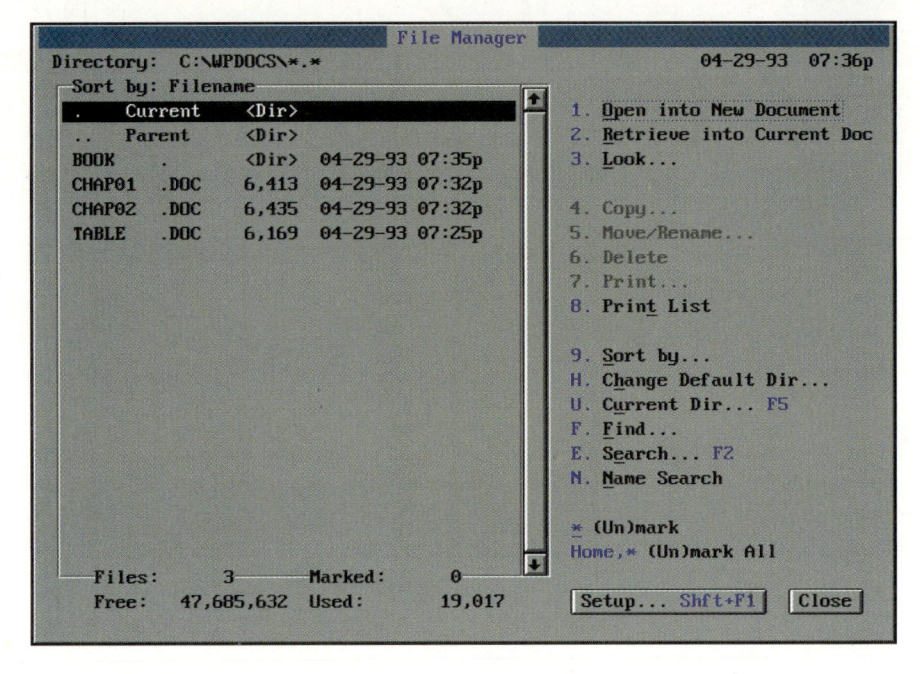

before

```
┌─────────────────────── File Manager ───────────────────────┐
Directory:   C:\WPDOCS\*.*                    04-29-93  07:36p
┌─Sort by: Filename ──────────────────┐
  .      Current    <Dir>              │  1. Open into New Document
  ..     Parent     <Dir>              │  2. Retrieve into Current Doc
  BOOK      .       <Dir>  04-29-93 07:35p │  3. Look...
  CHAP01   .DOC     6,413  04-29-93 07:32p │
  CHAP02   .DOC     6,435  04-29-93 07:32p │  4. Copy...
  TABLE    .DOC     6,169  04-29-93 07:25p │  5. Move/Rename...
                                           │  6. Delete
                                           │  7. Print...
                                           │  8. Print List
                                           │
                                           │  9. Sort by...
                                           │  H. Change Default Dir...
                                           │  U. Current Dir...   F5
                                           │  F. Find...
                                           │  E. Search...        F2
                                           │  N. Name Search
                                           │
                                           │  * (Un)mark
                                           │  Home,* (Un)mark All
└─Files:       3      Marked:     0 ──┘
  Free:   47,685,632  Used:   19,017    [Setup... Shft+F1] [Close]
```

Oops!

If you are changing the default directory and WordPerfect asks you whether you want to create that directory, you typed the name incorrectly. Press the Esc key to clear the prompt.

1. Start the File Manager.

   For help with this step, see *TASK: Start the File Manager*.

2. Press **H**.

   This step selects the Change Default Dir command.

3. Type **C:\WPDOCS\BOOK**.

   This step enters the name of the directory you want as the new default.

4. Press **Enter twice**.

   This step confirms the new directory. Each time you start the File Manager, WordPerfect will display the files in this directory. And whenever you save a file during this work session, WordPerfect will save it in this directory.

192   Easy WordPerfect for Version 6

after

[File Manager screenshot showing Directory: C:\WPDOCS\BOOK*.* with menu options including H. Change Default Dir...]

1. Start the File Manager.
2. Press **H** to select the Change Default Dir command.
3. Type the name of the directory you want as the default.
4. Press **Enter twice**.

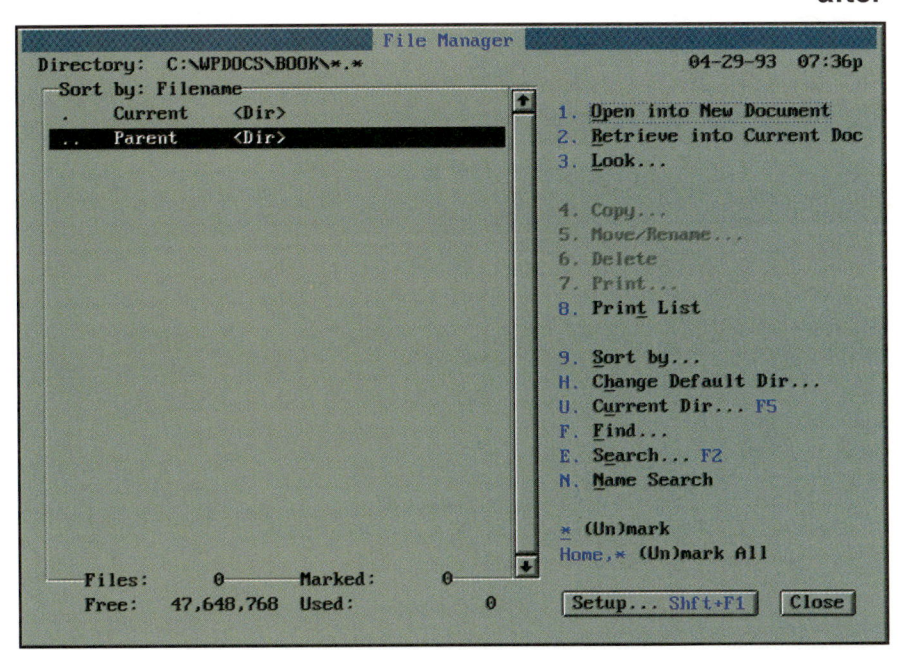

What is the "default directory"?

The default directory is the directory that WordPerfect uses to save and retrieve files, unless you specify a different directory.

REVIEW

To change the default directory

Create directory first

You should create the directory first, before you try to make it the default directory. See *TASK: Create a directory.*

More Files

193

TASK

Copy a file

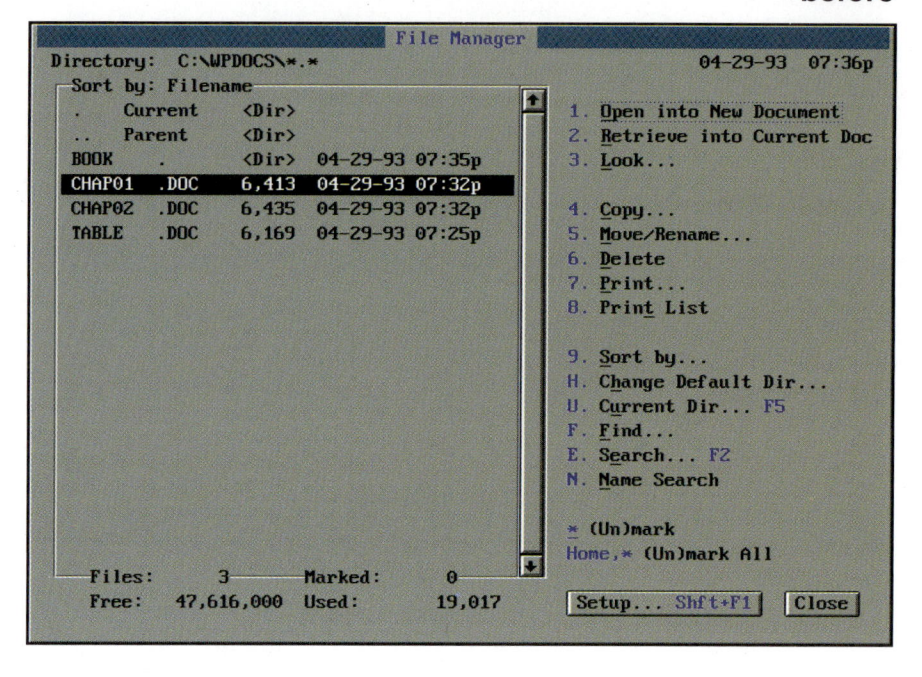

before

Oops!

If you don't want the copy you created, delete the file. See *TASK: Delete a file*.

1. Start the File Manager.

    For help with this step, see *TASK: Start the File Manager.*

2. Press the ↓ key until you highlight the file **CHAP01.DOC**.

    This step selects the file you want to copy.

3. Press **C**.

    This step selects the Copy command and displays the Copy dialog box.

4. Type **CHAP01.FIN**.

    This step enters the name you want to give to the copy of the file.

5. Press **Enter**.

    Pressing Enter makes a copy of the file.

194

Easy WordPerfect for Version 6

after

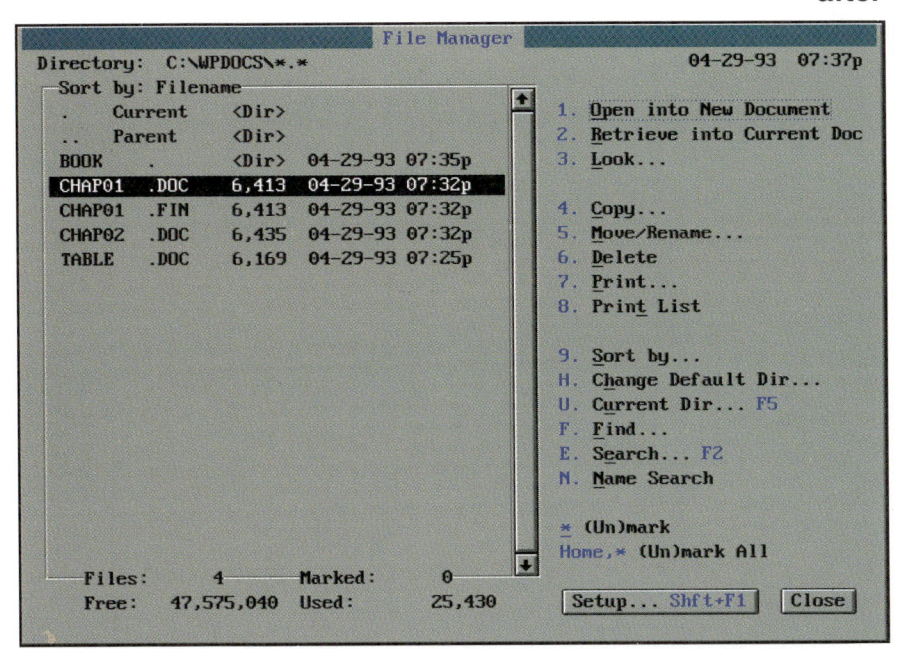

Copy to a different drive

To copy the file to a different drive, insert a disk and follow these same steps, but in step 4, type the drive letter (*A:* or *B:*) in front of the new file name.

REVIEW

To copy a file

1. Start the File Manager.
2. Highlight the file you want to copy.
3. Press **C** to select Copy.
4. Type the new file name.
5. Press **Enter**.

More Files

195

TASK

Rename a file

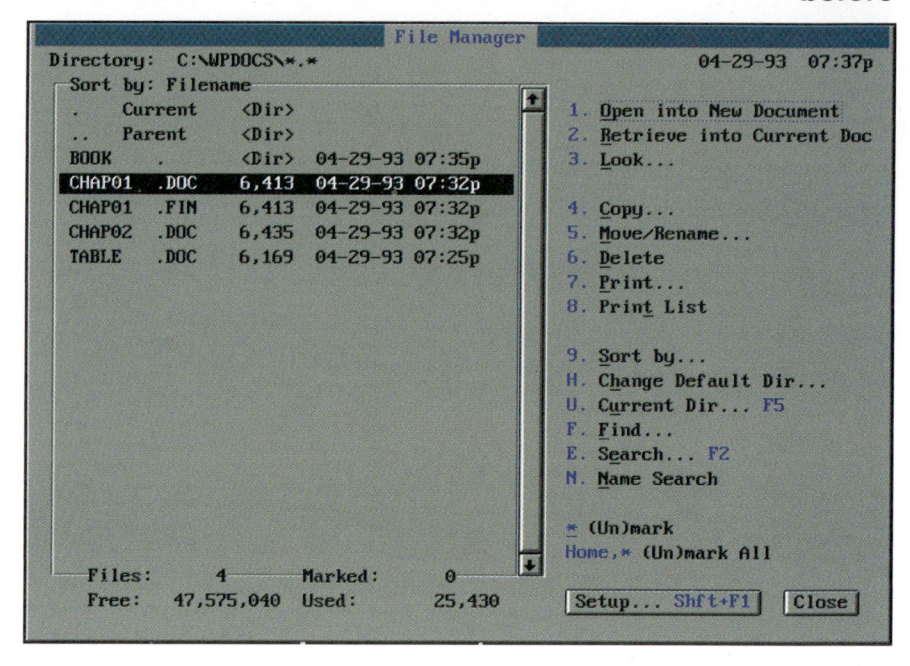

before

Oops!
To change the name again, follow this same procedure.

1. Start the File Manager.

   For help with this step, see *TASK: Start the File Manager.*

2. Press the ↓ key until you highlight the file **CHAP01.DOC**.

   This step selects the file you want to rename.

3. Press **M**.

   This step selects the Move/Rename command.

4. Type **CHAP01.DFT**.

   CHAP01.DFT is the new name you are giving to the file.

5. Press **Enter**.

   Pressing Enter renames the file.

196   *Easy WordPerfect for Version 6*

after

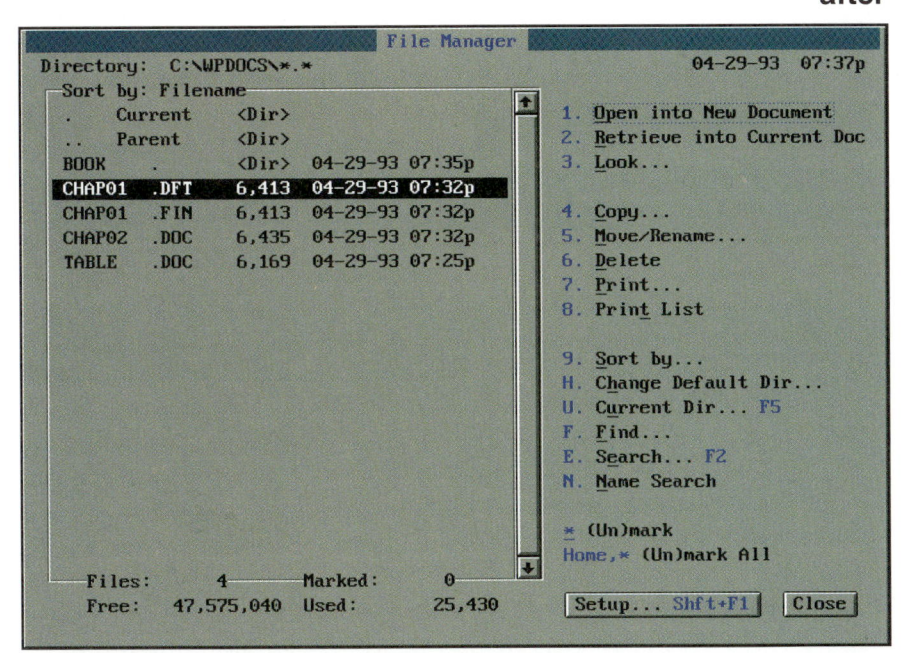

Move the file?

To move the file, type a directory name before the file name in step 4.

1. Start the File Manager.
2. Highlight the file you want to rename.
3. Press **M** to select Move/Rename.
4. Type the new file name.
5. Press **Enter**.

REVIEW

To rename a file

More Files

197

TASK

Delete a file

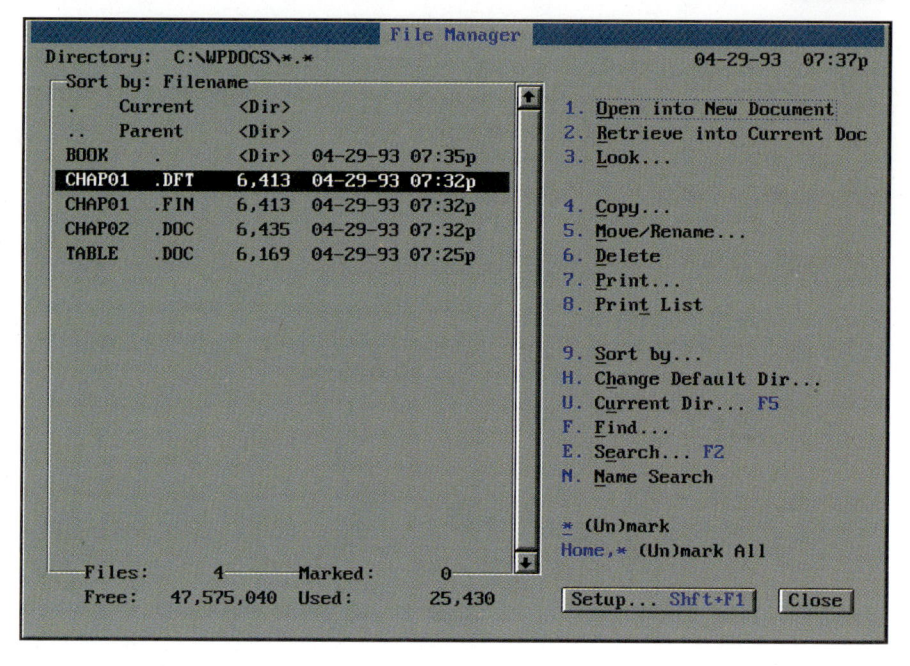

before

Oops!

If you don't want to delete the file, press N to select No in step 4.

1. Start the File Manager.

   For help with this step, see *TASK: Start the File Manager.*

2. Press the ↓ key until you highlight the file **CHAP01.DFT**.

   This step selects the file you want to delete.

3. Press **D**.

   This step selects the Delete command. You are asked to confirm the command.

4. Type **Y**.

   This step selects Yes and confirms the command. WordPerfect deletes the file.

Easy WordPerfect for Version 6

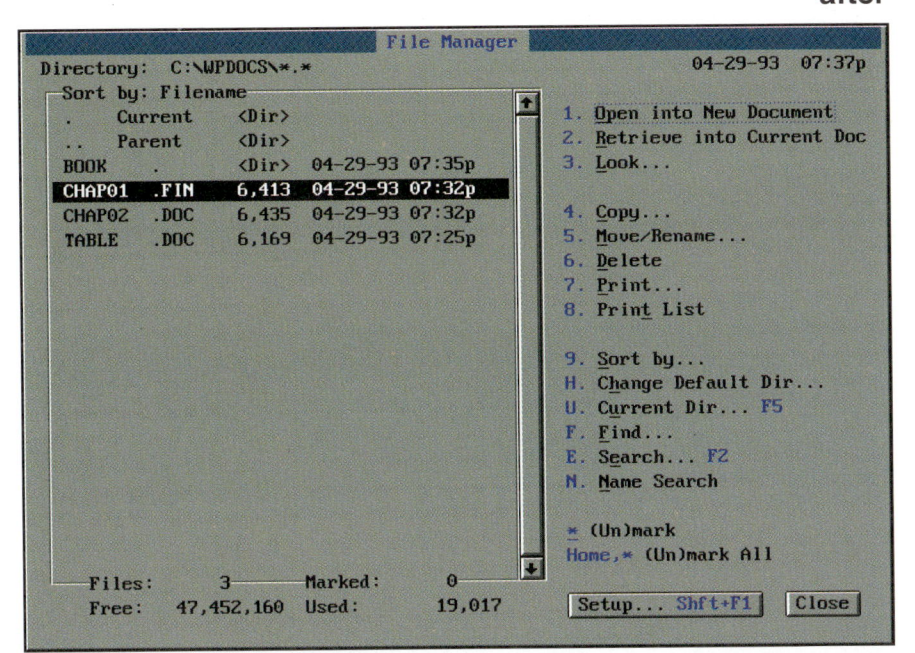

after

1. Start the File Manager.
2. Highlight the file you want to delete.
3. Press **D** to select Delete.
4. Press **Y** to select Yes.

Caution

You cannot undelete a file in WordPerfect. To undelete a file, you need a special program such as The Norton Utilities.

REVIEW

To delete a file

More Files

199

TASK

Find a file

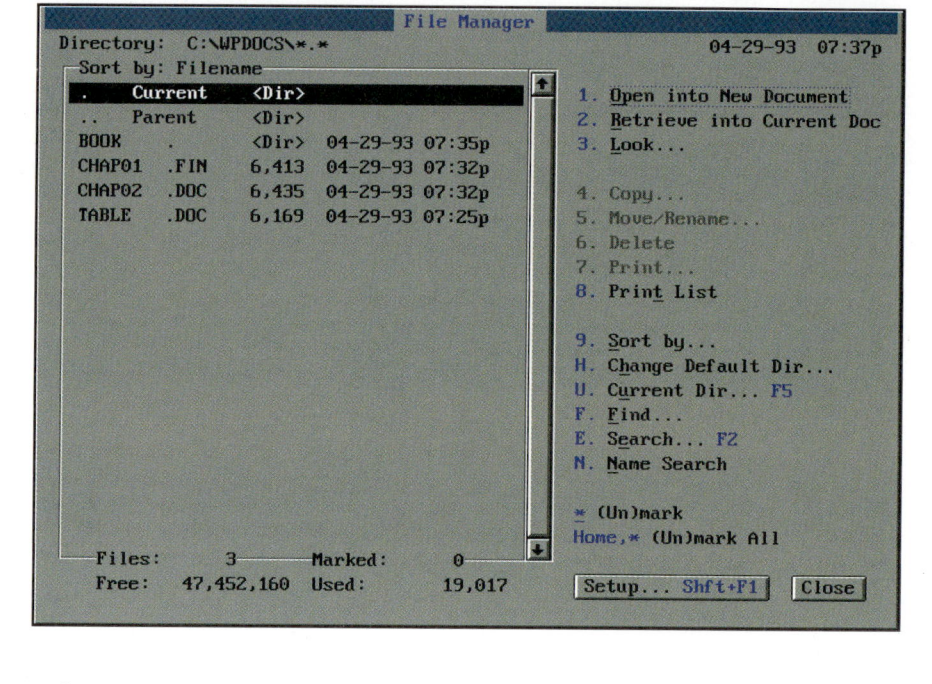

before

```
┌─────────────────────────────── File Manager ───────────────────────────────┐
│ Directory:  C:\WPDOCS\*.*                                04-29-93  07:37p  │
│ ┌Sort by: Filename────────────────────────┐                                │
│ │ .     Current    <Dir>                  │   1. Open into New Document    │
│ │ ..    Parent     <Dir>                  │   2. Retrieve into Current Doc │
│ │ BOOK       .     <Dir>  04-29-93 07:35p │   3. Look...                   │
│ │ CHAP01     .FIN  6,413  04-29-93 07:32p │                                │
│ │ CHAP02     .DOC  6,435  04-29-93 07:32p │   4. Copy...                   │
│ │ TABLE      .DOC  6,169  04-29-93 07:25p │   5. Move/Rename...            │
│ │                                         │   6. Delete                    │
│ │                                         │   7. Print...                  │
│ │                                         │   8. Print List                │
│ │                                         │                                │
│ │                                         │   9. Sort by...                │
│ │                                         │   H. Change Default Dir...     │
│ │                                         │   U. Current Dir...   F5       │
│ │                                         │   F. Find...                   │
│ │                                         │   E. Search...        F2       │
│ │                                         │   N. Name Search               │
│ │                                         │                                │
│ │                                         │   *    (Un)mark                │
│ │                                         │   Home,* (Un)mark All          │
│ └Files:     3────────Marked:      0───────┘                                │
│  Free:  47,452,160  Used:       19,017          Setup...  Shft+F1   Close  │
└────────────────────────────────────────────────────────────────────────────┘
```

Oops!

If you see the message `Not Found`, press Enter. Try the search again.

1. **Start the File Manager.**

   For help with this step, see *TASK: Start the File Manager.*

2. **Press F.**

   This step selects the Find command and displays a list of options.

3. **Press N.**

   This step selects Name, which tells WordPerfect to search for files by name.

4. **Type CH*.*.**

   This step tells WordPerfect to find all files that start with *CH*. The asterisks are wild cards that represent any characters. (For more information on wild cards, see Que's *Using WordPerfect 6,* Special Edition.)

5. **Press Enter.**

   This step starts the search. WordPerfect displays a list of every file that matches what you typed in step 4. You can copy, move, delete, open, or rename the files in the list.

Easy WordPerfect for Version 6

after

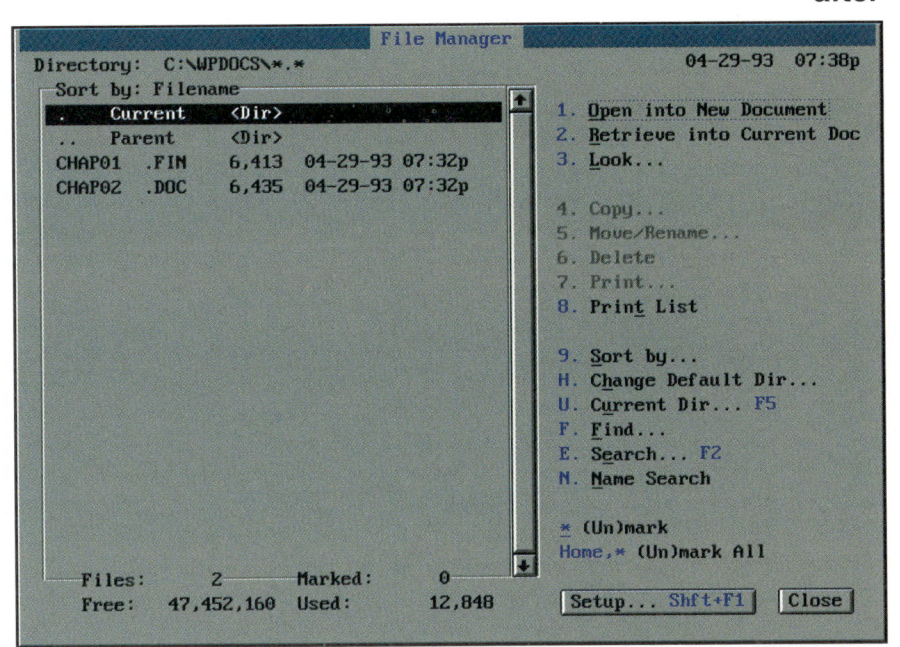

Go back to the original list

To return to the full list of files, select the `Current` directory at the top of the list and press Enter twice.

REVIEW

To find a file

1. Start the File Manager.

2. Press **F** to select the Find command.

3. Press **N** to select Name.

4. Type the name of the file you want to find. You can type wild cards if you want.

5. Press **Enter**.

More Files

201

Merging

This section covers the following tasks:

Create a merge letter

Create a form file

Enter text into a form file

Save the form file

Create a data file

Enter a record into the data file

Enter other records into the data file

Save the data file

Merge the files

TASK

Create a merge letter

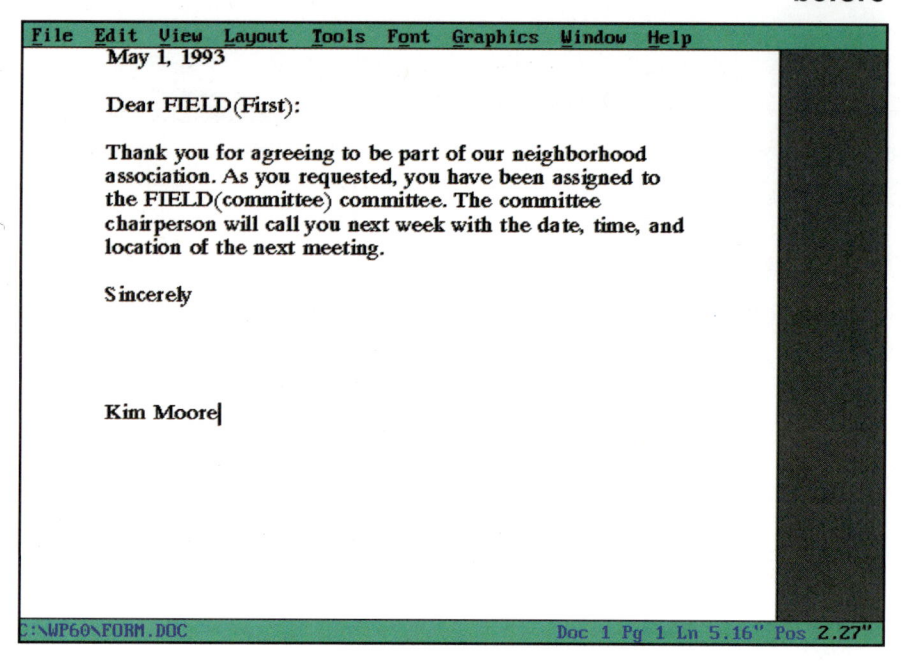

before

```
File  Edit  View  Layout  Tools  Font  Graphics  Window  Help
May 1, 1993

Dear FIELD(First):

Thank you for agreeing to be part of our neighborhood
association. As you requested, you have been assigned to
the FIELD(committee) committee. The committee
chairperson will call you next week with the date, time, and
location of the next meeting.

Sincerely



Kim Moore


C:\WP60\FORM.DOC                         Doc 1 Pg 1 Ln 5.16" Pos 2.27"
```

Creating a merge letter is an involved process. This task describes the general process and refers you to specific tasks for help on each step.

1. **Create a form file.**

    Two files make up a basic merge procedure: a data file and a form file. The form file contains the standard text you want to send to everyone on your mailing list, as well as the codes that control the merge. The data file contains changing information (such as the list of names and addresses) you want to insert into the form file. You create the form file first. See *TASK: Create a form file.* The Before screen shows a form file.

2. **Save the form file.**

    After you create the form file, save it. See *TASK: Save the form file.*

3. **Create a data file.**

    The data file contains the field definition and variable data—the specific information you want WordPerfect to plug into the form file. See *TASK: Create a data file.*

Easy WordPerfect for Version 6

after

```
File  Edit  View  Layout  Tools  Font  Graphics  Window  Help
          FIELDNAMES(First;Committee)ENDRECORD
     Carolyn ENDFIELD
     Recycle ENDRECORD
     Michael ENDFIELD
     Crime Watch ENDRECORD
     |




Field: First                              Doc 1 Pg 4 Ln 1" Pos 1"
```

> **Too confusing?**
>
> WordPerfect's Merge feature offers many options, which can make it a complex topic. This book covers only the bare essentials. If you want complete information, see Que's Using WordPerfect 6, Special Edition.

4. Enter the records.

    After you create the data file, you enter records into it. A record is one set of information you enter on a separate page. The merge will create a separate letter for each record. See *TASK: Enter a record into the data file* and *TASK: Enter other records into the data file*. The After screen shows a data file that contains records.

5. Save the data file.

    After you enter the records, you need to save the data file. See *TASK: Save the data file*.

6. Merge the files.

    The next step is to merge the two files. WordPerfect creates a new file that contains an individual letter for each record in your data file. You can save the new file or print it. See *TASK: Merge the files*.

TASK

Create a form file

before

[Screenshot of WordPerfect blank document screen with menu bar: File Edit View Layout Tools Font Graphics Window Help. Status bar shows: Dutch 801 18pt Roman (Speedo) — Doc 1 Pg 1 Ln 1" Pos 1"]

Oops!
If you make a mistake, abandon the document and start over. See *TASK: Abandon a document.*

1. **Start from a blank screen.**

   If you have a document on-screen, save and clear it. See *TASK: Save and clear a document.*

2. **Press Alt+T.**

   This step opens the Tools menu and displays a list of Tools commands.

3. **Press E.**

   This step selects the Merge command. You see a list of additional choices.

4. **Press D.**

   This step selects the Define command. Next you tell WordPerfect whether you want to create a form file or a data file.

5. **Press F.**

   This step selects Form and displays the Merge Codes (Form File) dialog box. The After screen shows this step.

6. **Press Esc.**

   This step closes the dialog box. You have just told WordPerfect that this document is a form file. Now you are ready to add text to the file. See *TASK: Enter text into a form file.*

206

Easy WordPerfect for Version 6

after

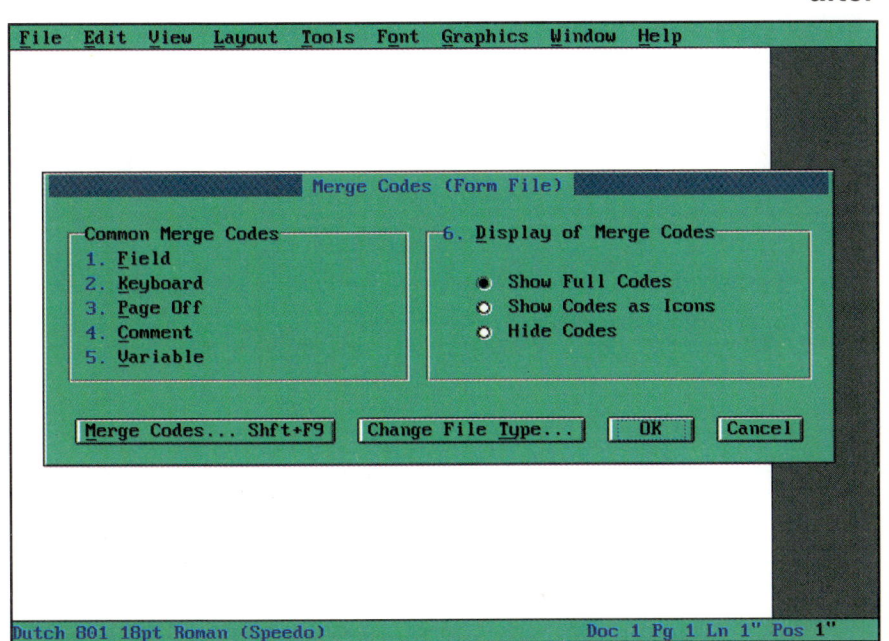

What's a form file?

A form file is the document that contains the text of your letter.

REVIEW

To create a form file

1. Start from a blank screen.
2. Press **Alt**+**T** to open the Tools menu.
3. Press **E** to select the Merge command.
4. Press **D** to select the Define command.
5. Press **F** to select Form.
6. Press **Esc**.

Merging

TASK

Enter text into a form file
(Part 1 of 2)

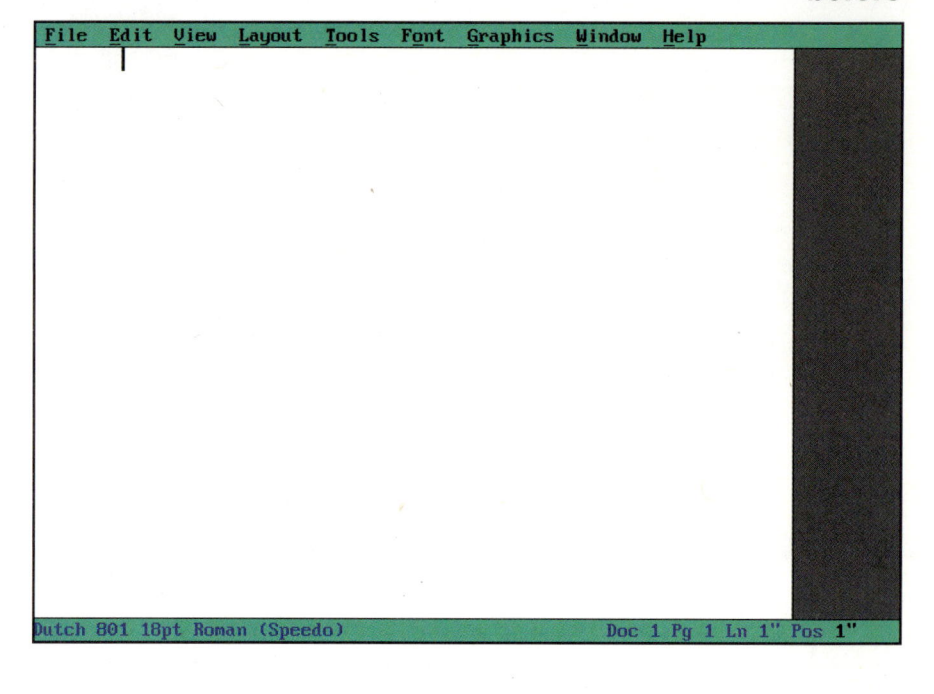

before

Oops!
Be sure to remember the field name you type in step 4. Later when you create the data file, you will need to define the fields you insert here.

These two pages contain the first part of this task. The next two pages contain the second part.

1. Type **May 1, 1993** and press **Enter twice**. Then type **Dear** and press the **space bar**.

   This step enters some text into the form file. The form file contains the unchanging text and the merge codes that tell WordPerfect where to insert the "changing," or variable, information. You are now ready to insert a field.

2. Press **Shift**+**F9**.

   This step opens the Merge Codes (Form File) dialog box.

3. Press **F**.

   This step selects Field Name and displays the Parameter Entry dialog box.

4. Type **First** and press **Enter**.

   This step enters a field for the first name and displays the field code on-screen. This code tells WordPerfect to insert the information in the first field of each record.

5. Type a colon (**:**) and press **Enter twice**.

   This step finishes the greeting for the letter.

208   *Easy WordPerfect for Version 6*

after

```
File  Edit  View  Layout  Tools  Font  Graphics  Window  Help
     May 1, 1993

     Dear FIELD(First):
     |




Dutch 801 18pt Roman (Speedo)           Doc 1 Pg 1 Ln 2.11" Pos 1"
```

1. Create a form file.
2. Type the text you want the form file to include.
3. Press **Shift**+**F9**.
4. Press **F**, type the field name, and press **Enter**.

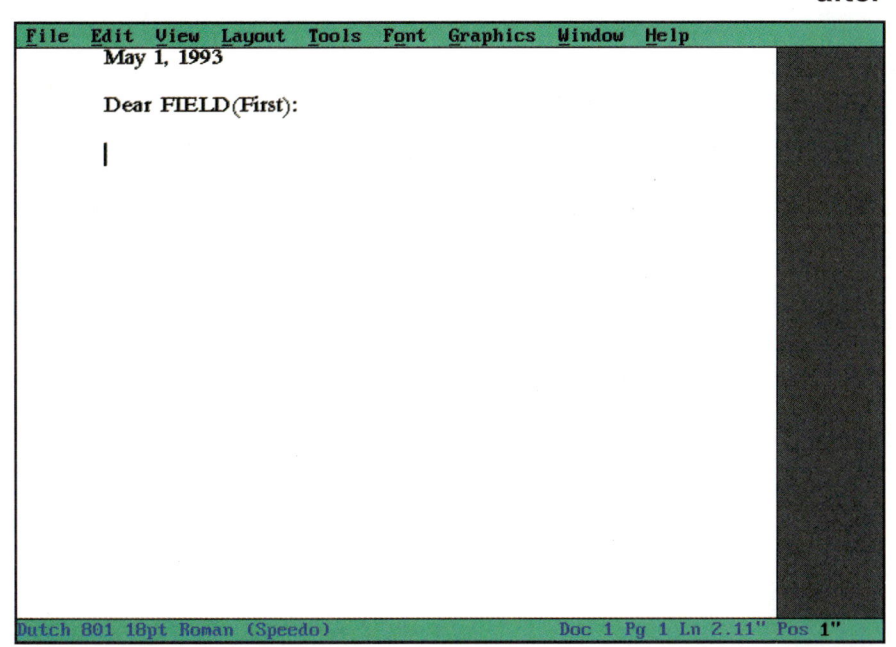

Delete a field
If you insert the field incorrectly, select it and press the Del key. Then try again.

REVIEW

To enter text into a form file
(Part 1 of 2)

Merging

209

TASK

Enter text into a form file
(Part 2 of 2)

before

```
File  Edit  View  Layout  Tools  Font  Graphics  Window  Help
   May 1, 1993

   Dear FIELD(First):
   |




Dutch 801 18pt Roman (Speedo)              Doc 1 Pg 1 Ln 2.11" Pos 1"
```

Oops!
Be sure to remember what fields you insert. Later when you create the data file, you will need to define the fields you insert here.

These two pages contain the second part of this task. The preceding two pages contain the first part.

1. Type the following text into the letter:

   Thank you for agreeing to be part of our neighborhood association. As you requested, you have been assigned to the

   This step enters more of the letter's unchanging text. Be sure to press the space bar after the word *the*. You are now ready to insert the next field.

2. Press **Shift**+**F9**.

   This step opens the Merge Codes (Form File) dialog box.

3. Press **F**.

   This step tells WordPerfect that you want to insert a field.

4. Type **Committee** and press **Enter**.

   This step enters a field for the committee name and displays the field code on-screen. This code tells WordPerfect to insert the information in the second field of each record.

210

Easy WordPerfect for Version 6

after

```
File  Edit  View  Layout  Tools  Font  Graphics  Window  Help
May 1, 1993

Dear FIELD(First):

Thank you for agreeing to be part of our neighborhood
association. As you requested, you have been assigned to
the FIELD(committee) committee. The committee
chairperson will call you next week with the date, time, and
location of the next meeting.

Sincerely



Kim Moore|


Dutch 801 18pt Roman (Speedo)           Doc 1 Pg 1 Ln 5.16" Pos 2.27"
```

Delete a field
If you insert the field incorrectly, select it and press the Del key. Then try again.

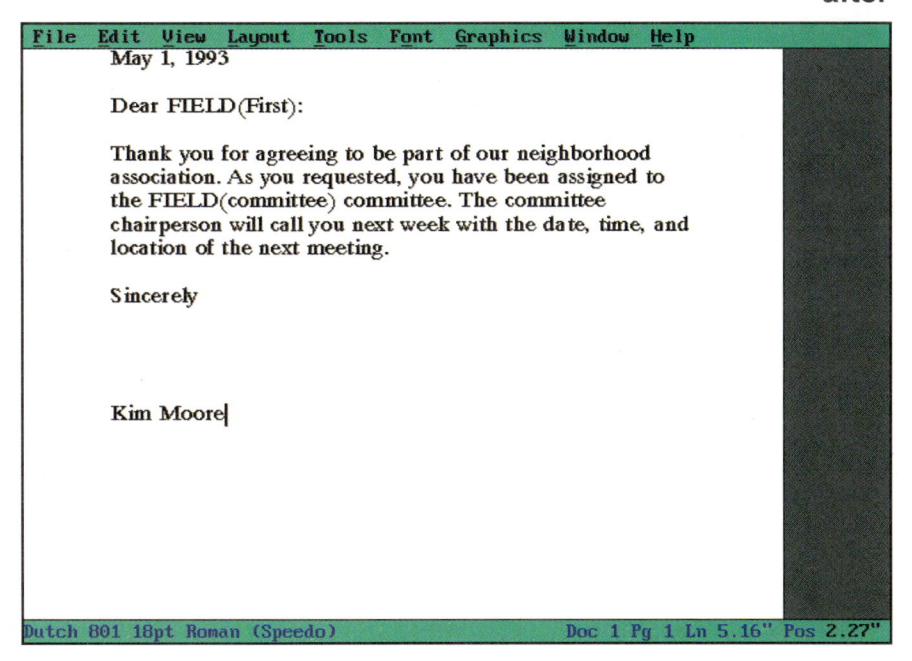

5. Type the rest of the letter:

   committee. The committee chairperson will call you next week with the date, time, and location of the next meeting.

   Sincerely

   Kim Moore

   This step completes the letter.

REVIEW

To enter text into a form file
(Part 2 of 2)

1. Type the text you want the form file to include.
2. To insert a field code, press **Shift**+**F9**.
3. Press **F**, type the field name, and press **Enter**.

Merging

211

TASK

Save the form file

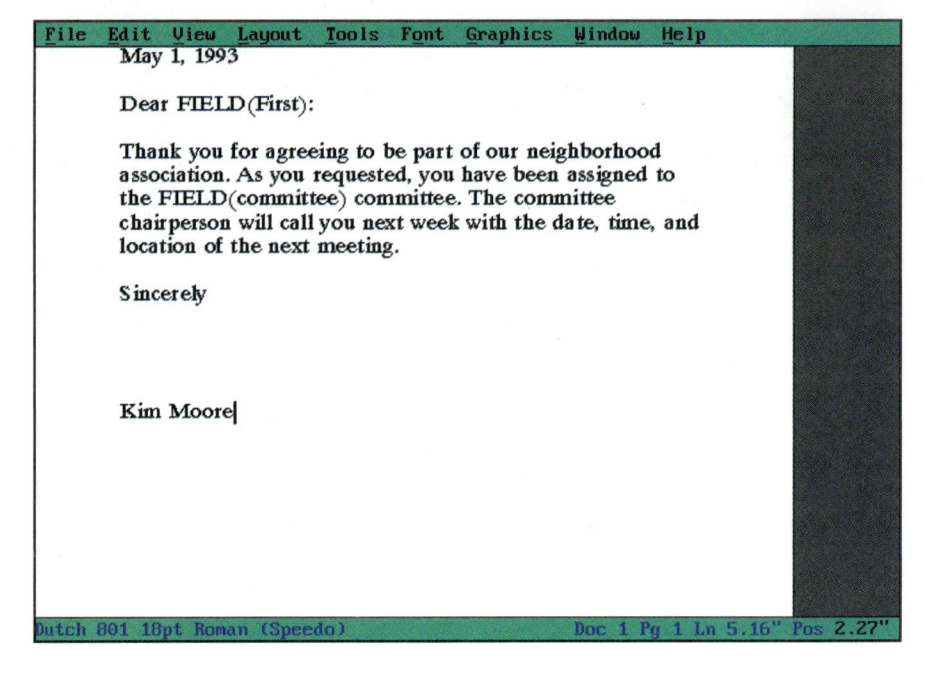

before

Oops!
If you don't want to save the form file, abandon it. See *TASK: Abandon a document.*

1. Press **Alt+F**.

   This step opens the File menu. You see a list of File commands.

2. Press **S**.

   This step selects the Save command. You see the Save Document dialog box, where you assign a name to the form file.

3. Type **FORM.DOC**.

   FORM.DOC is the name of the form file you are saving.

4. Press **Enter**.

   Pressing Enter confirms the name and saves the document to disk. For more information on saving, see the tasks in the section "Files."

Easy WordPerfect for Version 6

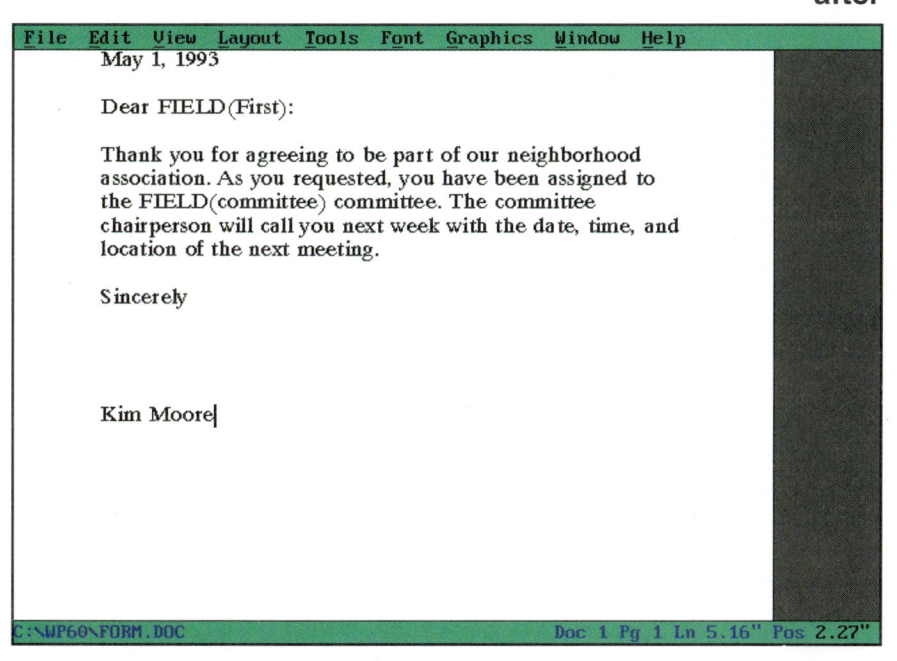

after

```
File  Edit  View  Layout  Tools  Font  Graphics  Window  Help
May 1, 1993

Dear FIELD(First):

Thank you for agreeing to be part of our neighborhood
association. As you requested, you have been assigned to
the FIELD(committee) committee. The committee
chairperson will call you next week with the date, time, and
location of the next meeting.

Sincerely



Kim Moore

C:\WP60\FORM.DOC                    Doc 1 Pg 1 Ln 5.16" Pos 2.27"
```

Save again?

To save again, press Alt+F and then S. You won't be prompted for a file name because WordPerfect saves the file with the same name.

REVIEW

To save the form file

1. Press **Alt**+**F** to open the File menu.
2. Press **S** to select the Save command.
3. Type a file name.
4. Press **Enter**.

Merging

TASK

Create a data file
(Part 1 of 2)

before

[Screenshot of WordPerfect blank screen with menu: File Edit View Layout Tools Font Graphics Window Help. Status bar: Dutch 801 18pt Roman (Speedo)   Doc 1 Pg 1 Ln 1" Pos 1"]

Oops!

If you don't want to create the file, press the Esc key to close the Merge Codes (Text Data File) dialog box.

These two pages contain the first part of this task: Select the document type. Turn the page for the next part: Enter the field names.

1. Start from a blank screen.

   If you have a document on-screen, save and clear it. See *TASK: Save and clear a document*.

2. Press **Alt**+**T**.

   This step opens the Tools menu and displays a list of Tools commands.

3. Press **E**.

   This step selects the Merge command.

4. Press **D**.

   This step selects the Define command. Next you tell WordPerfect whether you want to create a form file or a data file.

5. Press **D**.

   This step selects Data Text. You see the Merge Codes (Text Data File) dialog box. The After screen shows this step.

Easy WordPerfect for Version 6

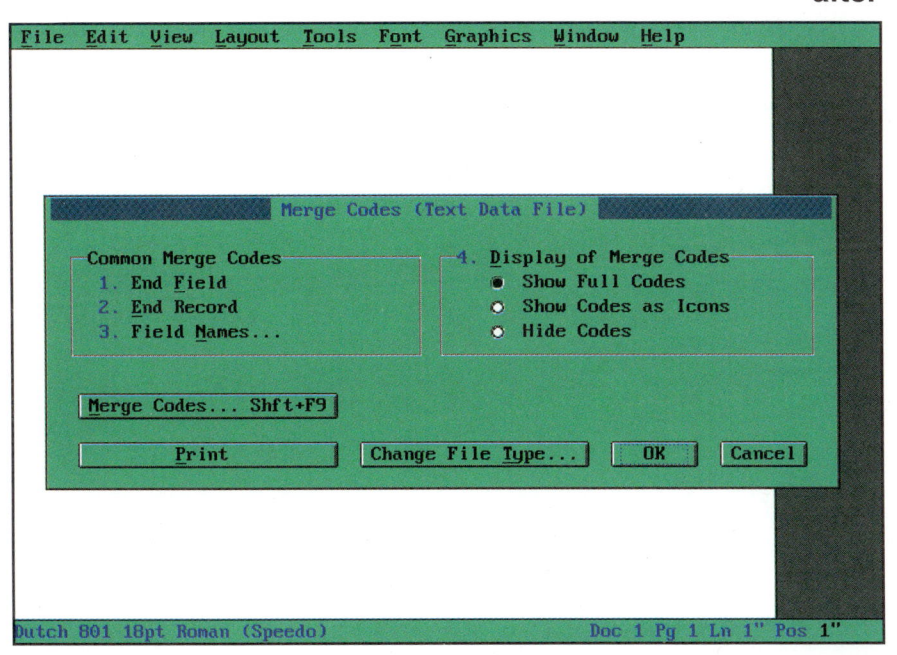

after

1. Start from a blank screen.
2. Press **Alt**+**T** to open the Tools menu.
3. Press **E** to select the Merge command.
4. Press **D** to select the Define command.
5. Press **D** to select Data Text.

What's a database?

The data file stores the variable information that you want to insert into the form file. Each piece of information is stored in a *field*, and each set of fields is called a *record*.

REVIEW

To create a data file
(Part 1 of 2)

Try a shortcut

Press Shift+F9 to select the Merge command.

Merging

215

TASK

Create a data file
(Part 2 of 2)

before

Oops!
If you don't want to add the fields, press the Esc key.

These two pages contain the second part of this task: Enter the field names. The preceding two pages cover the first part: Select the document type.

1. In the Merge Codes (Text Data File) dialog box, press **N**.

   This step selects the Field Names command and displays the Field Names dialog box.

2. Type **First** and press **Enter**.

   This step enters the first field name in the Field Name List.

3. Type **Committee** and press **Enter**.

   This step enters the second field name in the Field Name List.

4. Press **Enter**.

   This step closes the Field Names dialog box. The first page of the data file contains the field definition. WordPerfect automatically inserts a page break after the field definition. You are ready to enter specific records on this page of the data file.

216

Easy WordPerfect for Version 6

after

```
File  Edit  View  Layout  Tools  Font  Graphics  Window  Help
      FIELDNAMES(First;Committee)ENDRECORD






















Field: First                              Doc 1 Pg 2 Ln 1" Pos 1"
```

Add other fields

You can add as many fields as you need. And you can add other types of fields. See Que's *Using WordPerfect 6*, Special Edition, for complete information.

REVIEW

1. In the Merge Codes (Text Data File) dialog box, press **N** to select the Field Names command.

2. Type the name of the first field and press **Enter**.

3. Continue to type field names and press **Enter**.

4. When you are finished, press **Enter** to close the dialog box.

To create a data file
(Part 2 of 2)

Merging

217

TASK

Enter a record into the data file

before

```
File  Edit  View  Layout  Tools  Font  Graphics  Window  Help
         FIELDNAMES(First;Committee)ENDRECORD
```

Field: First   Doc 1 Pg 2 Ln 1" Pos 1"

Oops!

If you make a mistake when typing, correct it as you would in any other document. All of WordPerfect's editing features are available.

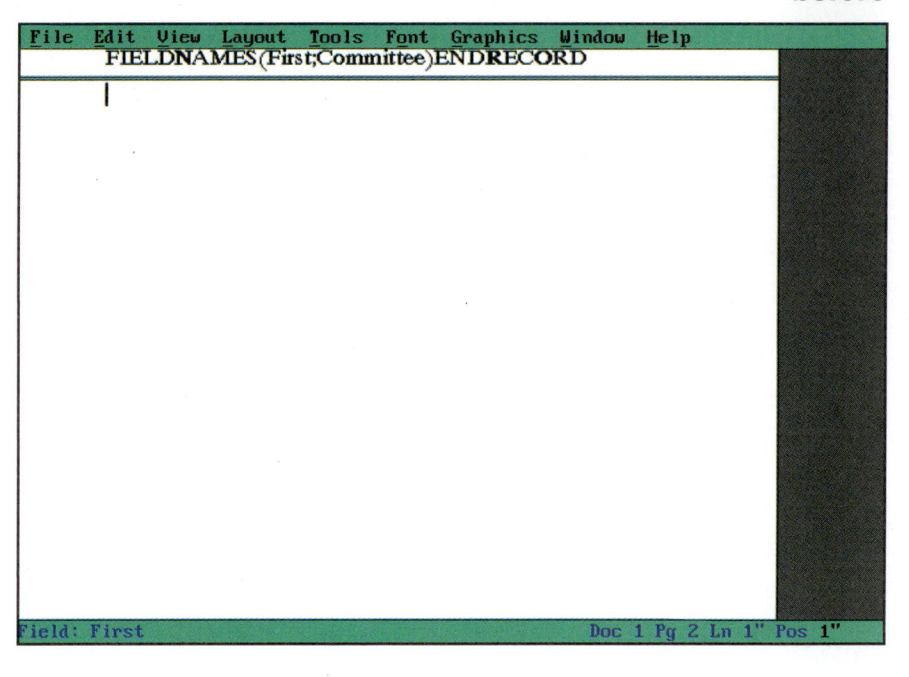

1. Type **Carolyn**.

   This step enters the information for the first field—the field called *First*. When you merge this data file with the form file, WordPerfect will insert this text into the form file.

2. Press **Shift+F9**.

   This step displays the Merge Codes (Text Data File) dialog box.

3. Press **F**.

   This step selects End Field and inserts a code that tells WordPerfect to end the field here.

4. Type **Recycle**.

   This step enters the information for the second field.

5. Press **Shift+F9**.

   This step displays the Merge Codes (Text Data File) dialog box.

6. Press **E**.

   This step selects End Record and inserts a code that tells WordPerfect to end the record here. WordPerfect automatically inserts a page break. Each record is stored on a separate page.

Easy WordPerfect for Version 6

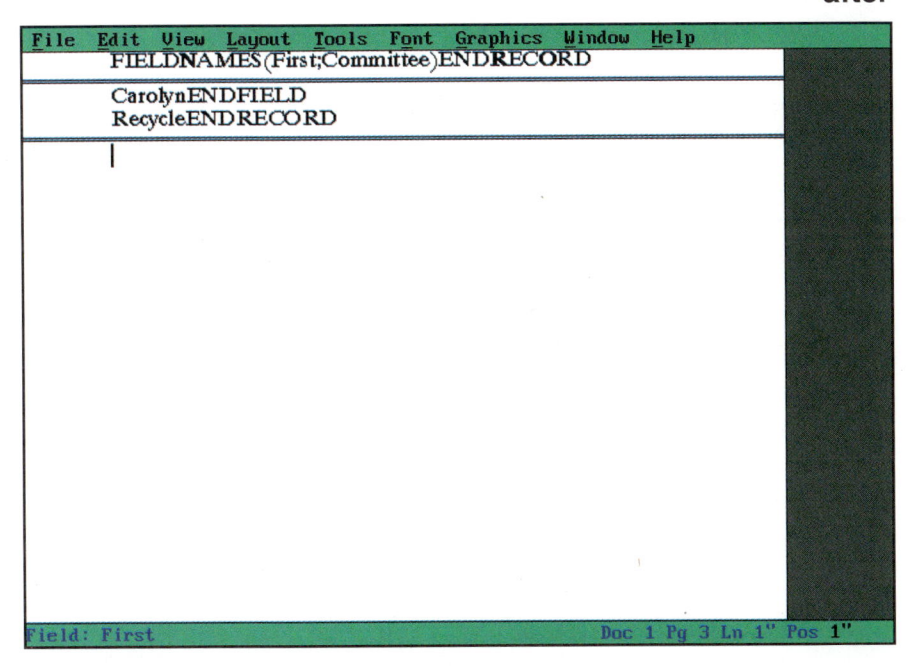

after

1. Type the information for the first field.
2. Press **Shift+F9**.
3. Press **F** to select End Field.
4. Follow steps 1–3 for all fields (except the last one).
5. When all fields have been entered, press **Shift+F9**.
6. Press **E** to insert an End Record code.

REVIEW

To enter a record into the data file

Merging

219

TASK

Enter other records into the data file

before

```
File  Edit  View  Layout  Tools  Font  Graphics  Window  Help
      FIELDNAMES(First;Committee)ENDRECORD
      CarolynENDFIELD
      RecycleENDRECORD
```
Field: First   Doc 1 Pg 3 Ln 1" Pos 1"

Oops!
If you make a mistake when typing, correct it as you would in any other document. All of WordPerfect's editing features are available.

1. Type **Michael**.

   This step enters the information for the first field of the second record.

2. Press **Shift+F9**.

   This step displays the Merge Codes (Text Data File) dialog box.

3. Press **F**.

   This step selects End Field and inserts a code that tells WordPerfect to end the field here.

4. Type **Crime Watch**.

   This step enters the information for the next field.

5. Press **Shift+F9**.

   This step displays the Merge Codes (Text Data File) dialog box.

6. Press **E**.

   This step selects End Record and inserts a code that tells WordPerfect to end the record here. WordPerfect automatically inserts a page break. Each record is stored on a separate page.

Easy WordPerfect for Version 6

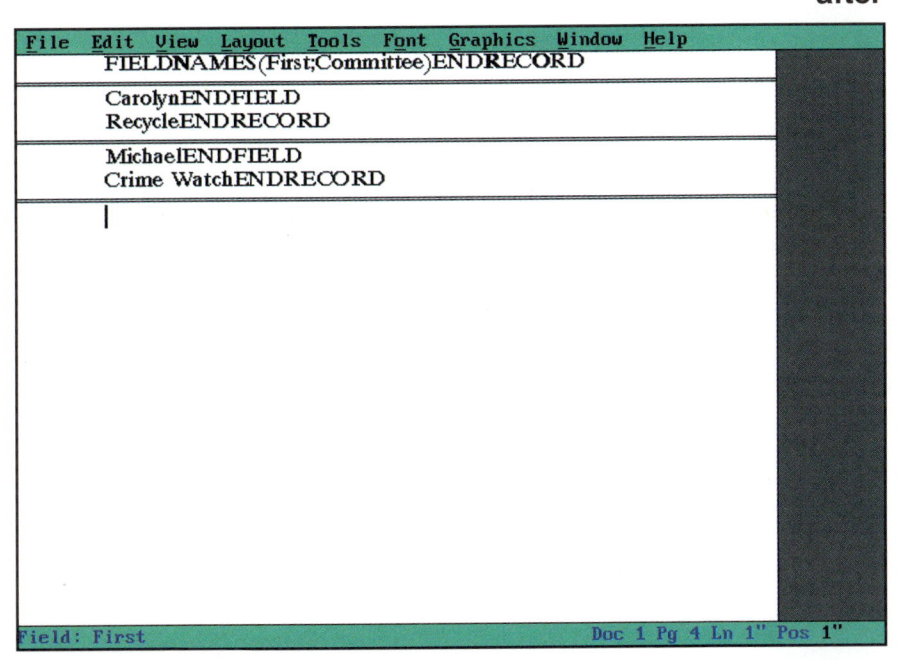

after

```
File  Edit  View  Layout  Tools  Font  Graphics  Window  Help
          FIELDNAMES(First;Committee)ENDRECORD
       CarolynENDFIELD
       RecycleENDRECORD

       MichaelENDFIELD
       Crime WatchENDRECORD
       |




Field: First                              Doc 1 Pg 4 Ln 1" Pos 1"
```

> **Delete a record**
>
> To delete a record, select the text and codes for that record and press the Del key.

REVIEW

To enter other records into the data file

1. Type the information for the first field of the second record.

2. Press **Shift+F9**.

3. Press **F** to select End Field.

4. Follow steps 1–3 for all fields (except the last one).

5. When all fields have been entered, press **Shift+F9**.

6. Press **E** to insert an End Record code.

TASK

Save the data file

before

```
File  Edit  View  Layout  Tools  Font  Graphics  Window  Help
      FIELDNAMES(First;Committee)ENDRECORD
      CarolynENDFIELD
      RecycleENDRECORD

      MichaelENDFIELD
      Crime WatchENDRECORD
      |
```

Field: First   Doc 1 Pg 4 Ln 1" Pos 1"

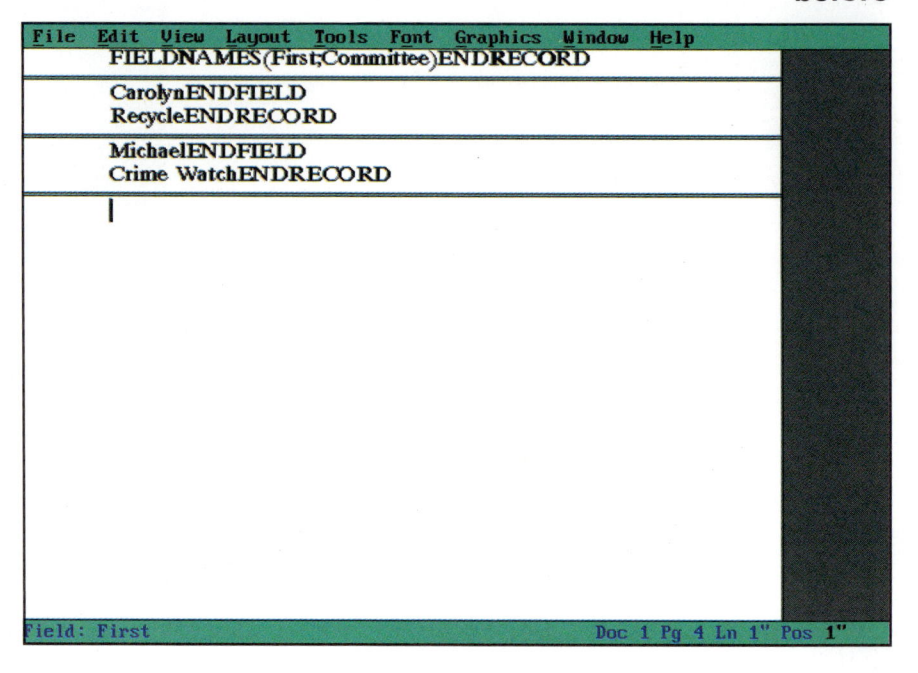

Oops!

If you don't want to save the data file, abandon it. See *TASK: Abandon a document*.

1. Press **Alt**+**F**.

   This step opens the File menu. You see a list of File commands.

2. Press **S**.

   This step selects the Save command. You see the Save Document dialog box, where you assign a name to the data file.

3. Type **DATA.DOC**.

   DATA.DOC is the name of the data file you are saving.

4. Press **Enter**.

   Pressing Enter confirms the name and saves the document to disk. For more information on saving, see the tasks in the section "Files."

222

Easy WordPerfect for Version 6

after

1. Press **Alt**+**F** to open the File menu.
2. Press **S** to select the Save command.
3. Type a file name.
4. Press **Enter**.

Save again?

To save again, press Alt+F and then S. You won't be prompted for a file name because WordPerfect saves the file with the same name.

REVIEW

To save the data file

TASK

Merge the files

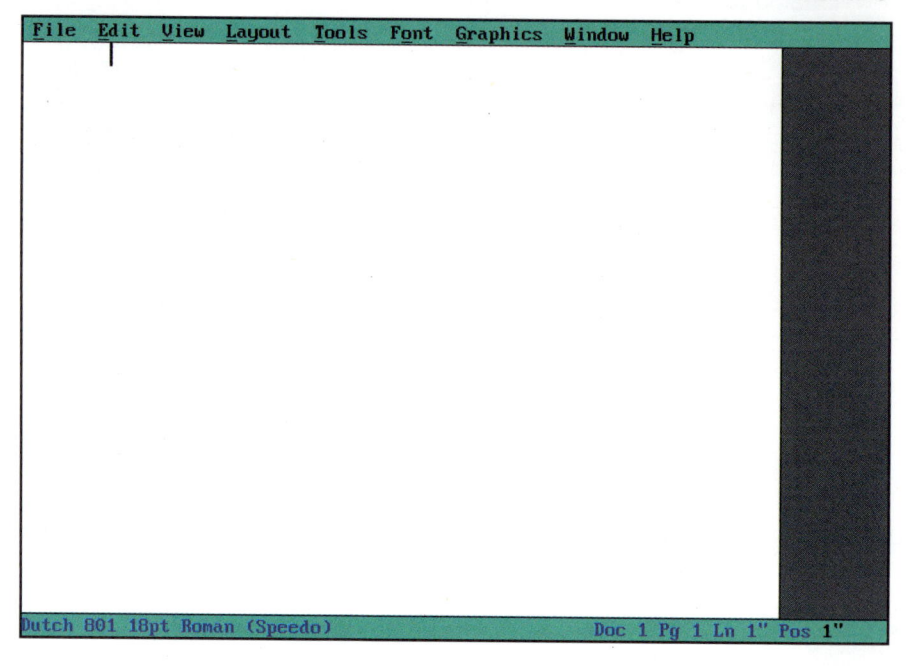

before

[screen showing WordPerfect menu bar: File Edit View Layout Tools Font Graphics Window Help; status line: Dutch 801 18pt Roman (Speedo)   Doc 1 Pg 1 Ln 1" Pos 1"]

Oops!

If the merge did not go as planned, check to be sure that you typed the file names correctly. Check each of the files to be sure that they are set up correctly.

1. Start from a blank screen.

   If you have a document on-screen, save and clear it. See *TASK: Save and clear a document*.

2. Press **Alt**+**T**.

   This step opens the Tools menu and displays a list of Tools commands.

3. Press **E**.

   This step selects the Merge command.

4. Press **R**.

   This step selects the Run command. You see the Run Merge dialog box.

5. Type **FORM.DOC** and press **Tab**.

   This step enters the name of the form file.

6. Type **DATA.DOC**.

   This step enters the name of the data file.

Easy WordPerfect for Version 6

after

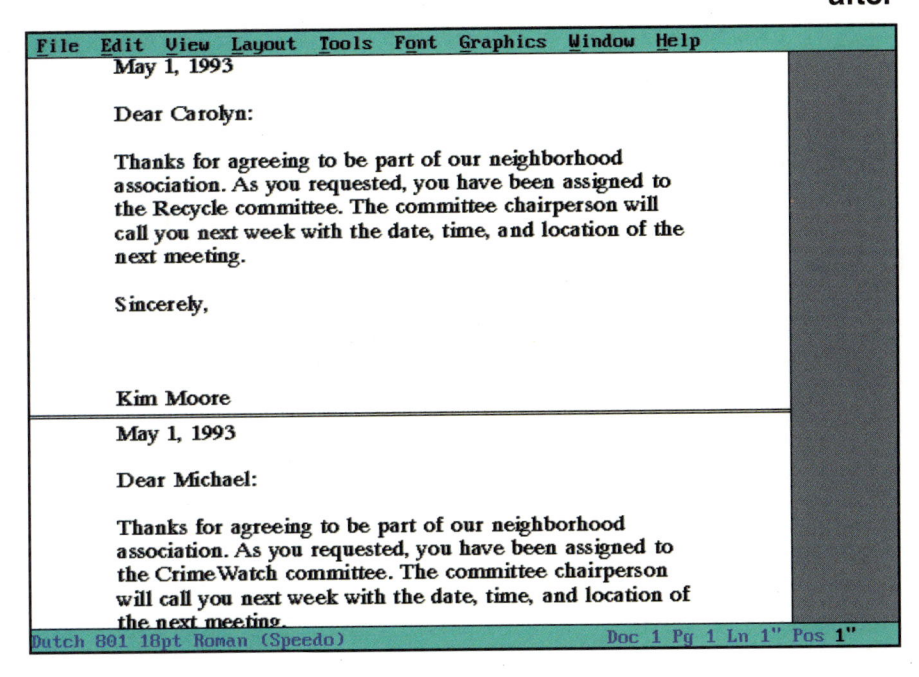

[Screenshot of WordPerfect document showing two merged letters dated May 1, 1993 — one to Dear Carolyn about the Recycle committee, signed Kim Moore; and one to Dear Michael about the CrimeWatch committee.]

A lot of options!

The Merge feature offers a lot of options. For complete information, see Que's *Using WordPerfect 6, Special Edition*.

7. Press **Enter twice**.

   This step merges the form file with the data file and creates a unique, specialized letter for each record in the data file. The text in each letter is identical to the text you entered into the form file, except that each field code in the form file has been replaced with the information you entered into the data file. You can print or save the letters. See *TASK: Save a document* or *TASK: Print a document*.

REVIEW

To merge the files

1. Start from a blank screen.
2. Press **Alt**+**T** to open the Tools menu.
3. Press **E** to select the Merge command.
4. Press **R** to select the Run command.
5. Type the name of the form file and press **Tab**.
6. Type the name of the data file.
7. Press **Enter twice**.

Try a shortcut

Press Shift+F9 to select the Merge command.

Merging

225

Reference

Guide to Using the Mouse

Where To Get More Help

Glossary

Easy WordPerfect for Version 6

Reference

Guide to Using the Mouse

A mouse is a pointing device you use to move the cursor on-screen. As you move the mouse on your desk, the mouse pointer moves on-screen. WordPerfect 5.1 and 6 allow you to use a mouse, but you do not need a mouse to use the program.

You can use the mouse for the following purposes:

- To move the cursor
- To make menu selections
- To block text

To use a mouse, you need to understand these terms:

Term	Meaning
Click	Press and release the left mouse button.
Drag	Press and hold down the left mouse button while you move the mouse.
Double-click	Press the left mouse button twice in rapid succession.

Moving the Cursor

To use the mouse to move the cursor, position the mouse pointer where you want the cursor to be, and click the left button.

Selecting a Menu Command

To use the mouse to select a menu command, click on the menu name. WordPerfect displays a pull-down menu. Click on the command you want.

For some commands, WordPerfect displays a submenu. Click on the command you want. For other commands, WordPerfect displays a dialog box. Select the options you want by clicking on them. Then click on the OK button.

Blocking Text

To use the mouse to block text, position the mouse pointer on the character that begins the text you want to select. Press and hold down the left mouse button as you drag the mouse over the block of text you want to select. When the text you want to block is highlighted, release the mouse button.

Where To Get More Help

As you become more comfortable using WordPerfect, you might need a more detailed reference book. Que offers several WordPerfect books to suit your needs:

Using WordPerfect 6, Special Edition

WordPerfect 6 QuickStart

WordPerfect 6 Quick Reference

Also of interest:

Easy DOS

Introduction to Personal Computers, 3rd Edition

Que's Computer User's Dictionary, 3rd Edition

Glossary

block   To select text while in Block mode. You can block a character, a word, a sentence, a paragraph, or any amount of text. After you block the text, you can perform different actions on it; for example, you can copy it, delete it, or enhance it.

carriage return   The method you use to end a line and start a new line. WordPerfect has two types of carriage returns: soft returns and hard returns. A soft return is inserted automatically by WordPerfect when you reach the end of a line. A hard return is inserted when you press Enter. A hard return ends a line and moves the cursor to the beginning of the next line.

centering   An alignment option that centers text between the right and left margins.

copy   An operation that duplicates a block of text. Text appears in both the original location and the location to which you copy the text.

cursor   A thin, blinking bar that marks the point on-screen where you begin typing text, deleting text, selecting a block, and so on.

data file   One of two essential parts of a merge operation. The data file contains the information you want to insert into the main document—the form file. WordPerfect stores each piece of information in a field and stores each set of fields in a record.

default settings   The standard WordPerfect settings in effect each time you start the program.

directory   A disk area that stores information about files. A directory is like a drawer in a file cabinet. Within that drawer, you can store your files.

document   All the text and formatting information you enter on-screen. WordPerfect and your operating system keep track of documents by storing them on-disk in files.

DOS An acronym for *disk operating system.* DOS manages the details of your system, such as storing and retrieving programs and files.

field The variable information that WordPerfect enters into a merge letter. You create the fields by entering them into a data file.

file An individual document, such as a report, memo, or letter, that you store on your hard drive or floppy disk for future use.

font The style, size, and typeface of a set of characters.

footer Text that appears at the bottom of a printed document. Footers can appear on all pages, only the even pages, or only the odd pages.

form file One of two essential parts of a merge operation (the data file is the other part). The form file contains the unchanging text of the document and the merge codes that tell WordPerfect where to insert the variable information (the fields from the data file).

hard page break A page break you insert to begin a new page at a certain spot. A hard page break appears on-screen as a double-dashed line.

hard return A type of carriage return you insert when you press Enter. A hard return ends the line and moves the cursor to the beginning of the next line.

header Text that appears at the top of a printed document. Headers can appear on all pages, only the even pages, or only the odd pages.

Help An on-screen feature that displays a description of different WordPerfect topics and features.

Insert mode A mode in which WordPerfect inserts new characters as you type and pushes existing characters forward. Insert mode is the opposite of Typeover mode.

left-justification   An alignment option that aligns text along the left margin.

margins   The white space left around the four edges of the paper (left, right, top, and bottom).

menu   An on-screen list of WordPerfect options. You can select a menu option by pressing the key that corresponds to its highlighted letter.

Merge code   A code that inserts a field or performs another action in a merge letter.

merge letter   A type of document that WordPerfect creates by combining variable information—such as a list of names and addresses—and a standard letter.

mouse   An input device, like a keyboard, that enables you to move the cursor on-screen, select menu commands, and perform other operations.

move   An operation that moves a block of text from one location to another.

path   The route, through directories, to a program or document file. For example, the path C:\WPDOCS\DATA\REPORT.DOC includes four elements: the disk drive (C:); the first directory (WPDOCS); the second directory, which is also called a *subdirectory*, (DATA); and the file name (REPORT.DOC).

record   The collection of fields in a data file. For instance, a record might store a set of information about one person.

Reveal Codes   The command you select from the View menu to open the Reveal Codes window to see the hidden codes that WordPerfect inserts into your document. These codes can indicate tab spaces, carriage returns, margin settings, font changes, line spacing, headers, footers, and so on.

Reference

right-justification   An alignment option that aligns text along the right margin.

search string   A set of characters, such as a word or phrase, that WordPerfect looks for during a search operation.

soft page break   A page break that WordPerfect inserts automatically when you have entered enough text to fill a page. A soft page break appears on-screen as a dashed line.

soft return   A type of carriage return that WordPerfect inserts automatically when you reach the end of a line. WordPerfect readjusts soft returns if you add or delete text.

status line   The bottom line of the WordPerfect editing screen. After you save your document, this line indicates the document's name. You also see information about the cursor's location.

Thesaurus   A WordPerfect feature that enables you to display synonyms and antonyms for a selected word. Synonyms are words with similar meanings. Antonyms are words with opposite meanings.

Typeover mode   A mode in which the characters you type replace existing characters. Typeover mode is the opposite of Insert mode.

word wrap   A WordPerfect feature that eliminates the need to press Enter each time you reach the right margin. Instead, WordPerfect automatically moves—or "wraps"—words to the next line.

Index

Easy WordPerfect for Version 6

Index

A

Alignment (Layout menu) command
    Center, 84-85
    Decimal Tab, 130-131
    Flush Right, 86-87
    Hanging Indent, 90-91
    Hard Page, 38-39
    Indent, 88-89
arrow keys, 11-12
asterisk (*) wild card, 200

B

[Back Tab] Reveal Code, 91
background paragraph shading, 136-137
Backspace key, 43, 51
blank lines, inserting, 34-35
Block (Edit menu) command, 46-47
Block mode, 46
blocking text, 229
blocks, 231
    capitalization, changing, 106-107
    copying, 56-57
    deleting, 50-51
    deselecting, 57
    moving, 58-59
    printing, 180-181
    retrieving, 122-123
    saving, 120-121
    selecting, 46-47
Bold (Font menu) command, 92-93
[Bold On] Reveal Code, 92
bold text, 92-93
borders
    pages, 142-143
    paragraphs, 134-135
breaks
    column, 172
    page
        hard, 232
        inserting, 38-39
        soft, 234

C

canceling retrievals, 122
capitalization of blocks, changing, 106-107
carriage returns, 231
Cascade (Window menu) command, 79
cells, 164-165
Center (Alignment menu) command, 84-85
centering text, 84-85, 231
    vertically on pages, 138-139
Change Default Dir (File Manager) command, 188-189, 192-193
Change Default Directory dialog box, 188-189
characters
    deleting, 42-43
    special, inserting, 156-157
Characters (Font menu) command, 156-157
Characters dialog box, 156-157
clicking, 228
closing
    File Manager, 184
    menus without selecting commands, 22
    Reveal Codes window, 82-83
[Cntr Cur Pg] Reveal Code, 138
[Cntr on Mar] Reveal Code, 85
[Col Def] Reveal Code, 170
column breaks, 172
columns, two in documents, 170-171
    typing text in second, 172-173
Columns (Layout menu) command, 170-171
commands
    Alignment (Layout menu)
        Center, 84-85
        Decimal Tab, 130-131
        Flush Right, 86-87
        Hanging Indent, 90-91
        Hard Page, 38-39
        Indent, 88-89

Block (Edit menu), 46-47
Bold (Font menu), 92-93
Cascade (Window menu), 79
Characters (Font menu), 156-157
Columns (Layout menu), 170-171
Contents (Help menu), 28-29
Convert Case (Edit menu),
   106-107
Copy (Edit menu), 56-57
Cut (Edit menu), 58-59
Date (Tools menu), 112-113
Exit (File menu), 66-69
Exit WP (File menu), 24-25
File Manager (File menu),
   184-185
   Change Default Dir, 188-189,
     192-193
   Copy, 194-195
   Delete, 198-199
   Find, 200-201
   Move/Rename, 196-197
Font (Font menu), 98-103
Go To (Edit menu), 40-41
Graphics Lines (Graphics menu),
   158-159
Graphics Mode (View menu),
   26-27
Header/Footer/Watermark
   (Layout menu), 148-155
Italics (Font menu), 96-97
Line (Layout menu), 132-137
Margins (Layout menu), 144-145
Maximize (Window menu), 78
Merge (Tools menu)
   Define, 206-207, 214-215
   Run, 224-225
New (File menu), 72-73
Open (File menu), 70-71, 74-75
Page (Layout menu), 138-143
Page Mode (View menu),
   146-147
Paste (Edit menu), 56-59
Print (File menu), 178-181
Print Preview (File menu),
   176-177
Pull-Down Menus (View
   menu), 23
Replace (Edit menu), 110-111
Retrieve (File menu), 122-123
Retrieve Image (Graphics menu),
   160-161
Reveal Codes (View menu),
   82-83
Save (File menu), 62-63
Save As (File menu), 64-65,
   120-121
Search (Edit menu), 108-109
Select (Edit menu), 48-49
   Paragraph, 48-49
selecting, 22-23, 229
Sort (Tools menu), 124-125
Switch To (Window menu),
   76-77
Tab Set (Layout menu), 128-129
Tables (Layout menu)
   Create, 162-163
   Delete Row, 168-169
   Insert Row, 166-167
Tile (Window menu), 78-79
Undelete (Edit menu), 52-53
Underline (Font menu), 94-95
Undo (Edit menu), 54-55
undoing last, 54-55
Writing Tools (Tools menu)
   Document Info, 118-119
   Spell Check, 114-115
   Thesaurus, 116-117
computers, turning on, 20
Contents (Help menu) command,
   28-29
Convert Case (Edit menu)
   command, 106-107
Copy command
   Edit menu, 56-57
   File Manager, 194-195
Copy dialog box, 194-195
copying, 231
   files, 194-195
   text blocks, 56-57
Create (Tables menu) command,
   162-163

Index

Create Graphics Line dialog box, 158-159
Create Page Border dialog box, 142-143
Create Paragraph Border dialog box, 134-135
Create Table dialog box, 162-163
creating
    data files, 214-217
    directories, 188-189
    documents, 72-73
    footers, 152-153
    form files, 206-207
    headers, 148-149
    merge letters, 204-205
current
    date and time, 20
        inserting, 112-113
    font, 11
cursor, 11, 231
    moving, 11, 229
cursor movement keys, 11-12
Cut (Edit menu) command, 58-59

D

data files, 231
    creating, 214-217
    entering records, 218-221
    merging with form files, 224-225
    saving, 222-223
databases, 215
date, current, 20
    inserting, 112-113
Date (Tools menu) command, 112-113
Decimal Tab (Alignment menu) command, 130-131
decimal tabs, 130-131
default
    directories, changing, 192-193
    Insert mode, 32-33
    settings, 231
Define (Merge menu) command, 206-207, 214-215
Del key, 42, 50-51
Delete (File Manager) command, 198-199

Delete Row (Tables menu) command, 168-169
deleting
    blank lines from text, 34
    characters, 42-43
    files, 198-199
    hidden codes, 83
    records, 221
    rows from tables, 168-169
    special characters, 157
    text blocks, 50-51
    words, 44-45
dialog boxes
    Change Default Directory, 188-189
    Characters, 156-157
    Copy, 194-195
    Create Graphics Line, 158-159
    Create Page Border, 142-143
    Create Paragraph Border, 134-135
    Create Table, 162-163
    Document Information, 118-119
    Exit WordPerfect, 24-25
    Field Names, 216-217
    Font, 98-103
    Go To, 40-41
    Line Format, 132-137
    Margin Format, 144-145
    Merge Codes (Form File), 206-211
    Merge Codes (Text Data File), 214-221
    Open Document, 70-71
    Page Format, 140-143
    Page Numbering, 140-141
    Parameter Entry, 208-209
    Print, 178-179
    Retrieve, 122-123
    Retrieve Image File, 160-161
    Run Merge, 224-225
    Save Block, 120-121
    Save Document, 62-65
    Search, 108-109
    Search and Replace, 110-111
    Search and Replace Results, 111
    Sort, 124-125
    Spell Check, 114-115

  Tab Set, 128-129
  Text Columns, 170-171
  Undelete, 52-53
dictionaries, 115
directories, 231
  changing default, 192-193
  creating, 188-189
  displaying different, 190-191
  WP60, 20-21
Document Info (Writing Tools menu) command, 118-119
Document Information dialog box, 118-119
documents, 231
  creating, 72-73
  displaying information about, 118-119
  double-spacing, 132-133
  duplicating, 64-65
  exiting, 66-67
   without saving, 68-69
  hidden codes, 82-83
  inserting
   graphics, 160-161
   page breaks, 38-39
   tables, 162-163
   text, 30-31
  open, viewing all, 78-79
  opening, 70-71
   multiple, 74-75
  overwriting text, 32-33
  previewing, 145, 176-177
  printing, 178-179
  saving, 12-13
   before exiting, 66-67
   first time, 62-63
   with new names, 64-65
  spell checking, 114-115
  switching between, 76-77
  two-column, 170-171
   typing text in second, 172-173
DOS (disk operating system), 232
double-clicking, 228
double-spacing, 132-133
dragging, 228
drawing horizontal lines, 158-159
duplicating documents, 64-65

E

Edit menu commands
  Block, 46-47
  Convert Case, 106-107
  Copy, 56-57
  Cut, 58-59
  Go To, 40-41
  Paste, 56-59
  Replace, 110-111
  Search, 108-109
  Select, 48-49
  Undelete, 52-53
  Undo, 54-55
editing
  footers, 154-155
  headers, 150-151
editing screen, 10
End key, 36
Enter key, 11, 34-35, 165
Exit (File menu) command, 66-69
Exit WordPerfect dialog box, 24-25
Exit WP (File menu) command, 24-25
exiting
  documents, 66-67
   without saving, 68-69
  Help, 28
  WordPerfect, 24-25

F

Field Names dialog box, 216-217
fields, 215, 232
File Manager
  closing, 184
  directories
   changing default, 192-193
   creating, 188-189
   displaying different, 190-191
  files
   copying, 194-195
   deleting, 198-199
   moving, 197
   opening, 186-187
   renaming, 196-197
   searching for, 200-201
  starting, 184-185

Index

File Manager (File menu) command, 184-185
    Change Default Dir, 188-189, 192-193
    Copy, 194-195
    Delete, 198-199
    Find, 200-201
    Move/Rename, 196-197
File menu commands
    Exit, 66-69
    Exit WP, 24-25
    File Manager, 184-185
        Change Default Dir, 188-189, 192-193
        Copy, 194-195
        Delete, 198-199
        Find, 200-201
        Move/Rename, 196-197
    New, 72-73
    Open, 70-71, 74-75
    Print, 178-181
    Print Preview, 176-177
    Retrieve, 122-123
    Save, 62-63
    Save As, 64-65, 120-121
`File not found` message, 70
files, 232
    copying, 194-195
    data, 231
        creating, 214-217
        entering records, 218-221
        merging with form files, 224-225
        saving, 222-223
    deleting, 198-199
    duplicating, 64-65
    exiting, 66-67
        without saving, 68-69
    form, 232
        creating, 206-207
        entering text, 208-211
        saving, 212-213
    moving, 197
    naming, 62
    opening, 70-71, 186-187
    renaming, 196-197
    saving
        before exiting, 66-67
        first time, 62-63
        with new names, 64-65
    searching for, 200-201
Find (File Manager) command, 200-201
finding, *see* searching
`[Flsh Rgt]` Reveal Code, 87
Flush Right (Alignment menu) command, 86-87
Font (Font menu) command, 98-103
Font dialog box, 98-103
Font menu commands
    Bold, 92-93
    Characters, 156-157
    Font, 98-103
    Italics, 96-97
    Underline, 94-95
`[Font]` Reveal Code, 98
fonts, 232
    changing, 98-99
    current, 11
    initial, changing, 102-103
    resizing, 100-101
`[Footer]` Reveal Code, 153
footers, 232
    creating, 152-153
    editing, 154-155
form files, 232
    creating, 206-207
    entering text, 208-211
    merging with data files, 224-225
    saving, 212-213
formatting
    blank lines in text, 34-35
    bold text, 92-93
    centering text, 84-85
        vertically on pages, 138-139
    fonts, 98-103
    footers, 152-155
    hard page breaks, 38-39
    headers, 148-151
    indents, 88-89
        hanging, 90-91
    italicizing text, 96-97
    margins, 144-145
    pages
        borders, 142-143
        numbering, 140-141

paragraphs
    borders, 134-135
    shading, 136-137
right-justifying text, 86-87
special characters, inserting,
    156-157
tabs
    decimal, 130-131
    left, 128-129
two-column documents, 170-171
underlined text, 94-95

G

Go To (Edit menu) command, 40-41
Go To dialog box, 40-41
going to pages, 40-41
[Graphic Line] Reveal Code,
    159
graphics
    horizontal lines, drawing,
        158-159
    inserting in documents, 160-161
Graphics Lines (Graphics menu)
    command, 158-159
Graphics menu commands
    Graphics Lines, 158-159
    Retrieve Image, 160-161
Graphics mode
    changing to, 26-27
    viewing font changes, 92-93
Graphics Mode (View menu)
    command, 26-27

H

Hanging Indent (Alignment menu)
    command, 90-91
hanging indents, 90-91
Hard Page (Alignment menu)
    command, 38-39
hard page breaks, 232
    inserting, 38-39
hard returns, 232
[Header] Reveal Code, 149
Header/Footer/Watermark (Layout
    menu) command, 148-155
headers, 232

creating, 148-149
editing, 150-151
Help, 28-29, 232
    reference books, 230
Help menu, Contents command,
    28-29
Help window, 28-29
hidden codes, see Reveal Codes
horizontal lines, drawing, 158-159

I-J

Indent (Alignment menu) command,
    88-89
indents, 88-89
    hanging, 90-91
indicators, 11
initial fonts, changing, 102-103
Ins key, 30, 32
Insert mode, 32-33, 232
Insert Row (Tables menu)
    command, 166-167
inserting
    blank lines in text, 34-35
    current date, 112-113
    graphics in documents, 160-161
    hard page breaks in documents,
        38-39
    special characters, 156-157
    tables in documents, 162-163
    text in documents, 30-31
[Italc On] Reveal Code, 96
italicizing text, 96-97
Italics (Font menu) command, 96-97

K

key letters, 22
keyboard shortcuts
    Block (Alt+F4), 47
    Bold (F6), 93
    Center (Shift+F6), 85
    Characters (Ctrl+W), 157
    Column Break (Ctrl+Enter), 172
    Copy (Ctrl+C), 57
    Cut (Ctrl+X), 59
    Decimal Tab (Ctrl+F6), 131
    Delete Row (Ctrl+Del), 169

Index

Delete Word (Ctrl+Backspace), 44
Exit (F7), 67
Exit WP (Home+F7), 25
File Manager (F5), 185
Flush Right (Alt+F6), 87
Font (Ctrl+F8), 99
Go To (Ctrl+Home), 41
Go To top of document (Home+Home+Home+↑), 40
Hard Page Break (Ctrl+Enter), 39
Help Contents (F1), 29
Indent (F4), 89
Insert Row (Ctrl+Ins), 167
Italics (Ctrl+I), 97
Menu (Alt+key letter), 22
Merge Codes (Shift+F9), 208
Open (Shift+F10), 71
Paste (Ctrl+V), 57
Print (Shift+F7), 179
Reveal Codes (Alt+F3), 83
Save As (F10), 65
Search (F2), 109
Spell Check (Ctrl+F2), 115
Undelete (Esc), 53
Underline (F8), 95
Undo (Ctrl+Z), 55
keys
    arrow, 11-12
    Backspace, 43, 51
    cursor movement, 11-12
    Del, 42, 50-51
    End, 36
    Enter, 11, 34-35, 165
    Ins, 30, 32
    space bar, 30, 36
    Tab, 165

L

Layout menu commands
    Alignment
        Center, 84-85
        Decimal Tab, 130-131
        Flush Right, 86-87
        Hanging Indent, 90-91
        Hard Page, 38-39
        Indent, 88-89
    Columns, 170-171
    Header/Footer/Watermark, 148-155
    Line, 132-137
    Margins, 144-145
    Page, 138-143
    Tab Set, 128-129
    Tables
        Create, 162-163
        Delete Row, 168-169
        Insert Row, 166-167
left tabs, setting, 128-129
left-justifying, 233
letters, *see* merge letters
[Lft Indent] Reveal Code, 89, 91
Line (Layout menu) command, 132-137
Line Format dialog box, 132-137
lines
    blank, inserting, 34-35
    horizontal, drawing, 158-159
[Ln Spacing] Reveal Code, 133
lowercase in blocks, changing, 106-107

M

Margin Format dialog box, 144-145
margins, 233
    setting, 144-145
Margins (Layout menu) command, 144-145
Maximize (Window menu) command, 78
menu bar, 10
menus, 233
    closing without selecting commands, 22
    selecting commands, 22-23, 229
Merge (Tools menu) command
    Define, 206-207, 214-215
    Run, 224-225
Merge codes, 233
Merge Codes dialog box
    Form File, 206-211
    Text Data File, 214-221
merge letters, 233
    creating, 204-205

data files, 231
   creating, 214-217
   entering records, 218-221
   saving, 222-223
form files, 232
   creating, 206-207
   entering text, 208-211
   saving, 212-213
merging form and data files, 224-225
messages
   `File not found`, 70
   `Not found`, 108, 200
modes
   Block, 46
   Graphics, 92-93
      changing to, 26-27
   Insert, 32-33, 232
   Page, 145-147
   Preview, 176
   Text, 26
   Typeover, 30, 33, 234
monitors, turning on, 20
mouse, 233
   operations, 228
Move/Rename (File Manager) command, 196-197
moving, 233
   cursor, 11, 229
   files, 197
   text blocks, 58-59

N

naming files, 62
New (File menu) command, 72-73
`Not found` message, 108, 200
numbering pages, 140-141
numbers, aligning at decimal points, 130-131

O

Open (File menu) command, 70-71, 74-75
Open Document dialog box, 70-71
opening
   documents, 70-71
      multiple, 74-75

files, 186-187
Reveal Codes window, 82-83
overwriting text, 32-33

P-Q

Page (Layout menu) command, 138-143
page breaks
   hard, 232
   inserting, 38-39
   soft, 234
Page Format dialog box, 140-143
Page mode, 145-147
Page Mode (View menu) command, 146-147
Page Numbering dialog box, 140-141
pages
   borders, 142-143
   centering text vertically, 138-139
   combining, 38
   going to, 40-41
   numbering, 140-141
`[+Para Border]` Reveal Code, 135
`[Para Box:FigureBox]` Reveal Code, 161
Paragraph (Select menu) command, 48-49
paragraphs
   blank lines between, 34-35
   borders, 134-135
   combining, 36-37
   selecting, 48-49
   shading, 136-137
   splitting, 36
Parameter Entry dialog box, 208-209
Paste (Edit menu) command, 56-59
paths, 233
`[Pg Border]` Reveal Code, 143
`[Pg Num Pos]` Reveal Code, 140
power switches, 20
Preview mode, 176
previewing documents, 145, 176-177
Print (File menu) command, 178-181

Index   243

Index

Print dialog box, 178-179
Print Preview (File menu) command, 176-177
printing
　documents, 178-179
　text blocks, 180-181
programs, troubleshooting starting, 21
Pull-Down Menus (View menu) command, 23

R

records, 215, 233
　deleting, 221
　entering in data files, 218-221
reference books, 230
renaming files, 196-197
Replace (Edit menu) command, 110-111
replacing text, 110-111
resizing fonts, 100-101
restoring deleted text, 52-53
Retrieve (File menu) command, 122-123
Retrieve dialog box, 122-123
Retrieve Image (Graphics menu) command, 160-161
Retrieve Image File dialog box, 160-161
retrieving text blocks, 122-123
Return key, see Enter key
returns
　hard, 232
　soft, 234
Reveal Codes, 233
　[Back Tab], 91
　[Bold On], 92
　[Cntr Cur Pg], 138
　[Cntr on Mar], 85
　[Col Def], 170
　[Flsh Rgt], 87
　[Font], 98
　[Footer], 153
　[Graphic Line], 159
　[Header], 149
　[Italc On], 96
　[Lft Indent], 89, 91
　[Ln Spacing], 133
　[+Para Border], 135
　[Para Box:FigureBox], 161
　[Pg Border], 143
　[Pg Num Pos], 140
　[Tab Set], 129
　[Tbl Def], 162
　[Und On], 94
　[Very Large On], 100
Reveal Codes window, opening/closing, 82-83
Reveal Codes (View menu) command, 82-83
right-justifying text, 86-87, 234
rows
　adding to tables, 166-167
　deleting from tables, 168-169
Run (Merge menu) command, 224-225
Run Merge dialog box, 224-225

S

Save (File menu) command, 62-63
Save As (File menu) command, 64-65, 120-121
Save Block dialog box, 120-121
Save Document dialog box, 62-65
saving
　data files, 222-223
　documents, 12-13
　　before exiting, 66-67
　　first time, 62-63
　　with new names, 64-65
　form files, 212-213
　text blocks, 120-121
screens, editing, 10
Search (Edit menu) command, 108-109
Search and Replace dialog box, 110-111
Search and Replace Results dialog box, 111
Search dialog box, 108-109
search strings, 234
searching
　for files, 200-201
　for text, 108-109
　　and replacing, 110-111

Select, Paragraph (Edit menu) command, 48-49
selecting
   blocks of text, 46-47
   commands, 22-23, 229
   files in File Manager, 186
   paragraphs, 48-49
shading paragraphs, 136-137
soft
   page breaks, 39, 234
   returns, 234
Sort (Tools menu) command, 124-125
Sort dialog box, 124-125
sorting text, 124-125
space bar, 30, 36
special characters, inserting, 156-157
Spell Check (Writing Tools menu) command, 114-115
Spell Check dialog box, 114-115
spell checking, 114-115
splitting paragraphs, 36
starting
   File Manager, 184-185
   programs, troubleshooting, 21
   WordPerfect, 20-21
status line, 234
strings, search, 234
Switch To (Window menu) command, 76-77
switches, power, 20
switching between documents, 76-77
synonyms, 116-117

T

Tab key, 165
Tab Set (Layout menu) command, 128-129
Tab Set dialog box, 128-129
[Tab Set] Reveal Code, 129
tables
   adding rows, 166-167
   deleting rows, 168-169
   entering text, 164-165
   inserting in documents, 162-163
Tables (Layout menu) command
   Create, 162-163
   Delete Row, 168-169
   Insert Row, 166-167
tabs
   decimal, 130-131
   left, setting, 128-129
[Tbl Def] Reveal Code, 162
text
   blocking, 229
   blocks, 231
      capitalization, changing, 106-107
      copying, 56-57
      deleting, 50-51
      deselecting, 57
      moving, 58-59
      printing, 180-181
      retrieving, 122-123
      saving, 120-121
      selecting, 46-47
   bold, 92-93
   centering, 84-85, 231
      vertically on pages, 138-139
   deleting
      characters, 42-43
      words, 44-45
   double-spacing, 132-133
   editing
      footers, 154-155
      headers, 150-151
   entering
      in form files, 208-211
      in second column of two-column documents, 172-173
      in tables, 164-165
   fonts
      changing, 98-99
      initial, changing, 102-103
      resizing, 100-101
   hidden codes, *see* Reveal Codes
   indents, 88-89
      hanging, 90-91
   inserting, 30-31
      blank lines, 34-35
   italicizing, 96-97
   left-justifying, 233
   overwriting, 32-33
   paragraphs
      borders, 134-135
      combining, 36-37

Index

selecting, 48-49
shading, 136-137
right-justifying, 86-87, 234
searching for, 108-109
and replacing, 110-111
sorting, 124-125
special characters, inserting, 156-157
spell checking, 114-115
undeleting, 52-53
underlined, 94-95
word wrap, 11, 234
Text Columns dialog box, 170-171
Text mode, 26
Thesaurus, 116-117, 234
Thesaurus (Writing Tools menu) command, 116-117
Tile (Window menu) command, 78-79
tiling windows, 78-79
time, current, 20
title pages, centering text vertically, 138-139
Tools menu commands
Date, 112-113
Merge
Define, 206-207, 214-215
Run, 224-225
Sort, 124-125
Writing Tools
Document Info, 118-119
Spell Check, 114-115
Thesaurus, 116-117
troubleshooting
overwriting text accidentally, 32
starting programs, 21
turning on computers and monitors, 20
two-column documents, 170-171
typing text in second column, 172-173
Typeover mode, 30, 33, 234

U

[Und On] Reveal Code, 94
Undelete (Edit menu) command, 52-53
Undelete dialog box, 52-53
undeleting text, 52-53
Underline (Font menu) command, 94-95
underlined text, 94-95
Undo (Edit menu) command, 54-55
undoing
centered text, 85
last action, 54-55
uppercase in blocks, changing, 106-107

V

[Very Large On] Reveal Code, 100
View menu commands
Graphics Mode, 26-27
Page Mode, 146-147
Pull-Down Menus, 23
Reveal Codes, 82-83

W-Z

wild cards, 200
Window menu commands
Cascade, 79
Maximize, 78
Switch To, 76-77
Tile, 78-79
windows
Help, 28-29
Reveal Codes, 82-83
tiling, 78-79
word wrap, 11, 234
WordPerfect
exiting, 24-25
starting, 20-21
words
deleting, 44-45
looking up in thesaurus, 116-117
WP60 directory, 20-21
Writing Tools (Tools menu) command
Document Info, 118-119
Spell Check, 114-115
Thesaurus, 116-117